The Girl with
Questioning Eyes

NEELESH RAGHUWANSHI

The Girl with Questioning Eyes

A Novel

Translated from the Hindi by

DEEPA JAIN SINGH

With an Introduction by

VASUDHA DALMIA

Published by

PERMANENT BLACK

'Himalayana', Mall Road, Ranikhet Cantt,
Ranikhet 263645

perblack@gmail.com

Distributed by

ORIENT BLACKSWAN PRIVATE LTD

Bangalore Bhopal Bhubaneshwar Chandigarh Chennai
Ernakulam Guwahati Hyderabad Jaipur Kolkata
Lucknow Mumbai New Delhi Patna
www.orientblackswan.com

First published 2012 in Hindi as
Ek Kasbe ke Notes
by Rajkamal Prakashan Pvt. Ltd.

This translation published by permission
of the author and the Hindi publisher

ISBN 978-81-7824-543-0

Typeset in Bembo
by Guru Typograph Technology, Crossing Republik, Ghaziabad
Printed and bound by Sapra Brothers, Noida, U.P.

Contents

Introduction

VASUDHA DALMIA

GANJ BASODA, WITH which this lively and delicate novel opens, is a sleepy market town situated on the northern edge of the rolling plains of Central India. It lies a little south of the Betwa, a major river of the area. A much smaller river, the Parasari, cuts the town neatly into two. The town as a whole boasts of several institutions which suggest its modernity. There are high schools for boys, and, more importantly, also for girls. There is a "convent" school for the better off; there is a girls' college; and surely also another college for boys, though it is not mentioned; there is a court of law and a bank.

Neither a village nor quite a city, Ganj Basoda hovers anxiously between the two. Its inhabitants are particularly careful to distinguish themselves from villagers, poking fun at the farmers who fill the town on market days. Rather like Hardy's Casterbridge, its status derives from its wholesale grain market – whence the Persian prefix *ganj*. For seven months in the year the town comes to life when its lanes fill up with farmers from the surrounding countryside. From March to June is held the market for wheat and gram, and from October to December for soya bean and *moong daal*. Ganj Basoda also has a busy railway station, an important crossing point for trains on the Bombay–Delhi line, as well as those running north to south, making possible the distribution of its produce all over the country. There are all-important quarries in the vicinity too, producing the stone the region is known for. They add to the dust, which swirls everywhere. It gets in the hair, in the nostrils, in the mouth. It covers hands and feet.

Regardless of the dust that colours their days, farmers, big and small, and townspeople, collect in the eatery – the dhaba – positioned to catch customers alighting from buses and those awaiting their arrival. The shops which line the road leading to the bus-stand and the colourful life of the street constitute the universe of the dhaba owner, Mohan Lal. He has fathered nine children, no less than eight of whom are girls. The tale of this lively, energetic, but ultimately tragic figure forms the backbone of this book, which sometimes reads more like the memoir of its narrator, Babli, than a novel. She is sixth in the line of Mohan Lal's eight daughters.

Mohan Lal presides over life in his dhaba. He sits on a *takht* – a raised wooden platform – set traditionally and invitingly in front of the dhaba, reading his newspaper, which links him both to the world outside and to his clientele, with whom he discusses the politics and social issues of the day, often setting the tone of the debate. He can preside only when one of his girls is managing the *bhatti* – the clay oven fired by coal and cowdung cakes – in which roti after roti is baked, where the daal is kept warm, as is the potato curry and a smaller vessel containing the green vegetable of the day. All side garnishings cost extra and are carefully calculated when the bill is presented: pickle, onion rings, and papad.

The space offered by Mohan Lal, supported by his wife Bhanwari Devi at home – Kakka and Bai to their children – serves as middle ground and public sphere of this little township. The social life of the dhaba may not quite fit the notion of what scholars call a "bourgeois public sphere", this being a concept posited by the German sociologist Juergen Habermas in 1962. There are some similarities nonetheless. The bourgeois public sphere is reckoned to have come into being in the course of the eighteenth century in Europe with the evolution of early capitalism and the start of a traffic in commodity and news. This was when the public and private spheres were, for the first time, thought of as distinct and separable.[1] The bourgeois public sphere was, naturally, constituted by the propertied and the educated: by jurists, doctors, professors, scholars; meanwhile the old burghers – the shopkeepers and craftsmen – were propelled downwards. This bourgeois public sphere claimed to represent *everyone*.

[1] Habermas 1989 [1962]: 11, 15.

Crucial within its composition was an informed and critical reading public that had begun creating what we now commonly call "public pressure" – compelling those in authority to justify their rule over the creators of public opinion and everyone else.[2] The "masses", supposedly represented by this reading public, were still largely illiterate and poor.

Looking at this scenario from a bird's-eye view, what seems visible is a top layer made up of Europe's royal courts and state institutions which legislated and exercised authority; a middle layer below this was constituted of the propertied and the educated with their patriarchal-conjugal middle-class families. This category of people, even as they constituted the bourgeois public sphere, also formed and projected the value of an intimate private sphere of interior thought processes. These were signposted by the new letter- and diary-writing culture – of private conversations with oneself as though addressed to another. Paradoxically and simultaneously, this form of writing contributed to the creation of public-spiritedness, to the coming into being of what Habermas termed the *Publikumsbezogenheit* (public orientation) of a bourgeois class.[3]

Informed though they were by their families, it was always the males who stepped out to constitute the new

[2] Ibid.: 23, 25.

[3] Ibid.: 28.

public spaces. Men filled the coffee-houses, theatres, clubs, and reading and discussion groups (*Tischgesellschaften*) where public opinion was created. In early-eighteenth-century England, these were the people whose opinions were embodied in *The Spectator* (1711–12), a periodical which its creators, Joseph Addison and Richard Steele, hoped would bring "philosophy out of closets and libraries, schools and colleges, to dwell in clubs and assemblies, at tea-tables and coffee-houses." Such were the people who debated the offerings of the moral weeklies and early novels that criticised the aristocracy and set up new moral and social codes for the newly emergent bourgeoisie. Once created, this public opinion helped shape the politics of the day. The latter part of Habermas' work is concerned with what he sees as the dissolution of this early public sphere, which began with the arrival of widespread industrialisation and the creation of newspapers owned by magnates, representing primarily their own narrower interests.

The newspaper-reading scenario presided over by the owner of an eatery in Neelesh Raghuwanshi's novel is of course contextually streets away from the European coffee-house. And yet in its substance, in the preoccupations of its characters, it is connected with what Habermas said about the coming into being of a public sphere. While the novel is focussed on a much later period and a completely different social stratum, it offers the occasion to look at a different public, formed largely by shopkeepers and craftsmen – precisely those excluded by Habermas' definition.

This subject – the constitution of a public sphere – is of particular interest to me because I happen to have written about the early public sphere in late-nineteenth-century Banaras, largely accepting Habermas' definition of the early capitalist public sphere.[4] The question I did not engage with at the time, but which was raised by critics and now comes strongly to mind because of Raghuwanshi's novel, is this: Did one social class alone inhabit, define, and demarcate what we call "public space"?

It has been pointed out that there were several competing publics and public spaces all along. These came into being as rural society began its transition to the urban, and as the idea of debate, discussion, and reasoned exchange filtered down to non-bourgeois subaltern groups.[5] Industrialisation, then, it seems plausible to conclude, did not destroy the public sphere; on the contrary, it widened it by including newer groups. The faster pace of urbanisation, the quicker spread of print culture, and the increased proliferation of newspapers led to the spread of literacy and oral argumentation. Thus were created a variety of public spaces and competing publics. Some of these new spaces began to be made up of

[4] Dalmia [1997] 2010.

[5] Eley 1994: 300, 306.

women.[6] And neat separations of the private and the public came to be eroded. Women, for instance, come to create their own forum, their common space in the lane – harking back to the days of the village well – where they meet to gossip, to give vent to feelings and frustrations, and in this way to contribute to the formation of social mores.

Even if the customers of Mohan Lal's dhaba are male, those serving them are male as well as female. For the older daughters of the family who help their father, the dhaba is also home; they often take their school homework there. Their social identity is partly defined by their work there. Their political opinions are formed by the conversations they overhear there. How can public and private be seen apart?

Raghuwanshi's work offers, then, a rare insight into a world that is neither of the village, nor of strongly defined caste occupations. Her novel is far removed, too, from what was so vividly depicted in Urdu/Hindi literature by Premchand, and by Fakirmohan Senapati and Gopinath Mohanty in Oriya writings: peasants, tribals, parasitic moneylenders, exploitative landlords. Nor is Raghuwanshi like the novelists and storytellers – the *nayi-kahanikars* – of the late 1950s and early 1960s who wrote of the lonely and alienated men and women in the urban middle

[6] Nancy Fraser has spoken of these as subaltern counter-groups, especially with post-bourgeois feminist groups in mind. See Fraser 1994: 122.

class.[7] Using not a word extra, nor an extraneous phrase, she achieves the rare feat not only of producing a pioneering literary work that lights up the individual lives of a warm-hearted lower-middle-class family as they mingle with a variegated clientele in a middling market town, but also of creating a forum or public space both outside the range of Habermas' thoughts and one that has never before been attempted or presented in Hindi literature with such penetrating insight, poignant empathy, and literary skill. The discussions that take place in the dhaba of this novel, the opinions formed there, can determine the outcome of parliamentary elections. They can and do exercise power in independent India with its guarantee of universal franchise.

My friend Deepa Jain Singh, whose work in the Indian Administrative Service took her to remote townships surrounded by villages, has responded in her translation of Raghuwanshi's novel as much to the re-creation of a world as it existed in the decade she was there, as to its author's sensitive literary prose.

Raghuwanshi is known primarily as a poet. Her work has the distinction of being part of a literary tradition peculiar to the region she comes from. Unlike the North, with its centuries-old Mughal cities, Madhya Pradesh inherited no major urban centre where patronage was

[7] Several of these writers are the subject of my most recent work: Dalmia 2017.

readily available for the arts. Yet, in its smaller cities and towns there has flourished the most unusual literary talent in the Hindi literary tradition, at least from the mid-twentieth century on. We have only to think of Gajanan Madhav Muktibodh (1917–1964), who was to acquire cult status after his early death, and his long poem "Andhere mein" (In the Dark), with its surreal landscape, its bloody pavements, its country lanes, and ruined step-wells. The magical worlds and uncanny displacements of Muktibodh's poetry deeply influenced another talented and whimsical poet and novelist, Vinod Kumar Shukla (b. 1937), as also the much darker poetry and long short stories of Uday Prakash (b. 1952).

Raghuwanshi's economical use of words and light touch are fuelled both by her poetic awareness as also by her work as a scriptwriter for Doordarshan TV in the state capital of Madhya Pradesh, Bhopal. In this novel, her powerful poetic prose lights up the intimacy of a family's life in which women figure as importantly as men. Kakka cannot exist without his wife; her occasional absence, when she visits her brother, disturbs the rhythm of his life, disrupting his everyday existence and the stoic calm with which he faces the heavy financial burden of keeping his eleven-member family clothed, fed, and educated. Raghuwanshi does not dwell on the family's poverty – of their single good meal of the day, of the single set of clothes for school and outdoor wear – even as she registers the shame of it for Babli and her sisters in detail. The sisters find clever ways to hide this poverty from their schoolmates.

The siblings are introduced in successive clusters – always in twos and threes – as they become the focus of family interest. Their names never overwhelm the reader. Asha, Usha, and Anni are the oldest three, married off one after the other into families where they toil and sweat, providing unpaid slave labour to the large clans they serve. Work is what they have always been accustomed to do, but once married they understand what it means to slog all day without the reward of family love and appreciation.

Babli, the sensitive narrator, carries on her older sisters' work once they leave for their new homes, though she cannot help fearing that she will be seen carrying the basket filled with *kanda*s (dried cowdung cakes) on her head by the tall, slim, smiling college teacher who hurries by regularly each morning, asking her whether the *bindi* on her forehead is placed exactly in the middle. Kakka is quick to notice how Babli hangs her head, how downcast she is, as she tries to hide her connection to the dhaba from the teacher. He reprimands her gently – one need never be ashamed of honest labour – and she notes how his protective shade spreads comfortingly over them all: "There were times, like this evening, when this strong-willed impenetrable man would mutate into a protective father, a banyan tree touching the sky."

Kakka is filled with remorse each time his married daughters come home, for then there is no escaping the bitter fact that their marital households have exhausted them, their lives reduced to a daily grind with no prospect of relief. Is this going to be the lot of his remaining daughters too? He is moved to make a public pledge, which he proclaims unabashedly to his disapproving clients: "Finally, having seen the state Asha-jiji, Usha-jiji, and Anni were in, Kakka decided he would think no further of the five of us marrying, at least for the time being. He'd first make us study, have us stand on our own feet, work. No! He would not tie us girls down like cattle tethered to a stake."

Shalu and Shiva are the next two who face the responsibilities of the dhaba, alongside Babli. What high hopes he has for this second trio! When the school results are announced he scans the newspaper for Shalu's roll number. Something inside him dries up when he fails to see her among those who have succeeded; he is like a well emptied of water.

Shalu disappoints him in another way later. Every evening she vanishes into the fields, as does handsome and friendly Rais Bhai of the nearby tyre shop. Shalu and Shiva are seen whispering in a huddle, conspiring to cover up Shalu's periodic absence from the dhaba. No storm follows, no torrent of rain, no lightning. One day, Kakka merely shuts shop abruptly, an event unknown to his daughters, and catches the next train to Nagpur. He has begun to look increasingly worn and old. Shalu and Shiva are both married off. Kakka falls at the feet of the bridegrooms' fathers – "Sa'ab, my daughters . . ." With their departure his dreams of seeing them become doctors are over. A blank page follows, left blank even in the book, of dreams that have failed the dreamer, of unwritten chapters.

The three remaining girls continue with their studies. Their brother, Bhaiyya (eighth in the line, he is seldom called by his name, Mukul), has large black eyes covered with dense long lashes. He has his father's figure. He is tall and broad chested, he has his mother's fair skin. But sleek good-looking Bhaiyya shows no trace of his father's quickness, his power and glow. Cosseted by his parents, his ways seem barely tolerable to his sisters. They watch impatiently as he eats his way slowly through an elaborately laid out meal. Not for him the mere state school the girls attend. He goes to the much more prestigious "convent" school, where, much to his father's and the nuns' despair, he repeatedly fails.

The colourful life of the bazaar leading to the bus stand carries on. There is attractive, mad Binny, who laughs so enticingly when she appears suddenly at the end of the lane. Who has given her those attractive bangles, that new sari? There is Old Hunchback Cheelgari who can howl through the day. There is a red bull hurtling through the lanes. And there is "Dedh Panv ka Signal" (One-and-a-half-legged Signal), a lame dog. All four, wonderfully odd, all finding protection and love, surprisingly often with old women. It is impossible to convey in a few words, the wealth and detail of social life as it whirls into and past the dhaba – the big, middling, and small farmers, the shopkeepers, the clerks and lawyers, their discussions, squabbles, antagonisms, and anxieties.

It would be giving too much away for me to outline the changes that follow – to the narrator, her beloved father, and their small town. It suffices to say that this is a world that Raghuwanshi knows from the inside and breathes life into in the way that only some novelists manage. Because of her skill, we sense that by the end of the novel subtle and imperceptible changes have made Ganj Basoda no longer the same town and Babli no longer the little girl she was when she began her story. Ox-carts no longer pull through the town's streets, it is filled now with the noisy tractors of bigger and middling farmers. The dhaba has changed. Pressed by Bhaiyya, their father has added a tandoor oven to his establishment; there are now ice cream, cold drinks, and liquor served surreptitiously. But Kakka cannot take to the new ways, he reverts to the old, he toils in solitude. He is getting old; he attracts pity. And then, one day, the unthinkable happens.

At the end of Premchand's *Godaan* (The Gift of a Cow; 1936), its protagonist dies broken and dejected. Kakka does not have the good fortune to die; he lives to see his world fall apart. A forum he once helped create, dissolves itself.

Our good fortune as readers is to be allowed into Kakka's dhaba, to become his clients and eat his rotis for the duration of Babli's memoir. What better tribute than to be able to say at the end of a novel, as I do at the end of this one: I felt the pulse of a world I did not know.

REFERENCES

Calhoun, Craig, ed. *Habermas and the Public Sphere*. Cambridge, Mass., & London: Massachusetts Institute of Technology Press, 1994.

Dalmia, Vasudha. *Fiction as History: The Novel and the City in Urban North India*. Ranikhet: Permanent Black, 2017, and New York: SUNY Press, 2019.

———. *The Nationalization of Hindu Traditions: Bharatendu Harischandra and Nineteenth Century Banaras*. New Delhi: Oxford University Press, 1997. Reprinted with a foreword by Francesca Orsini. Ranikhet: Permanent Black, 2010.

Eley, Geoff. "Nations, Publics, and Political Cultures: Placing Habermas in the Nineteenth Century", in Craig Calhoun, ed., *Habermas and the Public Sphere*. Cambridge, Mass., & London: Massachusetts Institute of Technology Press, 1994, pp. 289–339.

Fraser, Nancy. "Rethinking the Public Sphere: A Contribution to the Critique of Actually Existing Democracy," in Craig Calhoun, ed., *Habermas and the Public Sphere*. Cambridge, Mass., & London: Massachusetts Institute of Technology Press, 1994, pp. 109–42.

Habermas, Juergen. *The Structural Transformation of the Public Sphere*. Cambridge, Mass., & London, England: Massachusetts Institute of Technology Press, 1989. German original: *Strukturwandal der Oeffentlichkeit*. Darmstadt & Neuwied: Hermann Luchterhand Verlag, 1962.

1

KAKKA'S DAY STARTED between five and six every morning. The daily ritual of a bidi over, he'd have his bath. And with what care he bathed: he couldn't bear a single drop going waste. Every so often he'd fret over how much had gone down the drain and start an early morning argument with Bai.

Bai always suggested he visit the temple before leaving home for work, but Kakka would have none of it and headed straight for the dhaba. He had the keys of the dhaba in his kurta pocket and before seven each morning, in one swift swinging motion he flung open its cracked door and his kurta would find itself hanging on a nail. Strong and well built, Kakka bent daily to clean the oven of last night's ashes and then set about lighting it. He'd use all his lung power, blowing hard into the bellows. The whole dhaba filled up with smoke, but catch Kakka batting an eyelid! The next half-hour he'd put all his energy into lighting the oven. Ultimately the oven seemed shamed by his zeal into coming alive. What was more hot and blazing by the end of this ritual – Kakka or the oven? We, his children, never could tell. Red-hot and sweaty, Kakka was always such a sight.

By nine-thirty daal, potatoes, and green vegetables were cooked and ready. The vegetables were made in small quantities, often just enough to suggest their existence on the menu, in the proximity of the humbler daal and potatoes.

Kakka oozed sweat kneading the dough, his muscles shining, his copper-coloured reflection sparkling in the large dough-making platter. He'd add coal to the oven and then, his big laughter-filled eyes ablaze, settle down with his tea to read the morning newspaper.

We watched this everyday ritual. He never managed to finish the newspaper before the first customer arrived. Kakka by the oven, plate in hand, started his day asking:

"So, what'll you have?"

"Depends what you've got."

We knew what our father's response needed to be and muttered quietly, "There's daal, potatoes, okra, pickle, onions, green chilli . . ."

The moment the customer ordered, Kakka filled up a plate, passed it to us, put a griddle on the oven, and had a roti ready in no time.

The first morsel was always for the cow. Kakka never failed to put aside a mouthful for her in the closest corner before serving the first customer. With her huge shining black eyes, the cow was forever nearby. No-one had tethered her, she just knew it was time for the first sale of the morning and there she was! Only after he'd fed her that first offering would Kakka start his diurnal round, his day- and night-long working hours, those hard hours he put in to provide for his wife and us nine children.

On one such morning, Bai put a small basket of dried cowpats on my head. She did it so delicately – her hand touching my head, seeming to suggest she was carrying the weight, not I. At times like this her eyes welled up but she manoeuvred her sari subtly and wiped her eyes dry.

I was walking off with the basket of cowpats on my head when there was a "Hey! Listen, listen!" from somewhere behind. I turned around to see a tall, thin, dark-complexioned lady, books under her arm, hair still wet, hurrying to catch up with me. She seemed in a big rush, like she had to get to the seven o'clock morning college class to teach.

"Is my bindi properly centred? Just check."

I stood rooted and just about managed a nod. The lady rushed off smiling in the direction of the college. I stood transfixed, trembling under my headload. I'd seen her walk past the dhaba often, but the sudden assault of her question had got me all startled and confused. My turn to bear the headload of that cowpat basket came only maybe once every three or four days, and of all days *this* day had to be *that* day for a proper lady to come up and address me! She moved ahead, leaving me standing there all atremble with happiness and shame.

Kakka yelled from somewhere, "Move on . . . when d'you plan on reaching the dhaba?" I couldn't see the road but Kakka was soon well ahead of me. All I could see over that time was a grand teaching lady with books under her arm.

The moment I reached the dhaba, I began helping Kakka with the morning chores – getting the oven going, the vegetables ready. But that scene of the lady with those books under her arm and me gawping with my headload of cowpats wouldn't allow me to focus – despite Kakka's commanding tone and the crackling oven which shook the stupefaction out of me every now and then.

My mind still full of books and cowpats, that evening Kakka handed me a little steel jug and gestured towards the back door. I went over and emptied it, then realised too late the splash from it had sounded odd. I peered intently and discovered what I'd thrown out of the jug was milk. Scared, I said: "Kakka, there was milk in it . . . I thought it was full of water!" He jerked his head away, trying not to show his annoyance, and turned to light the fire.

It didn't stay dark all that long where we were. I was startled by a street light that came on, and then Kakka, standing close by, chided me gently: "What's to be ashamed of? . . . Carrying cowpats is good honest labour. *Arré*, she was off to work too, wasn't she? Hey, come on, stir the pot now and then!" And he sat down with his newspaper.

There were times when this strong-willed impenetr-able man mutated into a protective father, a banyan tree touching the sky.

A game began and continued in the family for days. No words were needed – there had only to be a basket of cowpats on my head for someone to shout from behind, *"Hey! Listen! Is my bindi properly centred?"* My breath would catch, I'd turn around and nod, *"Yes!"* Though I knew I was being teased and this was just a game, the thrill and embarrassment of it were still within me.

Each time I saw that lady I'd run for cover. She'd see me and smile.

Ours was no little town. It was a market town; people from the villages nearby called it a "market". One of our uncle's daughters said, taunting us, "Hey, you big-city types, don't you take us village folk to be fools!"

Once a year in the market a fair was held over the festival days of Ganesh Chaturthi and Durga Puja. The goddess Durga's fair was located in Jai Stambh Chauraha, near the power station. On the last day of the fair, an orchestra was called in which kept the whole town abuzz all night. Kids, girls, the older folk, everyone stayed up late into the night. The girls and the women – those whose houses were by the electricity station – spent all night on the roofs of buildings listening to that orchestra. Over such days we thought of them, perched on their vantage points, as the twice blessed. Men, and children too, got heavily involved in boisterous celebrations around the orchestra.

Bai's younger brother, Chhoté Mama-ji, lived right nextdoor with a few buffaloes and sold their milk. That year, on the last day of the fair, I was with him on the road, loving the orchestra. The tea shops were open, though it must have been two or three after midnight, and off I went with Chhoté Mama-ji and his friends to slurp some of that syrupy tea.

For the tea-shop owner, this was a big night. A long line of customers were awaiting their turn to get their lips into some of his tea. The problem was, his milk supply was close to running out. Naturally, he didn't want to shut shop in the middle of reaping this harvest of a lifetime! It was only once or twice a year that he wasn't gazing longingly out of his shop, craving customers, and tonight was one of those nights.

"Can you go milk a buffalo?" The tea-shop owner, eyes on fire, looked at Chhoté Mama-ji, at the boiling tea, at his customers – covering them all in one meaningful glance.

"Sure! For ten rupees a litre."

His eyes narrowed hearing that. ". . . Straight from five to ten, Brother?"

"Take it or leave it!" Chhoté Mama-ji retorted. "Give us our four teas, then just shut shop! Why not join the fun and enjoy the orchestra like us? Come on, stop showing off working so hard!" And with that Chhoté Mama-ji looked disdainfully at the man's queue of customers.

Having chanced upon a buffalo owner among his customers, there was no way the tea-shop owner was going to let the opportunity slip. "My boy will go with you," he said, "and if you dare mix even a drop of water in the milk . . ."

"I'll milk the buffalo in front of your boy. You're welcome to come along yourself . . ."

"Hah, you think I'm crazy or what? . . . Leave my shop now? Maybe you're all burning up seeing the money rolling in my way?" He looked like he wasn't exactly joking. Chhoté Mama-ji and his friends laughed out loud all the same. So did I.

The tea-shop owner's boy trotted along with us.

In the dark, where the pots and pans were, Chhoté Mama-ji started a clatter trying to find the right one.

"Oh, Patil Sahib! Switch on the light!" said the little perisher – he was no fool.

"What else am I trying to do! Can't find the blasted switch!"

Chhoté Mama-ji called out to me. "Hey Babli, come here!" I moved towards him in the pitch dark. He caught hold of my hand, pulled me towards him, then whispered: "Take this bucket and go straight . . ."

Even in the dark, Chhoté Mama-ji knew how to work wonders. In the midst of all the clattering he'd run the water and half-filled the bucket with it. While I walked straight to the buffalo, he lit a candle and yelled to the boy: "Come along, stand by the buffalo! The light's not working . . . the switch is behind all the pots and pans, I can't get to it . . . I can't move all that stuff, come along . . ."

The fellow came over and stood right beside us. I stood by him, holding the bucket, with Chhoté Mama-ji signalling every now and then that I should hold it tight. He hunched low to milk the buffalo and I squatted near him so my back was to the boy.

The boy stood there tense, eagle-eyed; I sat there, determined. In a little while the bucket was full.

"A full two litres of milk! Go quick, take it straight to your Seth-ji! His customers shouldn't have to leave without their tea . . ."

The boy ran off, clutching the bucket of milk.

I was delighted. "That was great fun, Chhoté Mama-ji! The orchestra should show up every day! We'd get to sell milk half mixed with water at double the price!"

Chhoté Mama-ji shushed me and thumped me forward.

Every fibre of my being was tingling. It's such fun duping the hell out of people! The milk spurting out of the buffalo's udder . . . the bidi sticking out of the corner of Chhoté Mama-ji's lips . . . me squatting with a bucket and making complete fools of the boy and his tea-shop owner!

A while later we went to the tea shop. "I say, Seth! What milk my buffalo gives," Chhoté Mama-ji said, letting out a thick black plume of bidi smoke.

"Why else would I give you twice the going rate!" The tea-shop man was seemingly high on making tea for his many customers and raking it in doublequick, and we were equally high on having given him a whole half litre less at double the price!

That morning, for the first time in my life, I heard the dawn birds chirp and wished the sun "Good Morning". After which, exhilarated and exhausted, we went off home and slept the sleep of the dead.

At times like these, Bai got furious. She disapproved thoroughly of my ways – hanging around with men, wandering aimlessly, gossiping late into the night. "No sign of being ladylike," she said, gnashing her teeth. Kakka muttered "Kids will be kids" and changed the subject.

And Chhoté Mama-ji? He made my life heaven just by letting me be with him, listening to the orchestra all night! Because it was *him*, Bai couldn't say much, else at the very mention of the orchestra she'd raise hell. It only required one sentence from Chhoté Mama-ji to shut Bai up.

"She was with me, Sister! She wasn't roaming around with anyone else! In any case, we only sat all night at the tea shop!"

Behind Bai's back, I was with him in Morse Code mode: "And how about the water-in-milk episode?"

Chhoté Mama-ji glared at me.

Actually, if Kakka'd heard the story of our adventure, he'd have guffawed! He may even have ribbed the tea-shop owner – "Hey, Brother! How come you were made such an idiot of last night?"

All day I tailed Chhoté Mama-ji. He'd keep his hide scarce in Kakka's presence and smoke his bidi behind the shop and make me stand guard at the door. Before he lit up he'd say: "If Lala-ji comes, don't stay standing! Sit down at once."

I'd accompany him on trips to buy oilcakes and bran and straw for the buffaloes. He'd get immersed talking to his friends and lose all track of time. Over our trip back home he'd say to me, "We'll tell your father we got held up at the straw sellers!"

Together we fed the buffaloes bran and oilcakes, Chhoté Mama-ji and I. Kakka'd say, "Feed them more oilcakes and less bran," but Chhoté Mama-ji did the opposite behind his back. He whispered conspiratorially to me, "Lala-ji doesn't understand. Why on earth should buffaloes get equal proportions of cake and bran?" Chhoté Mama-ji's views were always the opposite of Kakka's: he believed in buffaloes that gave more milk getting more oilcakes, and in those that gave less milk getting more bran.

Raees Bhai's welding workshop stood close by Kakka's dhaba. One day, Raees Bhai and Chhoté Mama-ji laid a bet on who could stare longest at the welding sparks on a tractor trolley – without, that is, blinking. Chhoté Mama-ji won, but a little later his eyes were swollen and red. When I got home from school in the evening, Mami said to me, "Hey . . . Just look what's happened to your Chhoté Mama-ji . . ."

Still in my school uniform, I ran across to Raees Bhai's shop and picked a fight with him.

Till his eyes got okay, Chhoté Mama-ji wouldn't let Bai leave, she had to be continuously by him all the time. Chhoté Mama-ji was a lazy and happy-go-lucky sort, while Kakka was industrious and hard-working. Chhoté Mama-ji was really scared of Kakka, whom he called Lala-ji – I think out of some respect and a fat dose of fear.

One morning, when Kakka happened to reach the dhaba really early, he found the buffaloes nextdoor missing. After a while he figured out what had happened: Chhoté Mama-ji had gone off to the village with his buffaloes. I went looking for them across the River Parasari, but it wasn't any use.

Then, one afternoon, I found Chhoté Mama-ji watching us from behind the paan kiosk. "Chhoté Mama-ji, have you got the buffaloes? Chhoté Mama-ji will you stay here now? I'll bring Kakka around. He'll let you sleep late, he won't yell at you!"

All the way back, Chhoté Mama-ji puffed on his bidi and kept humming and hawing; but ultimately he took Mami away and went off to their village.

In the evening, at teatime, Bai said cautiously to Kakka that Mami had gone missing too. Kakka was enraged. "Damn fool, shirker! Just watch – it won't be a month before he's sold off all his four buffaloes."

Which was exactly what happened: Chhoté Mama-ji sold the buffaloes and, by way of offering Bai an explanation, said, "Oh, Sister! They were eating us out of hearth and home and hardly giving any milk!"

Grandmother, sobbing, gave Kakka news of their village: "Grandfather's always yelling at Chhoté Mama for being a ne'er-do-well, but it has no effect on him. All his time's taken up playing cards with his pals!" I wanted to register my own complaint to Grandmother by saying "Oh, so even without an orchestra and buffaloes he's having fun in the village! He couldn't care less about me!" But I couldn't. I didn't know if Grandmother might take it ill and thrash the stuffing out of me. They didn't need to wash Chhoté Mama-ji's clothes now, but between the two of them Grandmother and Bai could wash me clean and hang me out to dry.

Over Kakka's absences Chhoté Mama-ji showed up stealthily, like a thief. And then all of us sisters would say to each other, "Don't tell Kakka he came, anyone."

Bai would feed him quick, and then he'd go up to the roof to smoke a bidi. I'd trail after him, but after a bit he'd leave. With him would leave my passion for the orchestra and milking buffaloes at midnight. But anytime I spotted a buffalo, an image of Chhoté Mama-ji floated up before my eyes.

I couldn't bear to watch Raees Bhai at his welding workshop and always turned my face away. He'd mock me: "Hey Babli! Why don't you call back your Chhoté Mama-ji! We'll help him start a welding workshop!"

"Hee hee!" I'd retort, bristling.

No way Raees Bhai could have had even the remotest sense of how much I'd lost with my Chhoté Mama-ji's departure. Every time the orchestra arrived near the power station, I took to stuffing cotton wool in my ears. Often, I wanted to ask Bai why Chhoté Mama-ji was so lazy, why he couldn't work with Kakka. But I was too scared to.

I used to run a mile from Bai anyway.

Also from my Phapphu, Kakka's sister. She was somewhat dark-skinned, so we'd tease her and she'd get irritated but still smile and say, "Have you seen your father's face? He looks like a jewel, doesn't he?" The image of him as a jewel made Kakka burst out laughing.

Phapphu always called me "Balo", which made me furious and stopped me wanting even to speak to her. Bai tried numerous times to tell her to call me "Babli", but would she listen?

Once, coming home from school with my friends, I saw Phapphu trotting along towards us with a bag on her head. I hid within a gaggle of my friends. She tried searching me out at the head of the group, and the moment the group got near her she began yelling.

"Hey, Balo! Hey, Balo!"

I ducked and moved ahead. But there she was, behind me.

"Hey, Balo! Hey, Balo! Can't you hear me? Are you deaf or what?"

I stopped. The girls turned around and saw a black dhoti up above the ankles, matched with a bright red blouse, bracelets and armlets, a thick necklace with a large locket, an ornamental girdle around the waist, anklets on feet, and chunky bangles to boot. And with all this, a bag balanced on her head! What a sight! This was some aunt! The girls screeched with laughter and went off. I yelled angrily at Phapphu: "What is it? Why did you stop me?"

She shot back, "Come come, take me to the bus. Here, hang on. You take this bag and give me your school bag. Child, I can't carry stuff any more! I tire easily now!" I dug in my heels and glared at her. She pushed me along into walking by her.

"Phapphu, please don't do this again . . . It embarrasses me."

"Hey, how come? . . . You don't feel embarrassed around your Kakka!"

I was sauntering along just fine, and she was urging me to get a move on. I was hoping she'd miss the bus and then I'd get Kakka to tick her off. As she got on the bus she handed me a coin and heckled me: "Go to hell! *Hee hee hee!*" She cackled madly and disappeared. Flushed with embarrassment, I went straight to the dhaba instead of getting home.

"My dear, she's your aunt, after all!" Kakka laughed just like his sister.

At home, Bai explained that our dear Phapphu had waited patiently for me a long while, but when she thought she was getting late she'd got up and said, "I know school must be over by now! I'll pick Balo up on the way." Even when leaving, she couldn't bring herself to call me "Babli"!

"What a name-wrecker of an aunt!" I swore between my teeth.

2

My oldest sister, Asha-jiji, had been married off into the nearby village of Kagpur. Off and on, to fetch her back home, Kakka would put me on the eight a.m. bus and I'd plonk myself by a window seat and go off happily to Jiji's in-laws, where I'd find her. She'd whisper questions to me, wanting all the dope on the well-being of our family. Head covered in a long purdah, she'd be making cowpats, plastering the walls with cowdung, and making rotis on a fire. Never quite free of her purdah, she'd churn buttermilk, and that made her bangles go jingle-jangle. I couldn't see her arms for those bangles. And slogging all day long . . . what a complete turnaround in Jiji's life!

What an absolute contrast from home, where she was always the bully, where she'd laughed and chatted but yelled at us too and kept us in line. She was more a friend than a daughter to Bai: their chatter was endless. We'd want to eavesdrop, but Jiji wouldn't let us.

"Don't mooch around listening, go out and play! C'mon, c'mon, out! Kakka's alone . . . he's bound to be in need of some helping hands!"

She'd give Bai all the village gossip – stories of every attic and every courtyard . . . this is what happened here, this is what happened there. She'd laugh more than talk, mouth wide open, so you could see the gaps between her teeth! There were times she laughed enough to choke while drinking water!

I teased her once by crying out, "Look! Look, everyone! See those windows between Jiji's teeth!" She chased me out of the house, brandishing a rolling pin. I stopped only when I reached Kakka at the dhaba. "Kakka! Bai and Asha-jiji are gossiping away and laughing like crazy but won't allow us near them. So we've decided to call Asha-jiji 'The One with Windows in her Teeth!'" Kakka was most amused.

In the evening, when we returned home together, he hollered from the door, "Hey, Asha! Asha! I say, gossip as much as you want, but this one here loves listening in . . . don't ruin her fun . . . she fetches you here and takes you back my dear, so don't you bully her!"

Jiji looked chastened. She smiled at him but glared at me, I couldn't quite figure out why. I could also hardly figure out how this sister of mine back home was the very same Asha-jiji I'd fetched – a woman transformed when at her in-laws'.

Her mother-in-law was a harridan, their whole village was in awe of her. People called her Indira Gandhi.

To me, when I visited to fetch her, Jiji would whisper while soldiering on with her work: "Go tell my mother-in-law you've come to fetch your sister." So I'd trot off and sit a while with Jiji's mother-in-law and then sound like I was just saying something by the way: "Oh, and I've come by to fetch Jiji . . ."

No response from Mother-in-law.

". . . So . . . can I take her along?"

Mother-in-law looked now like she badly wanted a change of subject.

I'd rush away from her glare, go to Jiji, and say, "Hurry up, get ready. Kakka said to catch the four o'clock bus."

Jiji wouldn't move. "Go ask her again."

So off I'd go again – and again and again – towards the stony silence of the dreaded mother-in-law. This time round she'd have a ruse all worked out to circumvent my pleas: "What d'you want me to say? Ask Laxman . . . ask your brother-in-law. If he says 'Yes', take her . . . happily!"

So then I'd go traipsing to the brother-in-law and he'd say, "If Bai agrees, sure, take her!"

Back in their attic I'd cling to the wall. Jiji, on the verge of tears, would hang on to my hand and say, "Just say goodbye to my mother-in-law and leave!"

"And how about you? Kakka sent me to fetch you home."

She'd look at me red-eyed and whisper, "Hurry up, you'll miss your bus." And then she'd be soundlessly sobbing and at that I'd burst into tears too. Finally, Brother-in-law would escort me to the bus stop and put me on a bus.

Without speaking to the driver or the conductor, I'd stare out of the window and cry helplessly, and the conductor would come up and ask, "Your sister didn't come? . . . Hey, you're crying?!" And the driver would swivel in his seat to look at me.

I'd pretend to stop crying, ". . . No, its only the wind getting in my eyes." So then all the way back they'd chat animatedly about this and that just to cheer me up.

The moment the bus got to our stop, Kakka came running and with a quick glance around asked, ". . . Where's she . . . what happened?"

"I won't go to Jiji's in-laws ever again. That Indira Gandhi won't let Jiji leave, and Jiji cries a lot . . . She can't even talk to me!" At times like these Kakka would wring his hands and mutter his frustration at Jiji's mother-in-law: ". . . She's hot-tempered, that woman!"

Each time Jiji managed to come home from her in-laws' she'd set about completing what she thought of as pending tasks. She'd teach us sewing, embroidery, knitting. If we made mistakes, she'd slap us around. She'd get us doing our school work. I once had the misfortune of getting what were called supplementary marks, so she sat me down with arithmetic. For every mistake I made she gave me one on the head – she was all geared up to make mincemeat of me! Bai yelled, "Let her be, Asha! Let her go to hell!"

"How can I just let her be? She'll waste a year dawdling this way!"

That evening, I got a half-hour off. It rained heavily. A whole lot of people decided to go in a bus to have a look at the overflowing Kakravade river. "The river's in spate, the river's in spate!" They went off yelling for all they were worth.

Kakka seemed to read my mind and told me to go along with them in the bus. So off I went and enjoyed myself thoroughly being in a crowd.

The river was brimful and all but spilling over. When I got back home Jiji screamed at me and everyone else ribbed me with – "Stop crying now or we'll have a flood inside the house!" And Jiji threatened me – "If you tell Kakka, just you wait and see what I do to you!" Sometimes when she slapped me about over my books I'd pray to God: "Oh God! Please, please let her mother-in-law never allow her to come here, *never*!"

One scene from what became a nightmare later is forever seared in my mind and unfurls in a ripple before my eyes every now and then, specially just when I'm starting to doze off. It is of a time when Kakka had fallen very ill – when he was, as they say, fighting off death. On that Diwali I imagined no dinner being made at home, and a pile of grain from offerings at the temple was all that gave us a little succour.

In my nightmare Sister Number Two, Usha-jiji, ran the dhaba during the time of Kakka's illness. She always wanted me around as support staff. I was barely able to keep my eyes open though she plagued me to stay wide awake. She splashed my face with water every now and then while I howled in bitter rage. So then she tried placating me and offered me some tea. Groggy with sleep, I kept her company. Other times she'd let me sleep on the bench and wake me only if there were customers, or when it was time to lock up and get back home.

Usha-jiji was one large bundle of timidity. She'd hang on to my finger in the dark and run along muttering a mantra under her breath, dragging me with her. The moment we reached home I'd cling to Bai and tell her I didn't want to go to the dhaba with Usha-jiji. Come next morning and there she'd be, dragging me back to the dhaba. And then all day I'd end up serving glasses of water or onions and pickle to customers while Jiji cooked and served. Come evening I'd plan on running back home, but Jiji would offer me what she thought was a deal: "We'll leave early today. I'll say a prayer and it'll drive your sleep away." There was no way Jiji could have kept me awake, or for that matter kept the darkness at bay! She couldn't even drive away my tears, however hard she tried.

Between the dhaba and our home was a red-coloured water tank, positioned just where it was invariably pitch dark. Jiji was scared stiff going past that bit of the road, but if she saw a cow or a buffalo anywhere close she'd walk past without a care. Dogs and bulls scared her stiff, though. Once, half asleep, I was walking along holding Jiji's hand when some pebbles fell on us. At this she began yelling blue murder – "Ghost! Ghost!" – and pulled desperately at me.

A long time later we came to know that some young ruffians had once pestered her. She kept all this kind of stuff hidden from our parents at the time. She spilled the beans about all of it much later, when we were older. At the time, though, Jiji had me petrified by pushing a scary idea into my head: "If you tell anyone about the pebble-throwing, ghosts will come into the house and carry Kakka off."

A long way away from the red water tank was a temple. Running up to it left Jiji panting for breath, so we'd stop when we reached it. After catching her breath she'd enter our house pretending nothing of note had happened en route.

On her wedding night, too, I heard Jiji intone some kind of prayer. She was leaving for her in-laws' after many arguments that had reduced her to tears. Even as she cried, she carried on the incantation under her breath. The wedding presents lay scattered all over the place, and Grandmother and Uncle were rushing around trying to organise things. Even as Uncle did all the running about, he kept one eye on Kakka.

Phupha-ji and Badé Mama-ji wouldn't leave Kakka alone, not for a minute! Chhoté Mama-ji seemed to have forgotten all about smoking and stood in a corner looking downcast and deeply stricken.

Kakka hadn't kept his word with the new in-laws, it appeared – or perhaps I should say since he hadn't the means he hadn't been able to keep his word. So Usha-jiji's in-laws were livid: "We're taking the girl off your hands but we'll have nothing to do with you," they said.

The bridegroom's party left around midnight, having partaken of precisely nothing. The first time Jiji was allowed to come back home was after two whole years of married life.

Asha-jiji and Usha-jiji tried keeping their tears hidden when speaking of their in-laws to Bai, who cursed the lot: "People of culture don't think this way of their daughter-in-laws' parents! A curse on them!"

Kakka had let Asha-jiji stay on in school till she was in Class 8. He'd wanted Usha-jiji to do her B.A. privately, but Usha-jiji hadn't wanted to carry on that far. Why she hadn't has always remained an unsolved mystery. Well, since it's never spoken of, where's the question of it being solved? Anytime anyone raised the subject, Jiji would blush and say: "Where's the need to bring up that rubbish, tell me? I need to understand it myself. What's the point chattering away about it for no rhyme or reason, eh?"

And as for Sister Number Three – Anni, a.k.a. the Buffalo – she simply wasn't ever interested in the world of scholarship, which is putting it mildly. All day she'd be out herding buffaloes. Asha-jiji would sit her down to study but she never could make her progress beyond a chapter called "Abbu Khan ki Bakri". That chapter defeated something deep inside her, it was the end of the road in her head. Hours of toil, and at the end of them all she could mutter was "Chapter 5, Abbu Khan ki Bakri". That was it. It was a chapter in her life and there was nothing more to be said about it. We'd all burst out laughing and she'd head straight off to sleep, exhausted by her effort.

Anni was married over a simple wedding during the rains to a chap from Barkhera village. The bridegroom's party sat all night in the verandah. We little girls tried feeding the bridegroom paan with red chilli in it, but he wasn't going to be tricked into having any of it!

Before she left for her in-laws', Asha-jiji explained a lot of the important facts of life to Anni: such as how she should live in her new home. What she should do. How softly she ought to speak. That she should remain silent as a tomb and not shoot her mouth off to anybody and everybody.

"Get up at four every morning," she said, "And sip your tea daintily. Don't slurp it noisily. Eat nothing that looks like you're gorging, that'll make it seem like you're from a house full of gluttons. Stay hungry, but don't ever stuff your mouth. And when you eat papad, eat it quietly. Don't crunch it."

Anni stared at Asha-jiji round-eyed: "How'm I supposed to eat papad without crunching it?"

Jiji gave up. "Anni," she thundered, "Don't eat papad at all, O.K.? Or you'll disgrace us all."

She had a long list up her sleeve and went on. "Remain in purdah. Touch everyone's feet, left, right, and centre. Bai-in-law's sister's feet, mother-in-law's sister-in-law's feet." Then she gave a lecture on how she should comport herself with all the village women who visited.

As Anni was leaving there was much lightning and torrential rain. She clung to Kakka and wept. It was as if the heavens wept with her.

After a while the rain stopped. But not Kakka. The morning's parting from his daughter had ruined the night's fun and frolic.

3

IN CLASS, ONE DAY, Saxena Behen-ji called me: "Come up here. Kiran . . ." – that was Anni's official name – ". . . has got married, has she? What does your brother-in-law do?"

I hung my head and played with a shirt button. "He has a kiosk selling toffees and biscuits and does a bit of farming."

"O.K. And where's Kiran? Here, or at her in-laws'?"

"She's here at home . . . at the moment."

"Tell her I want to see her. Tell her to come by to my place."

I nodded and went primly back to my seat, feeling puffed up with grandeur at Behen-ji having singled me out. For days I went around with a swollen head, looking down at my friends!

Anni's husband Gajendra Singh – my brother-in-law – could often be seen at the bus stand looking wistfully in the direction of the dhaba. I'd run across to him and he'd offer me toffees and biscuits. I'd shake my head in refusal and he'd say, "Give them to somebody at home." Sometimes he'd give me a paan to eat and another to take home. I'd often insist that he come home but he'd shoo me off with a "Not today. Tomorrow!"

Finally, one day, I managed to get him to come home. All the way to our place I was brimming over with the anticipation of how Bai and everyone else would be delighted to see me bring home a trophy. What happened was the exact opposite. It was like a snake had bitten everybody when he walked through the door. Asha-jiji gnashed her teeth and pulled me aside by my plait and hissed, "Why have you brought him here?" Bai held her head and cried, "There's no money in the house and the son-in-law has arrived for his First Visit. How'll the welcoming ceremony be done?"

After thinking through the havoc I'd wrought, Bai got up and went over to an aunt who lived opposite us. In a short while Bai and Asha-jiji, their heads decorously covered, brought water and tea to felicitate Brother-in-law.

He refused the invitation to dinner and cast sidelong glances in my direction. Anni sat there looking at me, smug and smiling, much like Goddess Lakshmi in the calendar. Bai put the required vermilion mark on Jija-ji's forehead, touched his feet, and presented him eleven rupees plus a coconut.

Brother-in-law said, "Come on Babli, I'll drop you off at the shop." All the way there I sat quietly on his cycle bar and didn't once twiddle the bell.

"So, how did that go off? You can see why I refused all those times."

"*Tring-tring-tring*!" Brother-in-law was vigorously working the bell.

Asha-jiji and Bai told Kakka the whole story. "He's as stupid as she is," she said, ". . . turning up uninvited, without giving us the chance to work out an auspicious time. Their whole village is full of utterly stupid people."

Kakka, chewing on a betel nut, looked at me and laughed out loud, "Why, you silly fool! Come, come and sit by me. The whole lot of you are being really hard on her! What does she know of this nonsense? Come on, make me some tea." Kakka had small white teeth. He was laughing delightedly through them. Watching him laugh, Bai and Asha-jiji smiled reluctantly – just about.

Anni was packed off to her in-laws' after a simple ceremony. Every three or four days I'd spot Brother-in-law at the bus stand and run to ask, "How's our Anni?" He'd smile: "How come you aren't asking me to come home today?"

All was going well when, suddenly one day, we heard Brother-in-law had disappeared. We waited a few days, after which Kakka put me on the bus to Barkhera. I found Anni sitting in purdah by her mother-in-law, head bent low. The mother-in-law was crying. She carried on weeping and gently comforting Anni. She fiddled with Anni's bangles and sighed like a willow. The day we were to catch our bus back, Anni's brother-in-law, Bhawani, was home. Anni signalled to me and handed me a bowl to give him. The moment he saw it, he bristled: "Listen, this ghastly gruel your sister's made! What's your mother taught her? She can't even make decent porridge?"

Had my brother-in-law run away because my sister couldn't make porridge?

On the balcony, Anni was very quiet.

I said, "Asha-jiji can teach you how to make a decent porridge." She held my hand and made me swear I wouldn't breathe a word to anyone at home about her "gruelling" time. Particularly not to Kakka.

A whole year later, one fine day, the brother-in-law showed up back home. He declared with a sneer on his face, "What's in this village for anyone?"

He'd changed completely and was full of tales about films. It was as if he'd brought Diwali with him. He knew the whole script of *Muqqaddar ka Sikandar* by heart. We sat around him and when he started reciting it was like the film was playing before our eyes. He'd found work in a cloth mill in Aurangabad and was back only so he could take Anni away with him.

Bai tied up a bundle of things to go with them: papad, pickle, flour, rice. She was worried over Anni being such a simpleton. "How'll she live alone in that big unknown city?" she moaned. The more she thought about it, the more worried she grew.

Brother-in-law took Anni away in a train. They'd be in that train the next two and a half days. We all trooped off to the railway station with Kakka. Anni was happy, but she was also weeping copiously. Brother-in-law glowed in a green shirt and dark glasses. Every now and then he said grandly, "What, What!" How shiny he looked!

The train began to move. He kept waving at us for a long while and then yelled, "Babli! O Babli! Next time we'll take you too!" I jumped up and down and waved wildly back. That day he looked like a regular film hero. For as long as we could see them, we stood there watching.

After the train left, the empty rail track seemed strangely unsettling. It felt like the train had left the track bereft – as bereft as Kakka. We'd never seen him look so forlorn. We'd seen Anni laughing at the train window, but it hadn't stopped Kakka's eyes welling up. Walking off fast, he left us all trailing behind. The train had left, but it felt like we were waiting there to will it back home.

Brother-in-law wrote to us off and on; Anni of course couldn't. We'd take turns reading his letters and Bai listened to each of us read each of them. God alone knows how many times those letters were read. One letter announced: "It's time for her delivery."

I had no clue what that meant. I read the letter many times but still couldn't figure out the meaning of that phrase. I trotted off to Kakka, who was sitting and gossiping with his friends on his takht. I stood quiet awhile, then took him aside.

"There's a letter from Brother-in-law. I can't make out what it says. You read it."

How the meaning of the word "delivery" dawned on me, I don't now recall. Maybe he said something to his friends and I caught on. The letter found its way into Kakka's vest pocket.

Jija-ji and Anni returned, Anni was being dropped off to deliver. Bai grumbled constantly about their ways. "For God's sake! What kind of made-in-heaven match is this? Both of them are such spendthrifts!"

Anni stayed home with her baby and awaited Jija-ji's return. Months later, Jija-ji came back once more, all the way from Aurangabad. We all thought he'd now go to their village – but no way! He'd now begun to speak in city slang. Bai tried to insinuate reform into his ear, but he responded sweetly: "Are we to destroy our lives living with the same twenty or twenty-five people around us and longing for the good things of life? When one uses soap and oil and dresses well, one's whole village laughs. There's no hospital in our village, in fact there's not one in the seven villages around! There are whole village clusters without hospitals. At the block headquarters there's that one school and one measly dispensary. When they open, when they close, who knows . . ."

Jija-ji was great at delivering monologues such as this. He followed them up with a strange *khu-khu* sound through his nose. "*Khu-khu* – see, Bai, our whole village is supposed to be treated by this one man, and the fellow's not even a compounder! He's learnt to give injections and dispense medicines just anyhow . . . and he's become our doctor! The whole village tries keeping him happy. If he's away, everyone with any kind of illness looks to the nearest town out of sheer desperation. What's the point in us coming into town every two or three days? Far better to just live in town. Most folks who live in the village have to keep getting to town for their supplies . . .

"*Khu-khu-khu* . . . I know one thing for sure, village life's pointless. It needs to end. Half the people in the world get to love life in town and the other half rot away in some village. People in town get stomach aches when they hear what our village life's like. What village life *is* there to speak of, anyhow? I know one thing for sure, Bai – those who sing the praises of village life should be made to settle in a village. Live in a village, Buddy, then you'll see how much you'll enjoy the life there! *Khu-khu-khu* . . . think about it, Bai. We're illiterate. At least in town our children will get an education. In the village, they'd grow up cowherds. There's only one village headman, plus a couple of big farmers. Not everyone can become big . . . for the rest, Bai, the village means a living death. One feels throttled just lying there on the balcony. How's anyone expected to spend all day in those fields? Plus . . . *khu-khu-khu* . . . village homes are dark and spooky. When the weather's cold, there's not a ray of sun on my balcony, Bai! I long for the winter sunshine . . . well, it's a mercy we men manage to go outdoors and take in some sun, but our poor women . . . Summer or winter, life's one long misery for them, *khu-khu* . . ."

He glanced sideways at Anni. She was staring open-mouthed at Bai.

Poor Bai. What could she say to that mile-long monologue? She only managed to squeak, "Hey, we're village folk too! We didn't arrive here from Bombay, you know!"

But Kakka lost his cool and rounded on his son-in-law: "Why, if you dislike being in the village, did you come back from Aurangabad? You should just have stayed there. You talk big, my friend, but you're frightened of hard work even at your age! Is this the time to be living off your folk? Your grandfather and great-grandfather may have managed, but in this day and age who's going to bother about you, eh? You want village folk to be ministering to your needs before their own? Come on, tell me, explain to me why you find the village so insufferable. My friend, will the city feed you just for sitting around in it? You know how to talk, but not how to *do*. All you do is strut around like some hotshot."

Jija-ji held his tongue, not even letting out a feeble *khu-khu*. But I could tell he was staring, eyes narrowed, at Kakka.

Another Jija-ji, the one from Kagpur, a.k.a. Jijaji-married-to-Asha-jiji, on the other hand, far from staring at father, never dared come anywhere near him. He chatted a lot with Bai, but with Kakka he was very cautiously deferential. Bai doted on him – the moment he arrived she'd blossom and bloom like a jasmine flower.

"So, the Barkherawallas are not returning home to Aurangabad now?" Asha-jiji, having stirred the pot, continued: "Thirteen years gone, and these ne'er-do-wells haven't a rupee to their names. Turned up with empty pockets! They may be sweet and simple-looking, but can they talk big! The moment their kids are grown, they land up here to plonk them on our heads. Think about it, Bai. We're the ones who'll have to settle their offspring. They're trying to make out as if only *their* land's been eaten up because of being endlessly divided and subdivided. Anyway, why's that a reason to raise such a storm? In the old days, every household in every village had no dearth of fields to plough. Now you can count large farmers on the fingers of one hand. Every second farmer's a small landowner, they're all running their households on pathetic incomes. It's people with *attitude* that're going to make one village emptier than the next. And who can't see that no-one becomes a sahib the moment they go off to live in a town?"

Asha-jiji was all wound up. Her annoyance cascaded down as an unbroken and uninterruptible waterfall. "*Arré* wasn't our land eaten up too? Our share just about exists . . . so, are we running away? Big hotshots they think they are! The way they talk, you'd think they went off to a town to open a jewellery store! And are villages supposed to just disappear because they say so? *Arré*, I'd sooner wish them worms in their mouths to stop them spouting nonsense . . . They just about own the clothes on their backs. But can they talk big!"

And Bai? She'd get a splitting headache.

Kakka got Jija-ji a shop close by on rent, and in this shop Jija-ji started a tea stall. The shop was near the law courts, so it did quite well, but of course Jija-ji wanted a swankier life. Being the happy-go-lucky sort, he'd developed a jaunty style of being. One day, he shut his tea shop at eight in the evening. Strolling along in his rakish manner while chewing paan, a cigarette between his fingers, he showed up at the dhaba and made himself comfortable. Surprised by his arrival, I said "*Arré!* You shut your shop *this* early!"

"Yeah! Why? You think I sit there all night?"

"At least keep it open till ten or eleven!"

"*Khu-khu* . . . what's the point when the milk's run out?"

"When did the milk run out?"

"At seven."

"You could've got more milk if the sales were going well . . ."

Irritated, he snapped his fingers and pulled for long at his cigarette. "What's the point of all this hard work?" he muttered. "Everything's going to get left behind here anyway. The more money one has, the more the nuisance. We came empty-handed, we'll go empty-handed. Don't think everyone in the world's like your father, willing to hang around till twelve at night in the hope of getting maybe one more last customer! Tell me, how many customers have you had in here so far? Eh? And your father's happy to stick around till midnight for *this* . . . there are all sorts . . . for some folks it's the done thing to just hang around waiting for a customer or two to show up! Babli, believe me, the time's not far when there's not even going to be one or two!"

Showing off, strutting about, he let fly countless such freewheeling hot-air homilies.

Jija-ji was all that Kakka was not. He wouldn't open his shop even on festivals, and there were times when he wouldn't open it even on a Sunday. Then, inevitably, he took to gambling. He sold off the little land he'd inherited as his share. It resulted in a lot of weeping and wailing and gnashing of teeth back home.

"He's left nothing for the kids. Why are we blessed with such relatives?"

If Bai had had her way, she'd have thrashed Jija-ji. On that particular day, Anni too had it in for her husband. "You haven't a rupee to your name now! My father didn't deserve a son-in-law like you . . . God knows what went wrong with his brains when he married me off to you."

"*Arré!* Your father married his daughter into a family of landlords. Just watch, soon I'm going to be the owner of a massive farm . . . we'll live in style in town, in a house of our own."

"Oh I see! And gambling's how you plan to make it happen? When's gambling done anything except ruin a man? It's going to make you bankrupt! Do you hear? *Bankrupt!*" When Anni spoke in anger, her eyebrows twitched bewitchingly.

The moment his land was sold, Jija-ji closed shop, took to full-time mooching, and developed himself as a professional layabout. His son Vijay re-started their shop. Debtors began appearing with threats – the milkman, the sugar seller, the kerosene supplier, and heaven knows who else that Jija-ji had taken stuff off against IOUs. After a bit, looking tired and woebegone, his son closed shop too. This did nothing to stop Jija-ji's gambling. It continued. One by one, things began disappearing from their house. And then, one day, Jija-ji himself disappeared.

Months later, he fetched up. This time he said he'd got a job in a factory far away, beyond Raipur. And again Anni was meant to be leaving with him. Bai ranted at Kakka when Kakka was safely elsewhere: "To hell with this fellow! His kids are all going to sit on my head! No place to live, no means of livelihood . . . Oh God, why don't You just carry me off . . ."

All day she went around cursing her luck.

Asha-jiji packed daal, flour, and papad for Anni. With eyes sore from crying, she explained a couple of things in earnest: "Learn how to save money; you have a bad habit of sponging."

"You don't get it, Sister! If I work and save, he'll never be able to give up gambling. He'll never do anything else if I earn. He'll just sit and eat and gamble away everything I have. You haven't a notion of his habits. He's just a complete and utter wastrel."

Simple-minded, guileless Anni, who'd never got beyond "Abbu Khan ki Bakri", had somehow managed to teach none other than Asha-jiji about there being more things in heaven and earth than were dreamt of in her philosophy.

Asha-jiji never said anything against our ancestral village. Early each morning she'd make cowpats, look after cows, and work like a spinning top all day long, even at the height of summer. She'd wear a long piece of cloth that protected her from the sun and shuttle between her in-laws' and our parents' home. Always in purdah, she was riddled with prickly heat. When home, if she so much as went to the toilet twice in the course of a day, Bai warned her of the importance of bladder control: "Asha, don't go in there in the afternoons. If you get into the habit, what'll you do when you're back at your in-laws'?"

In the village, Asha-jiji would go off to do her stuff really early in the morning, out in the open, and then get back to sleep for an hour or an hour and a half. Our neighbour watched her routine open-mouthed and regularly asked Jiji, her mouth gawping like a cavern: "Hey! How d'you manage to get back to sleep afterwards?"

Over the four months of the rainy season we'd have no news of Jiji. Only when she was back home with us could she breathe easy. Was it possible – though she'd never have admitted it – that somewhere deep within she too really longed to live in a town?

And Usha-jiji? She was the other sister who got her full quota of sleep only when she came back home. When she arrived it was like she became Kumbhakaran, impossible to wake. She slept like she'd never been allowed sleep by her in-laws.

And what of Anni, stuck with a romantic wanderer of a husband? A man neither fish nor fowl, neither villager nor citizen. God knows what world he belonged to, what doors he went knocking on. By the time Anni was able to come to terms with the opening and closing of one set of doors, he'd be off knocking on others. And knocking on doors with no latches, that needed neither opening nor closing.

Having seen the state Asha-jiji, Usha-jiji, and Anni were in, Kakka decided he'd think no further of marrying off the five of us that remained, at least not for the time being. He'd first make us work at our books, have us stand on our own feet, work. He'd never tie us girls down like cattle tethered to a stake. No!

4

SCHOOL TIMINGS WERE from seven in the morning to noon. One day the teacher announced: "From now on, you must all bring your tiffin to school, and during the recess we'll all sit and eat together. It'll be great fun!"

The girls shrieked in delight, "Yes, Yes! It'll be great fun!"

But we sisters weren't all that delighted. We managed without taking tiffin for a day or two. The girls all sat in a circle giggling and laughing, not really eating. We'd wait for them to finish and then join them in the playground. But our friends wouldn't let us be. "Share our stuff today," they said, "and remember to bring yours tomorrow."

"Oh, we don't feel hungry. We normally don't eat at this time and sometimes we eat and come." God knows how many excuses we made in quavering voices.

But Shiva wanted a way out of these daily unending arguments, so she thought up a stratagem. She got up early in the morning, took the rotis from the previous night's dinner, put them on the griddle, and re-heated them with a drop of oil – almost no oil in fact. She made the rotis so crunchy that no-one would be able to see them as mere rotis, they'd think them parathas. There was no tiffin-carrier in the house, so God knows where she found one part of that contraption and put the rotis in it along with some pickle.

I'd go off to Shiva's class and eat with her friends, and they'd say, "Shivani! What's this you've brought?" They'd eat from our tiffin and we from theirs. Shiva would look thrilled and smile at me with an air of triumph: "See what magic I've wrought!" she seemed to say.

Getting tiffin to school was an order, but bringing plain roti as tiffin was virtually a sin. Some of the girls brought parathas, one brought poha, another papri, one arrived with khurma, and some even brought in poori-halwa.

One day, after the tiffin break got over, I went back to my class and saw all the girls sitting and eating in a circle except one: she was sitting in a corner, hiding what she was eating, while the other girls strained to see what she had.

"Oh, she's got rotis, she's got rotis!"

The girl crouched in a corner and swallowed her rotis with her tears. I thought for a moment that I should tell her Shiva's stratagem, but then I was scared off by the thought that our secret would be out – and then what would become of us?

Oh my countrymen, shed tears
And remember the sacrifices of our martyrs.

When a loudspeaker boomed out this song annually on every Republic Day and Independence Day, we'd get poha and halwa for breakfast. Bai made excellent poha. On these two days Kakka would wake us up early, tell us to have our baths quick, and we'd get to school after wolfing down the poha and the halwa. After the National Anthem and Vande Mataram, there'd be morning prayers, and then "We shall Overcome". Clutching laddoos, we'd be off running back home. There we'd feed Bai a laddoo, and singing "We Shall Overcome", feed Kakka one as well. The rest of the year we had no breakfast. The only daytime meal we knew was lunch.

But Kakka understood our aspirations and attempted with all his might to support us. Possibly because of this, for our school uniform he got a cotton skirt stitched for each of us, and to go with it a terrycot shirt. "Wash them daily and fold and put them under the pillow," he said to Bai. Apart from the annual school uniform, he never failed to get all of us sisters a set of new clothes every year.

Anupma Somaiya was the daughter of a prosperous merchant. Everyone had school bags, but she had an aluminium box. It was a beautiful little box we all desperately coveted. She was a great friend of mine. Because of that box, a few other girls began bringing boxes rather than bags to school. I said to Kakka, "Can't you get us boxes like Anupma's?" He muttered something which culminated in "Not this year, next year." One time, when I raised the subject again, he said, "If you come first in class, I'll get you a box."

Anupma was very good at her books. She always came first. She wore beautiful clothes. She was getting tuitions.

I told Kakka all this and more about her: Anupma has this, Anupma has that. "Her books have yellow and khaki paper covers; they have bright-coloured stickers on them; she has a lot of notebooks; every Saturday she wears new clothes. Kakka, get me tuition. Then like her I'll come first!"

Kakka, never wanting when it came to a retort, said: "*Arré*, get a first division without tuitions! That's the thing to do."

Despite this, I managed to convince Kakka that this time round I'd get my clothes from Somaiya Seth's shop. Normally, we were taken to Kakka's favourite establishment, where he had a buy-now-pay-later arrangement, but he agreed to the Somaiya Seth shop on condition it would be just this once. I had to swear it was a one-off request and I wouldn't ask again.

We went to Somaiya Seth's to buy clothes. I couldn't find anything I liked. Kakka laughed and said, "Seth-ji, show us the clothes your daughter wears! *Arré* Seth, have a heart! Children copy each other, they're children after all! Our status isn't up there with yours, Seth-ji! So why show us down, my friend?"

I felt terrible. Really terrible. Back home I fought with Kakka. "Why did you have to say all that to him? He'll tell Anupma and what will she think of us then? From now I'm never going to tell you a thing. You just go off blabbing it to everyone!" I sobbed as I spoke.

Kakka only laughed it off and Bai muttered under her breath, "So, go on sending them to school! If they hang around with the daughters of wealthy merchants, what else d'you expect?" Then she turned on me and yelled, "And why can't you hang out with your own kind of girls, eh?"

"But Kakka also hangs around with bigwigs. They all come to the dhaba. Is Kakka a lawyer? Ask him, come on, ask him! So why does he talk for hours with Lawyer Uncle about court matters? We don't have any land but he still asks everyone about the harvest. Hey, Brother, what price did your daal and wheat go for?" I was so angry, I was mimicking Kakka.

Kakka laughed even louder, while Bai was livid. She banged the teapot on the floor: "If you're going to follow in your Kakka's footsteps, you'll spend your life weeping! You'll be carrying cowdung the rest of your life!"

I squealed, "Kakka!"

Bai continued to grind her teeth but didn't stop. "Arrogant family! If you weren't so arrogant I wouldn't have had to suffer days like this. It's arrogance that's consumed your whole family! Arrogance!" Seeing her enraged, Kakka's face fell.

Bai's anger surfaced every time Grandfather's antics came knocking on the doors of her memory. She could never get over the fact that Grandfather once had a huge amount of land in Sargauda village. All fertile land.

It was the time of the British Raj and, one day, a village revenue official arrived to collect the land tax. Grandfather fell into an argument with the fellow over the tax payable, and then, unable to tolerate his demands, got into a temper and slapped him. The result was that all the land he owned was confiscated and auctioned. And along with the land their house, their cattle, and all their moveable and immoveable assets. All auctioned.

At the end of which the only thing Grandfather was left in possession of was his arrogance.

Grandmother fainted, took to her bed, and never got out of it again.

With Kakka and my aunt on his shoulders, Grandfather then set off on foot. With the loss of his land, Sargauda village was lost to us. Grandfather walked somewhere between forty and fifty kilometres to his in-laws' village, Magakar, and never once put Kakka and our aunt down the whole way. But there was still no end to Grandfather's arrogance and Grandmother's grief.

Kakka came over from where they lived to the small town we're in now when he was about twelve, maybe fourteen. He began work as a porter in an oil mill. For two years he made rotis for himself under a tree on a makeshift fire and dried his towel on branches. He slept the nights in a cart over all that time. When the oil mill owner rented him a room, Grandfather, Grandmother, and Phapphu came over too. Even now, Phapphu often gently caresses Kakka's porter's back. From working as a porter, Kakka graduated to becoming headman of the mill for many years.

At some point later he started serving tea at the station and opened a sweet shop at Jai Stambh Chauraha. Grandfather grew into being his assistant by just sitting at the shop. The auctioning off of his land had left Grandfather with nothing to live on. Big hefty Grandfather was a broken man once his land went.

A few years later Kakka rented out his shop and took to selling country liquor in Masudpur, Rasoolpur, Baghrod, Harnakheri, and Masaur. He went bankrupt in this line of business. Finally, he dropped everything else he had going and opened his dhaba off the bus stand. The failed liquor business and the auctioned land were both taboo subjects, never brought up at home because even just the mention of them got Bai into a deep depression. "If we had the land today, why would our children be sitting in the bazaar and why would they be washing the used utensils of people of other castes? If the land hadn't been auctioned, Kakka would have been the proud owner of acres of fertile land."

Bai's sighs were long and heartfelt and invariably affected us as well. At Rakshabandhan, Kakka would buy eight simple strings. After a potato-poori-raita brunch he'd give us a four-anna coin and say, "Go get yourselves toffees from Munna's, you lot!" Our little brother demanded a toffee from out of that four-anna coin, but then he was the winner at every Rakshabandhan! All day he'd run around showing off, "Look! one, two, three, and here – all eight!"

He was bound to be a winner because no other boy in the vicinity had more than three or four rakhis displayed on his wrist. One time the neighbour Nisha tied a huge rakhi on the wrist of her only brother Karthik and they roamed around showing off the rakhi, which was made out of some kind of sponge and fake fivers tied to it on all four sides. That was some rakhi! It cost them a whole fiver.

For the first time, our Rakshabandhan was ruined. "The day we get hold of this fiver-laden rakhi, just you watch – both arms of our lil-brother are going to be covered!" Our stratagem was to tie the eight strings far apart from each other so that at least half his arm was taken care of, but not even that got us over the fact that Nisha had, with just one rakhi, managed to cover half her brother's arm!

The day after Rakshabandhan, the girls in school showed off their new clothes and told everyone how much cash they'd collected from their brothers. So and so Brother gave this, so and so Brother gave that; we did this, we did that. We really had fun etc., etc.

For some years we tolerated this tall talk. Then I just stopped going to school the day after Rakshabandhan and Diwali. We didn't get new clothes, not even at Diwali, and got gifted just a few crackers to burst, and even those were the cheap ones. How'd we talk about our festivities?

What would we say? That we loved Holi more? That the colours of Holi never failed to brighten our lives!?

And then there were days when the girls from school sauntered past the dhaba. What days those days turned out to be! If we spotted a girl, however far, we'd drop whatever it was we were up to and hide. Just thinking of what the girls would say if they saw us slaving in the dhaba would make us break into a sweat. Once, I happened to be serving food and Shiva was at the oven bellows and Kakka was making rotis. Neither of us sisters had gone to school that day. Girls from our school were walking past: Shiva dropped the bellows and crouched on the floor, pretending to play Ludo, while I hid behind the dhaba. Customers were yelling for rotis and Kakka shouted for me. I served them reluctantly, worried all the time I'd be spotted. I messed up the orders, serving one thing when another was asked for, forgetting to count the number of rotis eaten, who'd had which vegetable, who'd been served extra ghee, who extra onions, who papad, who'd had what extras – all the accounting went into a spin.

Customers fussed over paying up. Even after it was all over, I was breathing heavily, nervous as hell.

"Kakka, I feel very embarrassed. What if the girls from school or a teacher see us? The girls will really get after us. It's embarrassing for us to get to school all dress-ed up and then work at a dhaba. Kakka, either we go to school or we work with you in the dhaba. It's got be one or the other."

Was Kakka about to listen? He came towards me, tongs in hand. "Tell me, who exactly is going to come after you? Tell me. I'll come straight to your school. I'll talk to her father and to your teacher."

Of course, this was no solution to our embarrassment. Things came to a head when the sports tournament was held at the school. Various girls had come in from nearby towns to participate, and though I didn't compete in any of the sports events, I was heavily into hooting. For eight or ten of us, the main thing was to somehow make our school win by booing all our rivals so thoroughly that they'd be stymied while running and throwing their javelins and whatever else they were meant to succeed in doing. The result, however, was that all the hullabaloo and the raucous laughter led to a pitched battle. Things became so bad they almost reached the school principal.

Not even that stopped us continuing to create chaos by hollering with all our might. Soon, various girls recognised me and began pointing at me as the chief instigator of mischief. They pointed me out from a distance to their teacher: "There, there, that's the girl who's bothering us the most."

The day's sporting events ended and the school shut. We hung around for a while and, after planning strategies for the next day, proceeded home. When I approached the dhaba, instead of feeling happy, for some reason I began to feel like weeping. I couldn't go home, nor would my legs take me in the direction of the dhaba.

I hid behind a bus and from a distance watched the dhaba and Kakka and a few girls standing by him. Kakka looked like he was waiting for me. I wanted desperately to turn into a magician – into a wizard so adept that I'd make those girls disappear in a flash! And with them the school, the sports tournament, the bus stand, the town. I'd make the whole lot vanish into thin air. My magic would be of such magnitude that even Kakka and the dhaba . . .

Just at that moment Pappu, the rickshawalla, spotted me in my hiding place. "*Arré*, I was going to your house! Come on, hurry up! Your Kakka is calling for you. There's a huge crowd at the dhaba. What're you doing standing there? Can't you see how worried your Kakka's looking?"

I dragged myself to the dhaba and was going to run to its rear when the girls spotted me and laughed out loud. Kakka understood the whole mystery. He caught hold of my hand and took me to them.

"She's the one who's been bothering you, right?"

"Yes-yes !" they all shouted.

Their teacher laughed too: they were probably discussing it all before my appearance. Our school hadn't topped in any of the sports events and these girls were far ahead of us. Kakka said to me, "*Arré*, what's the point mocking them? Show what you can do on the sports field! That's what counts!"

At this the girls began yelling and screaming about their triumphs in the tournament. For a moment I thought this wasn't a dhaba, it sounded like the school playground, but I kept my mouth shut. Kakka brought us together in friendship: "Don't rib them any more," he said. "They're our guests. Don't ruin our town's reputation, my dear. Come on, come on, let me know who wants to eat what . . ."

They got so comfortable with Kakka and the dhaba they even began drawing the drinking water. For the next week they ate at the dhaba, and some of them started helping me serve customers. While they were there it was as if the dhaba belonged to them. When too many customers showed up, Kakka shooed them off: "Come after an hour or so! Can't you see, these girls are here right now. Don't hang around. Go on, move on!"

It was over this sports tournament that I managed to rid myself of the scourge of shame and embarrassment over my link with the dhaba. The episode trumped my shame. I stayed unsure, though, whether I'd scripted my own victory or whether Kakka had turned a lost cause in my favour.

He was just such a cheerful and large-hearted man, friends with a lot of well-off folk in the town, yet maintaining his reserve and mixing with them only when an important meeting or a wedding required his presence in their midst. Mostly he couldn't leave the dhaba, so a lot of his socialising and meeting took place at the dhaba. Big farmers, small farmers, poor farmers, really poor farmers, worn-at-heel farmers, really worn-at-heel farmers – all would be in attendance. Farming, relationships, monsoon or drought, good harvest or bad harvest, often it was as if his dhaba was the local town hall.

I don't really know why, but every second person in our little town liked coming to Kakka with their troubles and their woes. What's more, they liked following his advice. Which was also what Kakka expected from us. It was mixed up with his not wanting to see us deprived, or wanting for anything at all. And by ensuring each one of us attended school his status got a boost too. Running a dhaba well, especially with the help of his daughters, and supporting a large family single-handed, Kakka considered himself special and never worried about sounding boastful when proclaiming to all and sundry: "*Arré!* Look at me! Look at my kids!"

Which was also why there were no employees in his dhaba. We did all the work. His view of the matter was: "If we pay employees, what'll be left for us? *Arré*, either we eat or we pay an employee!"

As time passed the dhaba became the focus of our lives as well. How and when this happened I can't say, but it is connected in my recollection to the time we started going to school with a swagger, when we were able to smile at any girl who happened to be going from school past the dhaba – what's more, sometimes we'd even stop them for a chat!

Come peak summer, the school exams started. Kakka kept a caring eye on us: over those stressful times he did all the dhaba work himself. We'd totter home after an exam and head straight for the dhaba, he'd spot us from afar and yell, "*Arré*, you're back? How did your paper go?"

"Good! Very good!"

Sometimes it was embarrassing to talk this way with folk around, listening. If we made a move to assist him by picking up the tongs or the rolling pin, Kakka would hand us a four-anna coin: "Go off first, have a cold drink or cane juice or whatever you feel like!" Once, he got us lassi to drink, its taste lingering for days on my tongue and in my mind. He guessed we liked lassi best, so he'd get ice and then, using a portion of milk, pour a whole lot of water into a glass and beat the concoction into a froth for us to guzzle. Then, one or the other of us would be off home bearing lassi for Bai, Kakka's advice ringing in our ears: "*Arré*, stupid, take it easy! Don't run, else . . ." – followed by his laugh.

During these days of our exams, Bai was handed a headache: she had to give us regular doses of tea to stop us dozing off while studying late into the night after a stint at the dhaba, and if we looked like we were nodding off she had to yell and wake us up. "Bai, wake us up at four," we'd yell back, and fall into a deep slumber. She had a hard time getting us awake again. Once, she woke me up a bit sternly. Rubbing my eyes, book in hand, I went to Kakka and said plaintively, "She's very hard on us when she wakes us up. I don't feel like studying when she's this cruel."

Kakka said to Bai: "Don't ruin their mood during exam time! . . . It spoils their work rhythm . . ." She smouldered with irritation at this, and then Kakka grew fiery and yelled at her. "You'll remain an idiot, you illiterate! Why can you never understand simple things? The children are working day and night, and you . . .?"

This got her into a deadly sulk. The next day was my English exam but she didn't wake me for it at all. When I got up at a quarter to seven, I began hollering, "Bai, Bai! Oh Bai, why didn't you wake me up?" She didn't say a word, just stared at me.

Without tea, after just about splashing my face, I scurried to school. Kakka let Bai have another mouthful. She kept her temper, but when Asha-jiji came over next she caught hold of me: "Hey, you! You think your Bai's your servant? Just because you work at the dhaba doesn't mean you get to push everyone around. You better be worried about your papers, I'm not about to do your worrying for you. And next time you go tattling to Kakka . . ."

Jiji, taut with anger, carried on from where Bai had left off. "I say, Bai," she snorted, "working at the dhaba has given them airs. It's become a real problem in this house: I know it's difficult without them working in the dhaba, but they're growing up and how they're going to be married is beyond me."

"To hell with it! Are these children? No, they're the result of the sins of my past life! And as for Babli, your

Kakka has got her dancing on the tops of our heads. Mark my words, Asha, I'm saying this to you today: she's going to give us grief and give her Kakka grief, and we'll all come to grief. This girl's ways are the worst of anyone's in the house!"

So the situation was that Bai hadn't woken me up on the day of my English paper, and now salt was being rubbed in my wound by the grinding of her teeth each time she noticed my existence.

Meanwhile the exams were still in full swing. I was troubled day and night by my English paper having gone badly. Kakka understood my feeling and tried cheering me up to keep my spirits going. My friends would rib me with "What's happened has happened. Now focus on the future and box your pillow five times so you wake up exactly at five in the morning!" I did not find this specially amusing, but they did, to a point where they felt the need to sing out loud:

Oh dear, Oh dear!
You and us,
The lot of us,
All done in by English!
Let's all murder this English.

And then everyone cursed English and yelled, "What's happened has happened."

Once, through this period of English bashing, we found ourselves stuck in a traffic jam: broken-down trucks, bullock carts, rickshaws, hand-pulled carts, cycles, motorcycles, and us in their middle! We felt quite chuffed at there being traffic jams in our little corner of the woods. And then two in our group, Dharmila and Parveen, suddenly burst out laughing and clutching their stomachs squealed, "Look, look quick at what's written on that truck . . ." Painted on a ramshackle truck ahead were the words:

WHAT'S HAPPENED HAS HAPPENED

That little reflective remark on the back of a truck gave us much succour and peace of mind. "What's happened has happened, my friend!"

English was part of our curriculum from Class 6 to Class 11. When we were in Class 6 we learnt how to spell the word "car". What happened was that the teacher said we must learn the spellings on a list of words, and then asked the class monitor to test us all. Some of the words were infernally long and there we were, in one voice, the entire class, cramming spellings. Then, when the class monitor stood up to test us, the master made us shut our textbooks. Those who spelt a word right could sit down, but anyone who got it wrong had to stand in a corner. I was the first to be tested and was lucky enough to be asked the spelling of "car". In a fit of excitement and over-enthusiasm I cried: "C . . . a . . . – *car, car*!" Instead of completing the word by saying "r", I completed it by saying "car".

So the class monitor said: "Wrong, Sir, absolutely wrong!"

"You can't spell this little word? Even a four-year-old would have got it right! Go, stand in the corner."

I went sulking into a corner but was delighted to find, only a while later, that except for four or five girls the entire class was ranged alongside me. "There are far too many of you who can't read English" was all that Sir said to us in class that day. Yet somehow or the other we passed our way through all the way to Class 11. A couple of times I got what they called a supplementary result, and twice managed to get through by the grace of what were called grace marks.

Srivastava Sir didn't waste his time on girls like me; his focus was entirely on a handful of girls who sat right in front and understood proper English. As Sir explained things in class, their heads bobbed up and down non-stop.

"Yes, Sir! Yes, Sir!"

If Sir asked now and then: "Is that O.K.? Have you understood?" their heads bobbed even more vigorously. We sat in the back rows with our books open but all we could see was Sir's back and the girls' bobbing heads! We didn't understand a thing. And so in time we arrived at the settled conclusion that the best thing to do was laugh at them. We'd catch one or two English words in the class and then tease the girls in front just by going on repeating them. Sometimes, this caused them to burst into tears.

The one who bobbed her head the most was the class monitor, Yogeeta. She got wild: "This is great! Don't study at all yourselves and then bother those that want to, so they can't either. Don't act smart, you lot! Don't try any of this on us. You've got a complex because of English, a complex!"

"*Arré*, what's that?"

We were foxed. We couldn't figure out what she was saying. Nor did we want to ask either Sir or Yogeeta the meaning of that word, "complex". How could we have asked Yogeeta anyway? She was arrogant, and had we asked her it would have turned her head even more. Still, without knowing what the word meant, we started calling Yogeeta "Complex". She'd get horribly irritated, and the more irritated she got, the more we rubbed the word in.

How we managed to get through the night before the English paper, don't even ask! We tired ourselves out praying to all the gods there are! I'd pester Bai to help me pass via offerings at the temple. "Take a bowlful of flour to the temple. Pray for me. Over the whole time I'm answering my exam paper, please stay at the temple and sit with the Lord. Don't come home. If you do, I'm done for."

But let alone pray for me, she didn't even bother to wake me up. Both before and after the paper, Yogeeta and her friends just needed to look at us to laugh. High-pitched laughter it was, too.

I don't know who it was, but one of them said, "If

you touch a squirrel, you'll pass!" Well, that was it! The whole day I tried catching a squirrel to touch. Holding my breath, I'd inch up to a squirrel on tiptoe, but no chance! God alone knows the things I did to try learning English!

And, oh yes, Rawat Sir was good at his job. He worked hard trying to get us to learn English. The truth is, I tried very hard too: I listened carefully, but the moment we started on tenses, everything went haywire. He was very emphatic about tenses, but those tenses made my head spin. Steadying his spectacles, Rawat Sir would announce with gravitas: "If you don't learn your tenses, you won't learn English."

Well, I reckoned, if I'm not capable of getting something, how long can I go on running after it? With this thought I, and many other girls like me, bid a final farewell to the English language.

Around us we heard plenty about the pros and cons of English: "We don't want to learn the language of our colonial masters." The shallowness of this was staggering.

On the other hand: "*Arré*, English is the future. And child, you don't know English! What sort of education have you had if you haven't learnt any English? Say what you like, but you're not educated, child!"

But we felt far away from all this. Having dropped English, we were happy in our fool's paradise. We were consoled by hearing statements like "There's no-one more important in this world than your Mother.

And the same goes for the Mother Tongue. Learning an alien language is not acceptable. Do you understand this, or are you incapable of understanding?" With nonsense such as this we'd blast our English-loving colleagues. We believed no-one could possibly win the argument against us!

But when the time came for the English exam, it felt like I was wearing a noose round my neck. "What if I fail?" The very thought gave me a migraine. "Oh God, I'm not asking for too much – just pass marks, even grace marks will do. I won't ever depend on Bai again for doing well! I'll work all night. I won't let sleep get anywhere near me . . ." I'd mutter a thousand such things to myself.

Oh, forget it! Talking about English is like singing one of those unending ragas. Best to remember something uncomplex: "What's happened has happened."

5

THE FACT OF THE matter was that Kakka had decided he'd postpone every thought relating to marrying off No. 4, Shalu, and No. 5, Shiva, until later: he wanted first that they be educated and independent so that they might grow into working women.

Those days, the importance of studying anything at all was seen as synonymous with studying "Science". So Kakka made them both enrol for Science, and in Class 9 they specialised in Biology. Kakka sat on the takht surrounded by people and announced, "I say, Sahib, I've made both my girls take up Science. People are welcome to say what they like, Sahib, but I've decided I won't just marry them off. First I want them to stand on their own two feet. Marrying can wait. Do you follow? *Arré*, I won't push them towards a living hell." He held forth about his dreams, newspaper in hand. Those around him listened speechless, goggle-eyed. And why not, for wasn't Kakka opening up new vistas for everyone?

They were all soon convinced Shalu would become a doctor. In Class 9 Kakka got her an HMT watch. He'd begun saving for this gift the past many months and had calculated things just so – here were the Class 8 results and there was the right amount of cash for the watch. And he'd decided that, no matter what it took, each of us would get a watch after our Class 8 results.

Shalu went to school, watch on wrist, sometimes hair open, sometimes tied. She was beautiful: large, dark, almond-shaped eyes, thick and long black hair, shapely eyebrows, sharp nose, full cheeks. Her complexion was rosy as an apple. Shiva was slightly darker, her complexion the colour of wheat, which we exaggerated into a darker shade by calling her Blackie. One was all set to be the white doctor and the other was going to be the black doctor.

With all this tall talk, Shalu felt more and more emboldened. Her wrist with the watch on it took on a new shine. She said to us lesser little ones, "Hey, approach me from a distance and ask me the time." By way of response she'd look at her watch in the affected manner of a rich lady and tell us the time. She got us to do this many times a day and seemed to be evolving a style of her own just for looking at a wristwatch – her own unique way of telling the time. Definitely a show-off, was our Shalu, and because she knew she was beautiful, she strutted around an awful lot.

Kakka pampered her more than necessary. She'd throw her weight around because she studied Science and felt she could talk with Kakka's friends as an equal. Always first, always ahead. And yet her problems increased by the day. She'd come back after every Science exam and tell everyone how difficult her paper had been. The time came when Kakka finally asked:

"*Arré*, so how did your paper go?"

"Kakka, my paper went very well."

Butter wouldn't melt in her mouth. After her announcement of success, Kakka bought her a glass of lassi for five rupees which she drank in an outrageously flirtatious way. Gradually, Kakka started calling her Shalini instead of Shalu. Her name was Shalini, you see.

Shiva, on other hand, was secretive. She wasn't a show-off. The two of them were always competing. Shalu would hand out a small suckable mango to each of us and Shiva would be the last to get hers. Shiva always kept an eagle eye on each mango: she didn't quite blush, but her colour darkened, and with a grave faraway look, in a cold voice, she'd say, "You creep, you've given me a rotten mango. Who can eat this? Here, watch," and with that she'd chuck the mango on the road. We little ones were left staring, mouths agape, now at the splattered mango, now at Shiva.

In the little space that there was in the dhaba, we played kabaddi. If ever Shalu grabbed Shiva, she'd refuse to surrender by saying "Chi". The game would inevitably be abandoned, but the two of them wouldn't let go of each other and get into a regular scrap. We'd run after them and plead with Shiva: "Shiva, say 'Chi'! Come on, say it, Shiva, say 'Chi'." Shalu would tighten her hands around Shiva's neck and go on muttering "Kabaddi, Kabaddi", but Shiva just could not bring herself to utter "Chi" and end the game. The evening would go by in this fashion, till it grew time for Kakka and the customers to start showing up.

Shiva sat for hours at the oven making rotis. It didn't matter how many customers came, there was never a break in her roti-making rhythm. It was as if there was some magic in her hands. Shalu served the customers their meals, and we little ones served up the water and onions. Kakka washed the pots and pans, kept the oven going, kneaded the dough, and helped with making the rotis. When the line of customers grew short, or if there were no customers, he called Shiva out, "Child! Come and breathe some fresh air." She'd go on making more and more rotis and shoving them into a casserole.

I got along famously with Shiva. She often made my share of the rotis, but when the odd customer or two appeared Kakka would say to me, "Now the oven's over to you! Your turn." I'd look at Shiva, she'd call me fat and lazy, but then laugh and resume making the rotis. Kakka only managed to eat his own lunch around 3.30 or 4 p.m., by which time Shiva was sweaty and all but burnt out. Then it was my turn to make the rotis – an easier time of day because even if there was occasionally a customer or two, often there were none at all.

Shiva served Kakka his food most lovingly. The moment he started eating he'd say to her, "Come, come, sit down. Why not serve yourself as well?" When she sat to eat depended entirely on her mood. Sometimes she'd sit and eat with Kakka, other times later. Watching her eat I'd grumble, "How much are you going to eat, yaar? Stop now, Shiva, enough! You can't eat all that in one go . . . enough now, leave some for later. I'll make you just two more rotis. No more." Kakka gently scolded, Shiva merely laughed. Behind Kakka's back I'd glare at her and say, "That's ten rotis done. Enough . . . I'll make only five more." She'd hide some rotis. "How come ten? There've been only seven so far." Then I'd jump down from near the oven – "I say, please don't ask me to make rotis. Ask me to do anything at all, just not *this* . . ."

Shiva had more stories inside her than the oven had embers. And her stories, shining and shimmering like her complexion and the coal, took so many shapes that we could make neither head nor tail of them. She'd leave us stranded mid-stream anytime she felt like: "O.K., so tell me this. If you had to go into orbit, how'd you go about it?"

"With the help of a ladder."

"Hee-hee-hee."

I stood on tiptoe, stretched my arms all the way up, and said, "One on top of the other – many storeys high, and then we'd climb on to the roof . . ."

She stuck her thumb out at me, "And what if everything shakes and the storeys fall?"

That scared us. So one of us said, "Oh, O.K., in that case we'll go in a balloon."

She thought for a while and countered: "O.K., but would you sit in the balloon after the gas had been filled in it, or before?"

Someone said weakly, "With a ladder . . ."

"O.K., count. How many ladders would you need? Off with you. All of you, count together and then come back and tell me." The rest of the day we were stuck trying to figure out this basic problem of rocket science.

All kinds of weird things came into her head. During a lunar eclipse she grabbed my neck hard and rammed it next to her head. "Look, look at the moon. Look at it carefully." Still hanging on to my neck she said, "Look inside the moon, you'll see Lord Rama and Laxman. Look, look there. Broom in hand, a sweeper's running after them. Rama and Laxman are running away from him, they don't want to be touched by the sweeper . . ."

"Where, where? I can't make out . . ."

Squeezing my neck she said, "Watch carefully. Now look, there they are . . . !" After a while I spotted Rama-Laxman and even Babbu Uncle with a broom, he was running after them . . .

She said, "If the sweeper touches the Gods, the moon will disappear. Then it'll be pitch dark . . . Then nothing will be visible, nothing at all, no dhaba, no Kakka. But if Rama-Laxman manage to keep running around this way all night, the sweeper will tire and fall . . ."

"And what about our Babbu Uncle?"

"Quiet, quiet, don't speak. Just watch carefully."

We were up watching this drama she'd cooked up till midnight! What happened next, I don't know.

First thing in the morning, still rubbing my eyes, I asked, "Shiva! Shiva! What happened?"

"What're you Shiva-ing on about? Can't you see, Fatso, it's broad daylight."

On the auspicious Devuthni Gyaras, which was the eleventh day of the rising of the Gods, she gathered us all again and took us behind the dhaba.

"Today we'll chuck stones on the roofs of all the houses around. If we don't there'll be a quarrel at home. May all the quarrelling, mishaps, and hard times befall other people's homes today! Come on, chuck, chuck! Quick, don't wait!"

We rained stones on those roofs. The tin roofs made such a racket that all the shopkeepers came running out yelling, "What's happening? What's going on?"

Shiva hid us all in the coal mound. "It's us! It's us! Begone, fighting and quarrelling! Go on, go away fighting and quarrelling! *Phu! Phu!* Come on blow them away! Blow away all the fighting and quarrelling!"

Life was such incredible fun!

6

SHALU WAS DOMINEERING. She had a nauseating way of behaving like she was the family's head-girl, the self-appointed class mistress to us all.

Bai planted wheatgrass at home in little pots made of dried leaves. In due course, countless little stalks poked their heads out of the soil. Shalu explained their sprouting and growth to us in careful detail. Leaning over each other, glistening with water drops, the little stalks were a lovely sight.

On the day of their immersion in the river, Shalu and Shiva carried baskets full of those little pots of wheatgrass on their heads. When floating them into the water, Shalu left us little ones on the bank while Shiva and she walked halfway into the current to make the baskets move. In the process they got wet to their waists. Then, bearing the empty baskets and a handful of the stalks, they came wading back towards us.

We were not allowed into the river. In fact, because of the crowds at the bank, Shalu made us stand so far from the water's edge that we could hardly see the pots float away. The crowds by the river were always huge, group after group of people carrying baskets on their heads.

The river had so many little pots on it that the water changed colour.

Then we'd go off to other homes to exchange our remaining pots of wheatgrass, where we'd sometimes be given a four-anna coin, or samosas and sweetmeats and savouries such as balushahi, poha, and jalebis. Shyamlal, the banana-seller, always gave us a ripe banana each.

And Shalu, telling Kakka all this, kneeling before him, would say in her mock-preachy way: "Study hard; work hard. This time, may you all get First Divisions!"

"Why don't you get a First Division yourself, before you start advising everyone else? Who d'you think you are?" Shiva muttered this softly, but not softly enough to prevent Shalu hearing.

Grandfather owned a few books that he wouldn't let anyone touch. When we shut the dhaba and got home, he was always fast asleep. Shiva'd tiptoe past him and get some of the books, and then, in whispers, tell us the stories around the illustrations in them. One afternoon, Grandfather wasn't home. Shiva took advantage of his absence and the two of us got deeply engrossed in the pictures of a storybook. Seeing us poring over a book, Bai ticked us off and told us to get straight to the dhaba, but we wouldn't budge. We lost track of the time, and when we finally reached the dhaba Kakka gave us a solid scolding.

Shalu looked at Shiva, smiled, and said sweetly, "Till the next wheatgrass immersion, may your days be as blessed!"

7

MARCH, APRIL, MAY, JUNE – those were high-season months in the wholesale market; the remaining eight saw hardly any work in the dhaba. And besides, even within those eight months the four monsoon months were a complete write-off: we'd be hand to mouth and there was no book-keeping worth the name. It had to be very sensible living and eating for all of us at home.

To serve fresh food to customers was hard going. Very often what was left over would show signs of souring. What were we to do? We couldn't throw precious food away, and yet if a customer caught us dishing out stale stuff all hell would break loose.

To keep the dough going, Kakka repeatedly splashed water over it and kneaded it every half-hour. Customers would be served crusty rotis – because the rotis were delivered steaming hot, the bubbles in the dough from which they were made weren't visible and no-one guessed. In this way, our stale dough got used up. When the customer numbers went really low, Kakka, hating the thought of wastage, kneaded the flour several times a day.

The daal and vegetables too had to be boiled many times over – with the risk of them looking and tasting like the previous day's food reheated. Finishing food when its fresh is a great thing, but managing to keep fresh food from going stale is a much greater thing. And to make stale food look and taste so good that no-one can tell the difference – well, that's an art! Kakka knew all the tricks of this trade and watching him we picked them up as well.

He didn't fret during the times customers were scarce, he was content even to see a few. One such day, as he was asking Shalu about school and studies, the chat turned towards English. Shalu's school name was Shalini, Shiva's was Shivani.

Kakka said, "What d'you say for Shalini in English?"

This made Shalu clap her palm on her forehead in exasperation. "Kakka! My name's Shalini in English too."

"What? Nonsense! You aren't getting my point. Everything in Hindi has an English equivalent, so Shalini must be something else in English, surely?"

Shalu couldn't make him understand and he got very irritated with her: "You don't study English properly, child . . ." He thought his hard work was going down the drain and Shalu's face trying to get him to understand was a sight to behold!

One of the dhaba's regular customers, Girdhawal Sahib, happened to be around. Kakka and he were thick as thieves. He'd been out walking that day and had barely come in and sat down when Shalu went up to him and asked him in a hushed voice, "Babu-ji, how would you say 'Shalini' in English?"

He gave her a playful cuff. "Idiot! Is this what you're learning at school?"

She took a deep breath and jumped up for joy. "Kakka, Kakka! Ask Girdhawal Babu-ji! I was right!"

It took a long time for the penny to drop and after considerable cogitation on the subject Kakka said perplexedly, "*Arré*, in that case why's there such a hue and cry about the advantages of learning English? I mean if Shalini is only Shalini . . ."

Having passed this difficult English examination, Shalu decided she was too grand to be seen at the ration shop. People stood there in line for hours awaiting their turn – which never came, because the ration shop opened only for a very short time. In fact, it would often open for five minutes and then, without having sold a thing, close again.

The ration shop-owner was very tall – everyone called him Amitabh Bachchan – and treated with respect. He was always greeted with a "Namaste" and he swaggered around like a monarch. His shop had sacks full of wheat, sugar, rice, and any number of cans of oil, but more often than not he had no time for customers.

He was rather taciturn and wandered around with his hands in his pockets, or leant against a lamp-post deep in thought, alone in the crowd. He'd ignore the giant lock hanging in the front of his shop and unlock a little lock on the shutter at the back, and then condescend to provide a few waiting customers with some of his goods. In spite of these shenanigans, no-one dared take him on; in fact, everyone wanted to be friends with him.

The responsibility for getting stuff from his ration shop usually fell on Shiva and me. She'd say, "We'll have to do all we can to ruin this Amitabh Bachchan's movie. Just watch, I'll do it, or my name's not Shiva . . ." Shalu's refusal to get rations from the ration shop was fine with us.

But there was one other occasion when Shalu's nose-in-the-air ways really got her hitting the jackpot. That was when Kakka let her go off with her friends to Geeta Talkies to watch a movie. She was there a full three hours – but it was us at home who were the more excited! She'd dressed up beautifully; her black watchstrap looked lovely on her fair wrist.

What had we seen by way of films? Only a bioscope.

The bioscopewalla's call excited a whole lot of kids who arrived to trail after him: "Come and see Agra's Taj Mahal! Come and see Delhi's Qutb Minar!" Chanting his ditty, the fellow went diligently into each locality, but very few kids had the money to watch his show. Most just followed him around and hid their envy at the excitement of those lucky enough to watch. The locality kids had worked out a system: those who managed to cadge the money to watch the bioscope would provide those out of luck with a running commentary on what they were watching. Everyone stood in an animated queue to listen to the commentary. The fellow watching would start off narrating what he was seeing, and after a while his voice would start to trail away. Then the grumbling began: "Tell us! Tell us what's going on!" Fisticuffs would ensue and the bioscopewalla would scream and shoo us all off. Only those who had the means to watch were allowed to linger. So we'd move off and stand watching from a distance, waiting for the person who'd seen it all to come over and tell us all.

Soon after the end of this matinée, the bioscopewalla would start the next show: "Come and see Agra's Taj Mahal! Come and see Delhi's Qutb Minar!" He trilled this four or five times, and if no kids of means showed up he moved on to show his wares in the next neighbourhood. We followed him, chanting alongside: "Come and see Agra's Taj Mahal! Come and see Delhi's Qutb Minar! Come and see Meena Kumari! Come and see Bharat!" Singing and hollering, sometimes we ran ahead of him to try and sweet-talk kids with money in their pockets. In this way, with almost no money of our own, we saw the Taj Mahal, Meena Kumari, Bharat, and the Qutb Minar innumerable times.

And with just about the same amount Shalu managed to go and see a whole film! Shiva warned us all against pandering to Shalu's hi-fi attitude that evening: "Don't anyone dare! . . . Don't any of you dare ask that so-and-so about the film. It's the only way to stop this vain creature!

The moment we ask her about it, we'll never see the end of her airs and graces." But of course we couldn't help waiting eagerly for her return.

Shalu's affectations of superiority ballooned by the day. First thing each morning she took to scolding us over the littlest of things. When the baker passed by on his bicycle and we longed for his bread, she didn't just stop us watching him go past, she even stopped us standing at the door. "Why watch wide-eyed? Come on in! If you were ever to see bread being made, you'd know what a worthless unpalatable thing it is!"

"Yeah, just like you!"

The wheat seedlings swayed!

Shalu muttered: "You Blackie . . . you shitty Shiva! You're spoiling them all! You ought to be ashamed, thinking of food first thing in the morning."

8

THE DAY DAWNED when Shalu got into Class 10 and Shiva into Class 9.

Shiva was invariably late leaving for school: working in the dhaba till nearly midday, she was often close to tears because Shalu left for school before her. Shalu had worked out a division of labour at the dhaba which let her finish work quicker, so that she had time to get ready earlier. She went to school and got back from it in the company of friends, chatting all the while about their studies, the practicals, the tests. Even from a distance it was clear their group was oh-so-special, so distinctive. Shiva made a face each time she saw Shalu and her friends, snorting her opinion that they studied little and showed off plenty.

Shalu had worked out an expert trick to get away early. She'd go behind the dhaba, wash her hands and face, hand-comb her hair and plait it. Then she'd swirl around and ask, "Is it O.K.? Oh, look sharp, Fatty, or I'll make chutney out of you!" The work, of course, was unending, and finally Kakka would say to Shiva, "Go, girl! Go, go! I'll finish up here!" Shiva would run to the house, hurriedly wear her school clothes, and dash down to join the crowd of girls near the courthouse or the school.

Ours was the morning shift, theirs the afternoon one. After school, the three of us stayed with Kakka at the dhaba till late into the night. Kakka believed in not letting even a solitary customer leave till he'd been served. If a customer showed up around closing time, he'd take out stuff and feed him, then exclaim, "Oh good! Even at closing time we raked in a fiver!"

After about ten-thirty or eleven at night the vessels with leftover daal and vegetables had to be emptied and cleaned, as did the kneading platter. Kakka filled it with water and scrubbed it last, a difficult task because residues of dough were stuck to it and scraped our fingers, so this particular cleaning was something that Kakka preferred doing himself. For the rest, between us we'd divided the work of scrubbing and washing out all the pots and pans. After which the hand pump had to be worked to fill up the water tank for the next morning. Turn by turn we'd fill a bucket and pour water into the tank. Kakka did his best to see we weren't utterly exhausted and we, in turn, wanting to be of help, would go on insisting, "Kakka, let me do it! I can take care of it!"

If a customer arrived at this point, Shiva made the rotis and I did the serving. Kakka and Shalu carried on with the cleaning of pots and pans and the filling up of water. This done, Kakka peeled a whole basketful of onions for the morning's cooking, took out green chillies, and rinsed the coriander leaves. Occasionally he also prepared the garlic and ginger to spare himself doing them next morning. Our dinner happened after all this was over and done. Fried daal and thick rotis . . . Two of us served, two sat and ate. After which we reversed roles.

On exceptionally busy days Kakka gave me a rupee to buy myself savouries. I'd run down to Jai Stambh Chauraha, and, savouries in hand, come running back. Finally, it was time to shut the dhaba and head home. Bai was as usual awaiting our arrival. There were times we got back so late we'd see her looking out for us on the road at the turn towards our house.

Bai was always made unhappy by the thought that she had not managed to teach us girls how to be properly feminine. She wanted to see us behave like the other girls and worried herself silly over what was likely to happen to us once we were married and lived at our in-laws'.

Home was only for sleeping the night: we'd get home from the dhaba just before having to leave for school and were home only for as long as it took us to change and grab hold of our homework. Our studying often happened at the dhaba. When customers arrived, we'd shut our books; when there were none, we'd sit down and do our homework. Watching us study, Kakka grew emotional and did all the odd jobs himself. There was never a moment's rest in his life.

People watching us study complimented us, but Kakka reacted arrogantly. "I am the sole provider for a family of eleven!" he proclaimed. "My children lack for nothing. I'll give my life to see them well settled. There's only one problem I foresee, Sahib. It's having only enough to spend what you earn at the end of our daily grind. Not even savings enough to see us through an illness." His nostrils flared as he said this, his body giving out a sense of strength and suppleness. "My kids can slog. They work day and night with me. *Arré*, the more they slog the more they'll earn and have in their pockets to spend. I'll leave no stone unturned to make sure they're educated." This made us think we ought to focus more than we did on our school work. Shiva whispered, "From tomorrow we'll work extra and be a chapter ahead of the class." I nodded agreement. Looking at us Shalu wondered if Shiva was hatching yet another nefarious plot.

As for plotting, it was one of the brothers-in-law – Jija-ji from Siwni-Malwa – who was always at the receiving end. He tried all the time without getting anywhere. He'd go to Kakka and start off with, "Kakka, you should let the girls stay home now. They're grown up. It doesn't look good, watching them work at the dhaba."

Kakka was invariably short-tempered with him: "Why, Sir? If they sit at home, what's going to become of the dhaba? Am I supposed to run it alone?"

"Get helpers!" Jija-ji would respond in his all-knowing tone.

"In that case the helpers will eat what these kids eat! What nonsense your head's stuffed with! *Arré*, you think someone will swallow up my girls if they work here?" He found it difficult to keep his temper.

Jija-ji looked beaten but did not give up, he tried to get us to agree with him. "Listen! Kakka doesn't . . . so why don't all of you just stop working at the dhaba? Make any excuse you like – say you have to study, or say you're ill. Say what you like so long as you don't have to work in the dhaba." Shalu and Shiva looked at him wide-eyed; I went off and spilled the beans on what he'd been urging to Kakka, who cursed: "What a dolt! And thinks he's literate and modern!"

At this Bai turned on Kakka: "Oh, and aren't you the only forward-looking man around! The rest of us are all mad, are we? It's as if only you get to eat grain and everyone else manages on straw!"

"Of course! You're quite right, Bai! He doesn't eat like us! Daal fry and thick rotis! That's why he's dim-witted."

I quite liked adding my bit of fuel to their fire. I saw Kakka's purpose was to make us self-confident. He wanted the dhaba to be the source of our strength, not our weakness. By saying things like "Why be ashamed of what you do?" he was instilling ambition and energy in us – things he himself had in spadefulls. Whether it was something to eat or something to wear, he was always pushing us ahead and putting himself last.

His daily wear apart, by way of special clothes for going out he had only one yellow starched khadi kurta, white pyjamas, and a long shawl. These he wore maybe once or twice a year, for grand occasions. This set of clothes was always kept neatly folded in a small box. He took great care of them and when he appeared wearing them we'd all shout, "Look, how fine Kakka's looking!"

Shalu and Shiva looked after this set of clothes: Bai washed and those two ironed them. Access to the box containing them was restricted. Shalu didn't let us younger ones anywhere near this box of Kakka's finery.

For his daily wear, Kakka had two sets of lungi-vests. The vests had a clear trajectory: first a couple of holes, then the holes developing into maps of countries, and finally the countries shrinking into strings that were more string than country. None of this ever dissuaded Kakka from wearing them. Bai often ticked him off and told him to buy a new vest, but he ignored her. So, off and on, she darned what remained. Only when the vest was a nearly invisible set of loose strings and friends began looking at him in dismay – "*Arré*, Ramji, for God's sake, change your vest! There's no life left in it!" – only then, and with great difficulty, was a new vest bought. Shalu and Shiva would march off and buy it on credit without consulting Kakka.

Getting coal, vegetables, spices, paying the electricity bill – all these things Kakka did in his lungi-vest.

Once, a girl asked Shiva, "Hey, Shivani, why doesn't your Kakka wear clothes? He comes out in his lungi." Shiva's riposte came out pat: "Don't worry, soon your Kakka will be shopping in his underwear, it's getting so hot!" This had all the girls giggling.

9

AN INTERESTING STORY runs in the family about Kakka and the fan – he disliked letting it whirr at full speed. Every summer, the moment he saw it blow fast, he flew into a rage: "*Arré*, people either walk or run. There's a difference, isn't there? You're always running the fan at full speed – it'll stop working." And he'd slow it down.

To stop the daily bickering Bai reduced fan speed around the time Kakka was expected back, or sometimes out of sheer irritation she simply switched it off. At other times, Kakka switched it off himself – which happened the moment he rose from his bed in the morning. We yelled and groaned in our state of half-sleep: "*Arré*, has the electricity gone?!" His explanation was considerate – to the fan, that is: "It's been on all night, so let it rest awhile. Come on now, get up ... get up." This did nothing to dissuade us from carrying on grumbling, "We're sleepy! We didn't get to sleep till one! ... Kakka, you won't even let us sleep! ... God knows when we last got a good night's sleep." He'd count out the hours on his fingers and declare, "Eight hours is enough. You'll turn into Kumbhakaran if you carry on sleeping."

This kind of chatter got Bai's goat: "Curse his newspaper! He goes around sounding like some big leader . . . this good-for-nothing!" At this, Kakka's generous impulses would develop into hand-wringing: "Hey, listen, the farmers are in bad shape – they're getting no electricity. So they stand to lose a whole harvest . . . use only as much electricity as necessary. No need to waste it, is there? You people will kill a lot of poor farmers."

He was equally annoyed if we ran the taps too long or too hard. Bai liked letting the water gush, Kakka absolutely did not. If he noticed a bucket overflowing or a tap dripping, an explosion followed. If Bai's refrain was "Water! I need water", Kakka's riposte was a dissertation: "Oh, for God's sake! Are you going to carry water around in your fist? Use as much as you need, why waste it? Come on, let's calculate how many buckets this household needs." His fingers started enumerating each person's requirements for baths and laundry, and while he was at it one of us would interrupt him with "Kakka, a bucket's not enough for us! One bucket of water can't drive the sleep out of our eyes . . . we need a tankful!" Bai would sense an opportunity in our chorus: "Hear them! You think all you have to do is proclaim something and they'll agree! And there you were, preaching at me first thing in the morning!"

Sometimes, if things seemed to be getting out of hand, Kakka measured out water in tablespoons for each of us. I have no idea why he was so specific on particular days because the next day we'd use four times as much. "I say, today we'll have a proper bath! Yesterday Kakka drove us mad!" And with that we'd position a large tank to catch the tap's flow and bathe to our hearts' content.

10

ALL OUR SPICES WERE ground at home – red chillies, coriander, turmeric, garam masala. Bai found the going hard when the red chillies had to be done. First she pounded the masala in a mortar and pestle, then she ground it finer on a millstone. Chilli fumes percolated through every nook and cranny of the house and it was pretty impossible for us to sit around while she was hammering away at fingers of red. If she found us hanging about she was considerate and told us to head off to the dhaba. But despite the chilli in the air we liked just sitting around till she'd finished grinding all the masala into powder, turning our fond gaze now at Bai, now at her millstone.

Asha or Usha or Anni – whichever of them happened to have escaped their in-laws' – did what they could to take over the grinding. Eager and full of chatter, none of them liked sitting idle, and for my part I hastened from the dhaba to the house with a pot to get hold of some of the freshly powdered masala: "Bai! Hurry up, fill this up with chilli powder! There are customers waiting." Then I'd go scurrying back to the dhaba as fast as I'd come. If I found the house door locked during these fetching trips I banged on it; other times, if I found Bai gossiping with the women of the neighbourhood, I'd raise a hue and cry, "Bai! Bai! Come on, hurry! You saw me arrive, why haven't you got it done? I'll tell Kakka!"

There were also times I reached home to collect the masala – only to find Bai lying with a cloth wrapped tight around her head. She filled the pot with masala looking tired and asked, "How many customers . . .? How many customers today?" I'd go back and tell Kakka she had a cloth wrapped around her head and the moment he got free he'd hand me a four-anna coin and say, "Go! Go get a tablet from Munna's." I'd cross the road to the shop, hearing Kakka shout from the dhaba – "Hey Munna, Munna!" – and he'd tell the fellow to give me a tablet to take to Bai. Soon enough I knew the drill and told Munna myself, "Hurry, give me that headache tablet." He'd hand it over with a laugh.

At peak season, when there was a rush of customers, it took three or four trips back home to collect the masala and the pickle. At the end of such days Kakka counted out the takings and put them into his vest pocket while we crowded greedily around him: "If only we could get twenty bucks, *no* fifty bucks, *no* a hundred bucks, and more customers . . . Wouldn't that be just great!" Kakka only said, "Go on, go on! Everybody rest for a bit . . . play or study, do whatever you like."

I remember chortling with glee once, when I went to pick up cut-and-prepared garlic from the house, "D'you know, Bai, today there've been customers worth a hundred and fifty bucks! And more've queued up ... Come on, hurry up, hurry up ..." Bai stopped ladling garlic into the pan; she went and lit a diya in the alcove and stood there, hands folded. At night, chatting with Kakka and the rest, I mimicked Bai lighting the diya, at which she laughed and said, "Oh, this one's a born actress! How does she do it?" And Shiva added her bit of masala to the bonhomie, "Tomorrow I'll grind you up as well, with the chillies."

Oh, that Shiva!

Before I could retort Kakka said, "Come on! Come on! Get to sleep, everyone. There's plenty of work to be done in the morning – it's just these four months we have."

But was sleep possible over those days, when we lay thinking all night about the market? At harvest time the season was at its peak, there was little by way of night time, and we wanted the flow of chatting customers at the dhaba never to end. There was as much noise inside as out, the harvest's selling prices determined the level of the din.

Our happiness over those days was boundless. We ran about in a tizzy, serving customers, someone kneading the dough, another one running home with an empty bucket, a third rushing homewards to get daal, a fourth at the onions going *chop-chop-chop*, a fifth filling water at the hand pump. An invasion of customers ... and yet we never slipped up remembering the roti count . . . and there was Kakka washing piles of plates which we grabbed from him, wiping them, placing them to await the next round of customers. Not a table knew the interval between when it was vacated and when it was made ready by the quick swipe of a duster for the next round of customers. Rotis were flying about, and more and more daal was being fried before making an appearance. Papads baked on a fierce oven disappeared into thin air, not one was allowed to go waste. And as for the pickle, it was as if people were gorging platefuls of it with each roti instead of the other way round. And all the time the oven, in continuous competition with the sun, was winning. The sun decided to bow to the oven and just slipped quietly down.

Without those long queues of bullock-carts and huge herds of cattle our lives would have been a lot less meaningful, and the town's economy was entirely dependent on the grain market fed by them. Small shopkeepers, big shopkeepers, everyone's happiness depended on that market. Bullock-carts stuffed to the top, laden with sacks, meant happy farmers, happy traders, happy porters, and a delighted dhabawalla. The higher the harvest's sale prices, the more the demand for spicy masala-rich food. Such laughter, guffawing, merrymaking all around – not even the street theatre's noisy performances had much chance of being heard in the face of such a racket! For that matter the sun hadn't the ghost of a chance rising before people had risen for the grain market, and even those weren't the first folk in the queues because they'd been pipped by others who'd parked their bullock-carts and tractors and trolleys in queues that had formed the previous night.

The fun and merriment made each night seem without end. At Sironj Chowk, at the Railway Station, at Jai Stambh Chauraha, Gandhi Chowk, Savarkar Chowk, Mill Road – everywhere – it was an all-night jam session in full swing. Two o'clock at night was the same as seven in the evening, the bullock-carts all lined up from one end of the market and going all the way through the Mela Ground, the whole town decorated bright and colourful in their wake.

The May and June nights passed easily enough. And the afternoons? Porters, traders, farmers, shopkeepers – not one of them escaped being scorched in the open-air oven that was our town. But no-one ever gave up.

Under the searing sun, in the exposed area of the grain market, Ketan Bhai served cold water to farmers and porters and was affectionately called Adwa-ji. To tide folk over the summer he had cold-water dispensers installed at various spots. Plenty of people came by to assist him, and the cold water reached even those who were tied to the queue because of not knowing when their turn to sell might come.

"Such a big trader and yet so decent!" Kakka was full of praise for Ketan Bhai, well-wisher of farmers and supplier of cold water to the thirsty. Often, Ketan Bhai appeared at the dhaba. "How many cold-water dispensers should we have next summer? How many assistants to dole out water? How do we make sure the farmers manage through the day without difficulty . . .?"

"How do we make sure their grain isn't pilfered?"

"Maybe we need to take steps to stop shopkeepers raising their rates?"

"How do we deal with so many problems?"

"How do we improve matters between farmers and porters?"

Ketan Bhai, Kakka, and Diwan Singh Uncle were deep in such discussions and not even the arrival of customers could stop them. "Better first free yourself from all the work, we'll wind up too and get back." Uncle often tried taking on some of the dhaba work, but Kakka protested, "*Arré*, friend! Let me handle it! No, no, sit, take it easy. I'll be free in no time."

The work schedule of the grain market went vaguely this way:

March–April–May–June: Wheat and chickpea season.

July–August–September: Watch-the-rain season.

October–November–December: Soya bean and moong season.

January–February: Complete-silence season.

March–April–May–June: Long-queues season back again.

The bigger the harvest, the happier our days and nights!

Over the peak season, Rameshwar Uncle had his best mornings. He ran a tea-and-breakfast shop which was jampacked and the villagers congregating there were mostly in top form.

"You think you're casting pearls before swine, Brother? . . . With village folk, best to call a spade a spade, O.K.? . . . Just like piping hot pakoras, understand? . . . Come on, quick, give us a plate of pakoras and ladle that chutney over them . . . There's a long queue today, hurry up, else those jackals will steal a couple of sacks of my wheat . . . can't do without your pakoras though . . . Lusting after your pakoras is going to cost us dear!"

Uncle flattered folk as he prepared the dough. "Oh no, Brother! I'll go under first if things go wrong for you! Without your grain market I'm done for! You farmers are all there is! You're my life!" He was proud of his shop and his produce. No-one made tea, pakoras, and stuffed chilli like him. And he knew pretty well that once people tasted his wares they'd go nowhere else, they'd just keep coming back. So he'd start pushing out the idlers hanging around and cramming his shop: "Hey, hey, Brother! Come on, get up! Come on, come again after the market's over, you lot!" From where he sat at the oven he pushed plates towards farmers: "Hey, come on quick, take the pakoras while they're piping hot! Here's the chilli, big, just like your harvest! Sir, if you agree, a sweet . . .?"

"Oh, forget it! Here, give me water, fast! . . . After the market, I'll be back for your salties . . ."

The idling farmers were not about to be taken in by Uncle's stratagems to shove them off. A white headcloth wrapped around his hair, a fun-loving farmer would look first at Uncle's customers, eyes screwed, then at his companions. Then he'd look at Uncle and say: "See, we've cast our pearls before them, yet these market folk think of us villagers as swine! These fellows are too clever by half."

Uncle, bristling, putting batter into boiling oil – *chunn* – *chunn* – *chunn* – "*Arré*, Bhai! The pearls are yours and so are the swine! Only the marketplace is ours!" *Chunn chunn chunn* pakoras . . . *chunn chunn chunn* chilli . . . Uncle's very own music. *Chun-chun, chun-chun,* Uncle's wok on the fire. "Ah! What's up, Bhai? So cocky today! Last year same time you were lost for words, quite tongue-tied, weren't you?"

"Us farmers get done in by one thing and only that one thing: If our harvest's a winner we can take on the world. No one can beat us back if the harvest's a winner!"

"Oh, go on! Get to the market then, you clever chap!"

Right next to Uncle's shop was Roshan Paanwalla. He'd been listening a long time to the banter between Uncle and the farmers. Luckily for everyone, he hadn't put astringent white lime instead of the soothing red kattha in the paan! He was barely able to hide his excitement and the farmers egged him on, "There's still time before the market opens. Come on, have your say, spill the beans . . . Come on, out with it, or your stomach will go on gurgling."

"O.K., hear me out then! Just try and recall: What were you saying during the rains last year?"

"O.K. . . . let's hear what you remember . . ."

" '*Arré* Bhai, why such a downpour? A few drops of rain for a day or two, that's what's needed. This way the water just flows away, and believe me, a deluge doesn't help farms . . .' " – Roshan could mimic the farmers perfectly and was in full flow.

"*Ha Ha Ha!*" – everyone guffawed.

He had the floor to himself, he had everyone's ear. This puffed him up no end. ". . . And when it drizzled you were saying, 'Oh my God! What kind of drip-drip is this? If only it poured sheets, that'd be fun! A few days of non-stop rain! That's what it means – to rain! This drizzle's no use.' "

"You farmers don't know how to be happy! You want the rain to dance to your tune . . ." Roshan's acting had to be seen to be believed.

"Are you done? Have you finished? Forget about our earlier dues. We're giving you nothing. Our score's settled. And remove this board of yours saying Cash Today, Credit Tomorrow. If you can't remove it, here . . . let me do it. And listen, just close this paan shop of yours and go join an acting group. We'll happily shower you with a couple of hundred bucks each time you dance and sing!"

The farmers insisted on having their say! Dance would suit Roshan . . . or better still, shouldn't Roshan be taking on roles in epic drama? He needed to run off to Mathura the moment he realised the idea needed following up.

Striding forward to greater heights, Roshan continued: "O.K., if that's the case, hear me out on the topic of electricity. You see light bulbs in our shops and they drive you crazy. Going by your calculations, just one bulb's good for the entire bus stand! You want all the electricity for yourselves. It's you first, and the rest of the world can live on kerosene!" Roshan wasn't about to let the farmers off the hook, and yet none of them took offence. Because every last one of them was flourishing. "Hey, get lost!" they said to him, "Your comedy act will delay us for market . . ."

The farmers trotted off to the grain market with Kakka laughing his head off!

This was not an isolated instance of market-time revelry and banter. There were countless such tit-for-tat chats over which no-one let anyone get off lightly. God knows why the farmers felt the market-wallas saw them as simpletons and idiots; God knows why they thought town folk were cunning fellows who'd be cautious around them. Crazy – given how both sides were joined not at the hip but at the stomach!

If anything, we market-wallas were much more dependent on the farmers. We thought of them as clever and intelligent villagers. It seemed to us that the farmers, having been cheated for centuries, were learning fast how to resist being duped and refusing to be treated as simpletons any longer. It was now time when more or less any of these villagers might say to us town folk: "Look here, my good man, we farmers are pretty sharp . . . and mature! Maybe it's you bunch that need to wise up to us . . . If you think we can be fooled, it's certainly you lot who're the real idiots!"

11

THE ANNUAL FAIR was always held across the river. The bridge had to be crossed to get to it. I was terrified of the ferris wheel. Once, Shiva forced me to sit on it. She said, "When the wheel starts descending from high up, I'll cover your eyes."

The ferris wheel had four eight- to ten-seater cabins, and on that particular day girls from the neighbourhood were already in them. The moment the wheel started moving I began hollering, "Shiva, Shiva!" She tried to calm me down.

"Look, look at the fair! How high up we are!"

I opened my eyes and realised how impossibly high up we were. In a state of sheer panic, I shut my eyes again. When the wheel started moving faster, I began yelling, "Help! Help! Kakka! I'm dying! . . . I'm going to die today, Kakka!"

The faster the wheel went, the louder I yelled. So the ferris wheel's owner brought it to a halt. I clambered out and scurried off to a corner. Shiva looked at me and laughed, I looked at her and shuddered.

After her ferris-wheel ride, she began dancing with the girls: "That was great fun! How we enjoyed that ride!" They laughed and danced, ". . . It was like we were going to die any minute! . . . Now, my dears, we're going on that ferris wheel every day for the next seven days!" The fair meant the ferris wheel – and only the ferris wheel – to them. Shiva curled her arm around my shoulders and calmed me down. "If only you had a little more guts," she said.

I was okay watching the others go up and around on the ferris wheel, but there was no way I was ever going to get on it again.

The next day, Shalu and our little brother and I went off to the fair. Shalu picked our little Bhaiyya up and walked over the bridge with him. After dropping him off at the other end she came back, held my hand, and helped me across. Except on the very odd occasion, we always went to the fair with no money on us.

This time there were two quite astonishing things at the fair – an electric merry-go-round, and Vasu's gulab jamun. The gulab jamun weighed half a kilo and would have needed five or six customers to eat it all. People were betting left and right on anyone taking on eating that gulab jamun single-handed. And to top it all, Vasu had put up a board saying "Eat one, get one free!" That year, his gulab jamun and the merry-go-round made for an astonishingly new sort of feeling at the fair.

The merry-go-round was huge and very high and had cabins, each cabin with its own tubelight. Holding Bhaiyya by the hand, we stood around it gawking. The moment it started turning, a chant began in the crowd,

"Hoo Ha Hoo Ha, Ho Hey Ho, Hey Hey Hey . . ." The people watching had as much fun, if not more, than the people on it!

Suddenly, Shalu and I screamed, "Bhaiyya? Bhaiyya?" When had he slipped away from our grasp? We looked frantically around and finding him nowhere, burst into tears. People stared at us crying – but only momentarily, because their eyes were riveted to the merry-go-round and they were too distracted to pay us much heed.

In a flash, the fun of the fair vanished for us. There was now an encompassing darkness. We began to see familiar faces in the faces of strangers. Every woman looked like Asha-jiji, Usha-jiji, and Bai from behind. The merry-go-round's height and brightness and speed and noise only magnified our fears. We started screaming for Kakka.

Then, I don't know how or from where, Om Bhaiyya from the bus stand spotted us. Shalu said to him, "Our little brother's lost! He was right here, but we don't know where he's disappeared."

"Stay here. I'll get your Kakka."

And away went Om Bhaiyya. The two of us hung on to each other for dear life, shouting "Bhaiyya! Bhaiyya!" all the while. Off and on we were shoved aside by waves of people and lost each other's grip, but we managed to stick to where we were and grabbed each other's hand again and again.

A while later, Kakka arrived. He was still in his lungi-and-vest. "What happened? What happened, girls?"

"Kakka, we were right here standing by the merry-go-round, holding Bhaiyya's hand . . . but don't know where he disappeared . . ."

Taking us along, Kakka went to the man in charge of the mike, and soon the mike-walla said stentoriously into his instrument, "A kid's got lost. He's wearing a grey shirt and shorts . . . He's about two and a half or three years old. Anyone who finds the boy, please bring him to this stall."

And the noise! The Circus, the Well of Death, the Gate of Hell, the Haunted House, and now "A Child's Lost . . ."

"Bhaiyya! Bhaiyya!" Shalu's voice was ringing out everywhere, maybe her voice would draw him to us . . . but she was drowned out by all the noise.

Some people arrived from the bus stand and began a search. Shalu hung on to my hand. We were half running after our Kakka, who'd occasionally turn around reassuringly, "Don't worry. Don't worry, my dears."

And then, at once, Shalu screaming for sheer joy – "Bhaiyya! Bhaiyya! Bhaiyya!" She left me, grabbed our little tyke, hugged him hard, lifted him into her arms.

He'd been standing in front of the merry-go-round all this time. Kakka had moved further on in his search, so I went running after him. "Kakka! Kakka! Bhaiyya!"

The little fellow, oblivious of it all, was trying even now to wriggle out of Shalu's lap to gawp again at the merry-go-round. And Kakka laughed – his happy laugh. He went off to inform the mike man at his stall, and to look for the fellows from the bus stand. Shalu continued clinging to Bhaiyya. He was now cuddled up with her. Keeping our distance, we bade goodbye to Vasu of the gulab jamun.

Back at the dhaba, absolute silence prevailed – it was open but empty. A crowd had gathered around it. Mohan Uncle said, "Found your little brother? Silly girls, you've only got this one brother, and if you'd lost him . . ." He smirked.

Kakka made us drink some water and sat us under the fan.

Bai knew nothing of what had happened – she only found out at night when we closed the dhaba and were back to tell the tale. Half awake, half asleep, she stared at us open-mouthed. Bhaiyya, sleeping next to her . . . he'd been lost . . . and she'd had no idea!

We were now relaxed enough for Shalu to start off with her teasing: "D'you know, when Babli was crying, her nose was swollen like this . . . she was bawling like this . . ."

"Were you looking for your Bhaiyya or watching Babli's nose? Vamoose, vixen! Who told you to go to the fair in the first place? If Bhaiyya hadn't been found . . ." – as always, it was Shiva to my rescue.

12

WHEN TEACHING THEM to cook vegetables, Kakka made Shalu and Shiva stand a little away from the fire. Those two-hour classes were also a lesson in how to tolerate the hellish heat of the oven. How often and precisely when must the onions in the pot be stirred; when must water go in and how much was optimal; what should the distance be between pot and flames to stop the spices burning; the ideal time for the pot to be put on the fire and removed; how the pot needed to be on the fire and yet not quite on it – in these many ways Kakka showed how the oven needed to be controlled.

After sautéing the onions he'd say, "Look! Look!" and both girls would bend forward. He'd put the turmeric in and while sautéing whatever was in the pot he'd splash a drop or two of water into it. Before putting in the crushed coriander he'd stress his next instruction: "Look, girls! If there's too much coriander, the vegetables will turn black."

A whole lot of red chilli powder would go in next, and then, with all three spices in, he'd take his time stirring the mix. Now it came time to bung in the potatoes, and finally the chopped tomatoes. What a lovely sight the vegetables made, all simmering delightfully together! And the fragrance! – it wafted over the whole dhaba. Kakka always knew how much salt to put into his vegetables, his measure was invariably exact. Then, the pot lidded with an aluminium plate, he'd say, "Understood, girls?" After which he sat on the takht and cooled himself with a handmade fan. "Go, fill a glass of water and the jug," he'd say to me, keeping an eye on the vegetables slow-cooking over a low fire as he carried on reading the newspaper with his other eye. Meanwhile Shalu and Shiva had questions: "O.K., tell us, if we happen to put too much salt into the vegetables? . . . What then? Come on, tell us, what do we do then?"

"Not such a big problem . . . Pour in a whole lot of water and let it all boil. No reason to worry."

Trying to trap the steam coming out of the vegetable pot with the palm of her hand, Shiva yelled, "Vamoose, Blackie!" Shalu removed the cover from the pot at once, but it did nothing to stop Shiva. "If Kakka weren't here, I'd show you . . ." I screeched, "Look, Kakka! They're squabbling . . . spoiling for a fight!" Kakka stayed resolutely absorbed in his newspaper. He really enjoyed reading it.

Between the dhaba and Raees Bhai's shop was a narrow lane. Every time a bus stopped at the stand, passengers strode into this lane to pee. The awful gut-wrenching stench made us sick to the gills. Ubaid, Jamshed, Shalu, and Shiva decided to teach the peeing populace a lesson. To do that they had to have a plan, and finally they hit upon one which worked: the moment anyone squatted to pee we stole up and poured water on them from the window above. They were horrified, they looked around, and we chucked more water over them. They yelled, "Hey, what's this?", and one of us yelled back, "Is this any place to pee? Go on, get lost!" Then a second, third, fourth, and fifth was targeted . . . How much water we chucked, on how many people, how many pissers we managed to stop, how many not, and how many actually took the drenching – often we'd be able to count, often the numbers were so large we couldn't keep track.

Ubaid wrote on the wall they liked targeting, "Look, here's a donkey urinating" and drew a half-donkey-half-man picture on it. In spite of all this, people still sat themselves right there to pee, possibly because it was a good vantage point from which to keep an eye on the bus. Some of those that got soaked grumbled and swore and went off, others complained to Kakka and Uncle. At such times we hid behind the dhaba.

Then, one day, an aggressive chap raised a huge hue and cry. The neighbouring shopowners joined the fray. There was a lot of cursing and shouting. The fellow most enraged said, "If this were a proper city, your kids would be boycotted. They'd get no marriage proposals. What kind of village boys and girls go around watching men pee and chuck water on them?" After this fracas, we stopped dousing pissing men. The moment a bus stopped we congregated at the entrance of the lane and shouted, "Not here, Not here." We allowed no-one to enter the lane to pee.

Right next to Raees Bhai's shop was Sindhi Kaka's, where meat was cooked, as well as daal. Not that anyone went there to eat daal. Once, Sindhi Kaka was heading to the maidan, mug in one hand and bidi in the other, for his morning ablutions. He was almost by the river when Shiva called me, "Look Babli, look!" First we laughed. Then she said, "Go, run off . . ."

And how I ran! Shiva shouting, "Faster! Faster!" I ran fast, slipperless, and almost bumped into him. Before he could figure things out, I snatched the mug from him and dropped it. "Hey, Hey," he shouted, turning. I ran back, with Sindhi Kaka in hot pursuit. Shiva had disappeared. He caught hold of me and socked me one on my back. I had to touch my ears, beg his forgiveness, but even while forgiving me he smacked me one more.

Sindhi Kaka wore spectacles. Looking at him, I wondered how he slept at night, how he turned while asleep, and whether when turning in his sleep his spectacles broke and the glass . . . Shiva lay down and explained it all properly: "See, here's the bed and here's the pillow. Near the pillow, here are the spectacles. Before going to sleep, he probably takes them off and when he gets up he puts them on again."

"Yeah! But then how does he find his spectacles?"

Shiva used her hands to grope around the pillow, "Like this . . . Like this . . ." I had assumed that people who wore specs were blind as bats without them.

Bai kept many fasts. Mostly she ate no food at all on such days, but occasionally she had semolina mixed up with potatoes, peanuts, green chillies, powered red chillies, sea salt, fresh coriander. It made a deliciously colourful khichadi which she shared with all of us. During her fasts she was beset by the most awful headaches. On one such occasion, Asha-jiji was home. Trying to figure out the reason for Bai's headaches she said, "Why do you stay hungry? Finish eating your mishmash."

"Don't badger me, Asha. What good will a bit of semolina do? And anyway, your Kakka doesn't always get it, does he?" Bai was irritated. But Asha-jiji, arms akimbo, said, "So, why do you make the whole lot in one go? Why don't you save some for later?"

"*Arré*, so that all of you can enjoy some of it!"

"So large-hearted of you! As if the others don't get to eat rotis!" She was seriously angry. She caught hold of each of us in turn: "Well? Why have the lot of you set your eyes on Bai's food?" She was a bit like that hot red chilli on Bai's dish, was our Asha-jiji. She could powder us into submission.

Bai started us all off on a fast on Mondays in July–August. For Shalu and Shiva it was every first Monday. The moment it was time for food, both piped up, "Kakka, we won't eat today. It's our Monday fast."

"You fools! How can you be taken in by such nonsense? Come on, eat! All this fasting is a heap of rubbish. Tell me, do you plan to work day and night without food?"

Even before those two were made to start fasting, we were familiar with the rituals associated with fasts, and of the fact that Kakka was as firmly opposed to them as Bai was for them. Kakka, it was clear, got thoroughly exasperated by the whole business.

Mondays in July–August became a real pain at school too. The girls grew extra chirpy over this time, they'd clutch their stomachs and say, "We plucked bel leaves, had our baths, went to the temple with our hair still wet, and were oh-so-hungry! And then we ate bananas and peanuts! We felt a bit better after that!"

Some of them ate sweet stuff despite the fast. Because of all this confusion we decided to keep just the nine-day fast when Durga Puja came around. When my very special friend Punita asked, "You're on a fast, aren't you?" I said: "No! In our family, only Bai fasts, no-one else does."

Surprised, she asked, "No-one except your mother? Not even your older sisters?"

"No, no-one! Our Kakka gets furious if we fast."

"Where's the need to tell your Kakka? We don't discuss

such things with our father. No girl does. Ask any of them."

So all the girls in class now knew I didn't fast. Then the whispering started – and grew louder. Shiva and Shalu went through the same experience. And then Shiva had a brainwave: "So what? We forgot the first Monday. We can start from next Monday!"

Shalu hesitated. "And Kakka?"

"You have to manage Kakka. No-one else can handle him the way you can! So, go on, start working on him."

And, most affectionately, Shiva pushed Shalu towards Kakka.

The result was that we started fasting on Mondays in July–August as well. The first day, we had our baths and went off to the temple. There was a lovely breeze. We were all carrying jasmine flowers and our hair flew in the breeze. We were close to the temple when there was a sudden gust. We tried to stop the flowers flying off our hands but a few fell into the gutter. Baby-didi from the neighbourhood was ready with a prediction: "Oh look! This is what's called Fate! Poor things – Fate has the gutter in store for them, not God."

"Tch tch tch," sighed everyone around, "The poor flowers . . ."

Those days, I was ill with hunger. I'd have to sit down clutching my stomach. Shalu and Shiva tried keeping my spirits up, "Just a little while more, a little more time, now! Just a little, quite little . . ."

Kakka would look at our dismal faces, laugh, and hand us some money, "Go get a banana from Shyamlal." The three of us would break our fast in the evening, around four or five, but we'd be hungry again by eleven at night. I'd go to serve the customers with Shalu and Shiva saying, ". . . Hey, Hey! Don't eat anything on the sly. You're not hiding a roti, are you?"

One Monday, Shiva packed a roti and vegetables for me to take home. "After midnight, the new day starts. Eat this at five past twelve . . . Babli, since you can't manage five Mondays, you do the first and the last. You'll only get a fat husband, that's all!" But since I still couldn't cope, I suffered a lot of snide remarks. When they grew unbearable, I went to Kakka and stood quietly before him, and then he yelled at them all.

Shivratri was a boisterously busy affair in our locality. People went off to Udaipur in whatever conveyance they could find. Kakka's view was, "If you want to see Udaipur, go some other day. Where's the need to go today? What will you ever manage to see or enjoy caught up in this kind of crowd?" But Bai wanted to go to Udaipur every year, and though we couldn't manage that, one year we did finally get to Udaipur.

What an incredible blend of architecture and sculpture! Stone fortifications and stunning statuary! The Rani's well, the temple gates! Beautifully sculpted broken statues, but still managing to reveal how attractive they must have been once.

The folks around chattered away without trying to listen or understand anything about the things they were seeing. They glanced at the temple and exclaimed, "Our very own Udeshwar temple, and just like Khajuraho . . . even better . . ." Others responded aggressively to this, "Oh, no! Khajuraho is something else! People come from all over the world to see it."

"Oh well, if the same people could only hear of this one, they'd turn up here too. No big deal! If we publicise it properly . . . Unless you make a racket, nobody knows a thing in this day and age . . . so it's necessary . . ."

These were the sorts that turned Shivratri into a noisy affair. They semed hell-bent on not seeing anything and not letting anyone else see anything either.

Later, we all broke our fast by the side of the Kevtan river. That was the moment we saw poori-aloo and mango pickle . . . mouth-watering stuff! At sundown, everyone genuflected and turned towards the temple and prayed to Lord Shiva. The temple appeared to be aglow. All around us was the poetry of sunset, land and sky becoming one on the horizon. Low clouds, the shadow of the sun, and the temple on the river water, the water shimmering, cries of *"Om Nama Shivaye, Om Nama Shivaye, Bhola Sabke Saath, Ganesh Hamare Saath!"*

On tracks with potholes, innumerable tractor-trolleys bumped along, large letters painted on them:

"If you want peace, spare us pain."

"Dream not, look straight ahead."

"Overtake when there's space."

"Overtake if you have the guts, or take it easy."

"Ask only from him who will happily give."

"Tell only him who will tell no-one."

The charms of Shivratri were so intoxicating that it was ages before we came down to earth.

We didn't listen much to Bai. She'd go on yelling and shouting and we'd go on ignoring her, so she took it out on us when she washed our hair. Sunday was the designated day and Saturday evening we'd hide the clothes-washing mallet; who knows, she might use it on us more than on the clothes! We called Sunday our "head-bashing" day. After Bai had washed our hair, we handed her the mallet and scampered off to the dhaba, laughing and shouting, "Head-bashing complete!" Those of us who'd been given the hair-wash were presented before Kakka at the dhaba as the Bashees of the Day. He'd say "*Arré, yaar!*" laugh, and pull the Bashees onto his lap.

I didn't know how to plait my hair. Which is why every morning, on school days, I ran after Bai. She invariably had her hands full with odd jobs. We did nothing around the house; we'd even ask her for a glass of water and not think of putting the glass back where it belonged. Schooltime was when I needed Bai to plait my hair.

Shiva managed to plait her own any old way, but I just couldn't. Bai grumbled a lot and it worried me to think thoughts like – When I grow up and start working and live far away from Bai, who's going to plait my hair? At one of the houses in the neighbourhood was a house-help who came to clean utensils. Watching her, I hit on a solution: when I grew up and started working, I'd keep a house-help who'd plait my hair.

At assembly in school the girls liked teasing each other about their hairstyles: "Yours is really crooked today! Look, it goes like this, then like this! My dear, today yours is well on its way to Bombay, yes!"

Once a week we were allowed to come to school in whatever clothes we chose. Every time a girl wore new clothes, all the girls yelled "New-pinch, New-pinch" and pinched her like hell.

"New-pinch! New-pinch! What colour? What colour?"

Till she recited all the colours she had on her, the pinching wouldn't end. Rajkumari pinched so hard she could make any poor girl in new clothes cry. When fighting, or when annoyed with a fellow student, the wearing of new clothes gave us a great excuse to take it all out on her. If a girl showed off too much in her new clothes, we all proceeded to sort her out with "New-pinch!" Among us sisters, though, the new-pinch opportunity was a rare thing.

If it began raining while we were at school, we'd all

shriek with delight. When school ended we hung around at the door and pushed each other out. The moment the rain got heavy we dashed homewards since home wasn't far from school. None of us took umbrellas to school, we enjoyed getting wet. Besides, carrying umbrellas was embarrassing. In any case, we couldn't carry umbrellas to school since we had no umbrellas at home.

During the rains we ran up and down between the house and the dhaba. The dhaba roof was a sieve during the monsoon and we had a hard time keeping a couple of benches dry for customers. Water dripped, *drip-drip-drip*, on everyone's heads. We loved the sound. During heavy thunderstorms the tin roofs often flew off. Kakka would climb up onto the roof and place loose plastic sheets to cover it. The tin of the roof was so flimsy we held our breath all the while that Kakka had to go up and down on it.

Over the rainy season, the grain market stayed shut. It was the time of long waits for customers, and when the odd customer finally arrived we'd all get involved serving him. When the rain was disastrously heavy, the drain in front of the dhaba choked, so then there were no customers at all; often a whole day went by with not a single customer. On such occasions Kakka heated and reheated the lentils and vegetables and sniffed at the dough to check it hadn't gone off.

One year, the Parasari burst its banks. Half the dhaba was flooded. Kakka lifted Seema, Bhaiyya, and myself and put us on top of the oven because the water was almost up to our necks. Kakka, Shalu, and Shiva were busy trying to save what they could. Both were waist-deep in water, Kakka rapidly passing stuff to them which they carried on their heads, across the drain, to safety. A strong wind made the rain seem calamitous. The wading girls screamed, "Kakka! Kakka!" in terror, and he chanted "Careful, girl! Careful girl!"

Between the three of them they hoisted all that could be carried to safety. Then Kakka took Seema and me on his shoulders and Shalu and Shiva joined hands to make a seat for Bhaiyya – this way we all got across. Then the three youngest among us stood guard over our belongings while the other three went to and fro till everything got home.

Kakka went off and on to check on the situation at the dhaba and came back looking grim each time. Mercifully, the flood did not disrupt life in the locality. Three or four days later the rain stopped, the flood waters receded, and the dhaba reopened.

On bleak days such as these we ate the lentils and vegetables meant for the dhaba's customers. Bai made rotis on the stove and all of us sat around it, or more truly around her, and ate.

When the river overflowed, the townspeople gathered to watch the floods in wonderment and awe, but it puzzled us how they could look so bedazzled – because for us the floods meant Bai's sad face and Kakka lifting us onto his shoulders to carry us to safety. In the rains, the Parasari was a boon for the townsfolk but a bane for those near the bus stand. The river waters had receded from the dhaba, but the rain had not let up. For days we watched the river in spate from atop the college boundary wall: "If it continues non-stop till nightfall, the water's bound to enter the shops again."

"*Arré*, Bhaiyya Mohan, our Parasari is as great as any river! See, how she rolls!"

This was Om Bhaiyya, squeezing water out of his shirt, swaying from the branch of a tree by the river.

Rameshwar Uncle, never one to keep his mouth shut, gazed wide-eyed in the river waters for green chillies and coriander, and said sarcastically, "Hey! The river's only looking this good because of the flood waters! Mostly it's only a stream and half the time it's bone dry!"

"So what d'you want it to do, roll around all year this way? We'd all starve without food and water, and how would you pay your creditors?" Mohan Bhaiyya was all worked up and ready to pick a fight.

"Hell, no! These rivers know when to be in spate, and when to do other things. They're far smarter than you!"

Bespectacled Sindhi Kaka explained it all to us . . . though in the midst of all that chattering we feared a few of us might topple off the boundary wall and into the water.

Shiva said of Sindhi Kaka, "Y'know, Uncle should get wipers for his spectacles, like the ones on bus windscreens!"

Om Bhaiyya was settled on the boundary wall, legs dangling. Roshan sat on his shoulders and sang hymns to the river. The moment Vakil Sahib walked into the dhaba, Kakka summoned us all back. Mishra-ji, the Vakil Sahib, talked a lot but could explain nothing. His ramblings went roughly like this: "Listen carefully to what I say. Four hundred years ago, by the banks of the River Betwa, lay Vasudev Nagar. The city was destroyed by floods. The population had to scatter. You know how our town came into existence? Let me explain. All the pandits settled in Rajinder Nagar and Pandapura. This is now what we call the town. The Rajputs settled in Pathaar Mohalla. The rest in Mirzapur and Balaut, and the painters in Budhepura. You know how the name Basudeva came about? It's a gift of those painters.

"This is all coming down from the Vedic civilisation. Now, don't all of you get worked up about the meaning of civilisation! If I was to explain all those intricacies, my jaw would give way. And believe me, you wouldn't understand anyway, not even if you sat here the rest of your lives. But listen, the Vedic people made a lot of gold jewellery . . . used gold thread to embroider their clothes. Gold was worked into their clothes! Very fine, very delicate! Basoda! . . . meaning one who gives 'vastra' . . . but not any old ordinary clothes of the kind that you and I wear, they had zari-embossed clothes. Pushan Dev was the original weaver of that kind of cloth."

Everyone was deeply engrossed in Vakil Sahib's meanderings till someone interrrupted his flow: "And how about our wholesale market . . .?"

"Your market was begun some eighty or ninety years back."

Straightaway, a third person piped up: "You're talking of the grain market, right?"

"Oh dear! Hey, you fellows talk like such absolute idiots. If not the grain market, what d'you think I was referring to? The vegetable market? Use your brains, you lot, not just your hands and legs. O.K.? Apart from the grain market, what do we even have here?

"Basoda's glory is the grain market . . . And yes, after they made the Delhi–Mumbai line go past here, we've all prospered. No-one would've known you existed without it . . . the world contains thousands of small towns . . ."

"And . . . Vakil Sahib, what of our river? Look at its fierce avatar now! Tell us a little about the Parasari, and about the Betwa . . ." Even those who never spoke had now begun edging their irons into the fire.

"Enough for today. I'll tell you about the Betwa some other day. It's late, I'd better get to the courts to see what's going on."

Before Vakil Sahib could step out to go off to the court compound, the crowd rose to see the G.T. Express, which had been stalled by the rain. "Come on, Come on! Let's take a round of the station. As it is, the G.T. never stops here – now that it has, let's go and take a look . . ."

". . .Yeah, let's see how the station looks in the rain now that the G.T.'s parked in it . . ."

The evening spreads itself over the station and the birds are in full song. It's almost as if the crackle and laughter of evenings the world over starts here. A small platform, four or five stone benches, and two water taps on either side, people greedily drinking water while chatting about the world!

The sound of the train echoed through the town; it was as if she wanted every household to know she'd reached the platform, or would shortly. And yet the locals never let on that they'd heard her arrive. If an outsider said, "Hurry up, come on! The train's come!" or "Hurry up, the train will soon leave", the locals stared at them as if looking at the Eighth Wonder of the World! They said lovingly – though outsiders could have misconstrued it as arrogance – "*Arré!* How can it go without you? We'll put you on it. Don't worry, it'll take everyone."

The moment that train stopped, whole swarms of locals ran up with buckets of water. Their aim was that no-one, not one person, should have to go without water. At the height of summer afternoons, having drunk cold water from our taps, those train travellers started singing like birds: they peeped out of train windows, read out the name of our town – Ganj Basoda – and as the train left they waved at the people who'd quenched their thirst.

In peak summer the only thing, cold water apart, that could conceivably entice a traveller to look out of the window was the parting from a beloved daughter who'd just been married. The railway station at Ganj Basoda was a regular venue for weeping Kakkas bidding good-bye to their newly wedded daughters. It seemed to us that even the birds wept on these occasions and flew alongside the train, telling the departing daughters to take heart . . .

But then, what else was there at that forlorn station – other than a little water? Even the Grand Trunk Express looked to us like a passenger train. Sure, the travellers in the G.T. looked a bit different – and they in turn probably saw us as scarecrows.

In the middle of that torrential rain, chatter about the river was extraordinarily heart-warming! Vakil Sahib talked non-stop and didn't like being interrupted. A book under his arm, his tongue would begin wagging faster than a happy dog's tail: "About two miles from Sagar Mandi, near Mangraud, where two streams meet up with the Betwa, the Betwa turns east and fetches up at Village Sakrauli. That's it. Right there the Betwa turns south and then moves eastwards. It crosses our Sironj–Basoda road right there.

"Our Basoda is based two miles south of the Betwa. About three miles further down the Betwa's right bank touches the Parasari flowing in from the east and then moves up north. The Betwa's current is so strong it beats even some of the great rivers. Which is why no-one could dam the Betwa! Till 1887 the Betwa was self-willed and unrestrainable. But then the dam at Paricha made people realise the good that can come of it, that the Betwa could be a life-giver. Then in 1910 the Sukwa–Dhukwa Dam got built, and in 1952 the Mata-Tila Dam."

Rounding it all off, Vakil Sahib said: "O.K. Did you lot realise that our Basoda spreads out four ways? Right in the centre of the town is Jai Stambh Chauraha. To its east is the Railway Station, westwards is the town and the market area, while up north is Bareth Road, and south of the square is Tyonda Road."

"Yeah! No-one gets lost in our town!"

One smack on Roshan's head from Vakil Sahib and then the class dispersed!

After everyone had left, Kakka said, "*Arré, wah!* These are knowledgeable people. It's a different world among these intellectuals. Very interesting, so enlightening! These people know how to gab about absolutely everything! Such well-read people, these . . ." Saying all this, it seemed his entire body was radiant with happiness! "Shalu," he went on, "pay attention, child, when he speaks, he's full of learning . . ." And Shalu's expression suggested she already knew every last thing that Vakil Sahib had said.

Shalu's affectations really got Shiva's goat, she couldn't stop herself: "Listen, Sourpuss! You can start lecturing us too from tomorrow. You can teach us what the colour of water is, about the sound of water, the smell of water, the water's temperament, enmity with water, relationship with water, and even what water tastes like. Kakka will be happy!"

"No! First I'm going to teach you to swim in the river using a tube!"

"You can't even drink a full glass of water, how're you planning on facing the river?"

Taken aback, Shalu couldn't figure out whether she should take on the challenge of the jug of water or the challenge of the tube . . .

Kakka, of course, got along famously with Vakil Sahib. After hearing those stories about the river and Basoda we understood why. But the bottomline for him was still the lack of customers at his dhaba during the rains – it was very difficult for him to handle that. Watching those moving passengers in the train we always yearned for them to stop a while and eat at where we waited.

13

THE COURT HAD ITS seasons too. The red-brick court house had black-coated lawyers and, trailing behind them, poor farmers. The courts were always packed with farmers. If someone happened to say to a farmer, "Hey, granddad! How come you're caught up in all this? Who's done this to you?", the old man responded as if the questioner and the other hangers-on were there to decide his fate. Often, it seemed this was a rehearsal for the real thing! "No, no, Babu-ji! I'm stuck in a land dispute. My younger brother's really stupid. What can I say? He listens to nobody. He's off his rocker!"

When the farmers were exhausted by the goings-on in the court house, the peepal tree provided them succour. They sat in its shade and ate their dry rotis and washed them down with water from a nearby tap. Then they rolled their towels into pillows and curled up, lying with their eyes open in the shade of the tree, watching the court house. God knows how many poor litigants were given a little relief by that peepal tree! Every half-hour the farmers went into the court house, and when they came back empty-handed the peepal tree was still around, waiting right there. Farmers whose appearance at the court house was required every week or two took out crunched-up five-rupee notes from their bags, then put them back in, repeating the act again and again. If yet another court date was announced, they'd beg Vakil Sahib to expedite the case.

Before Vakil Sahib could reach the dhaba, this variety of litigant farmer would go off to Rameshwar Uncle and place an order for tea and snacks. Inspite of places on the bench, he'd squat on the ground. From a vest under a dirty kurta he'd fish out one of those crumpled notes. Kakka's heart would melt at this sight, "This chap . . . he can't afford even a cup of tea . . . has to swallow dry rotis with water . . . he's half dead himself but feels he must feed Vakil Sahib tea and snacks . . ."

The endless litigation that plagued farmers' lives disturbed Kakka very deeply. "Tope, you'll die going in and out of the court house! Go fetch your brother and make him meet Vakil Sahib. Arrive at some compromise, you fool! And if you can't cope, fetch your brother here. I'll show him how to listen, that brother of yours! And here, keep your money."

Then he'd yell – "Hey Rameshwar!" – and persuade Vakil Sahib to reduce his fees by half.

Farmers tired out by the law, teary-eyed, caught buses back home in the hope that they would in time be rid of the ritual of going back and forth to the court house. These were men who bowed before the court house from the bus stand, almost as if bowing to the river. No words of prayer, but men trembling, their eyes wet. What were they begging for from the gods they imagined in that court house?

14

EVERY DIWALI, A COAT of paint was lathered on the table and chair in Pramod's shop. We argued with Kakka, "... this time round we'll paint our tables and chairs too." He stayed non-committal while we fought over who was going to do the painting. Shalu mostly carried the day – he'd say "She's the oldest and the most sensible. So she's the one who's going to paint."

At home and at the dhaba, it was lime wash. We all wielded the brush and were soon covered in lime. Eight or nine at night meant bath time, after which Bai rubbed coconut oil all over our skin. Her fingers were burnt by the lime over the painting days and some years it was so bad they bled. Bai was always a stickler for cleanliness and work clumsily done she could not bear. She painted so well herself that people thought the house had been professionally done. It did tire her out, though, and made her crabby, and she'd yell at us for no reason at all.

The process of whitewashing involved her being up on a ladder and me standing below with a pot of the lime wash. As she climbed higher I'd take a step or two up in tandem. Bhaiyya and Seema held the ladder firm. She also made us fetch and carry while the lime wash was getting done, all the while worrying about us slipping and falling.

Once, she said something to Bhaiyya that he didn't understand. This irritated her, and then God knows what, something set us giggling. Bai said something again, and again Bhaiyya didn't understand. Really angry now, she yelled, "He's an idiot, like his father!"

None of us could bear anything said against Kakka, but Bai never could fathom this, and her mutterings progressed to a litany: "God knows what clay this whole family of mine is made of . . . Who can bear children like these? *Arré*, you lot are a curse on me from my last life! A curse!"

This made us too scared to utter a word, and often when her ranting went on and on, we were near tears. That particular evening, when Kakka came back home, Bai's painting fatigue had left her bristling with anger. Kakka asked laughingly, "What Rajjo . . . are you worn out? . . .", but she said nothing in reply. Bhaiyya said, "Kakka . . ." and lunged to hug him, whereupon I piped up, "Kakka, Bai was telling Bhaiyya that . . . that . . ."

At this point Bai angrily swung the paint brush, covering everyone with lime wash. Some of it splashed and fell on Kakka as well.

"Don't go on this way with the kids, my dear . . . control your anger, Rajjo," he said.

"*Arré!* Since when has lime splash begun talking?"

The way she was looking at me now was how she was looking that time . . . like Grandma looked when ticking off her younger son.

"Kakka, Bai was telling Bhaiyya that . . .?"

Sometimes I wonder if that question mark changed into some other punctuation mark – could it have? I often ended my sentences with an exclamation mark instead of a full stop. Shalu twisted my ear many times, but Shiva's full stops and question marks were, like her, proper.

"*Chhook-Chhook-Chhook ko-ko-ko*" – green flag – "*Chu-churr-churr*" – platform – and the train stops. When Shiva the engine stopped, we "coaches" stopped too. Pretending to be a smoking engine she'd ask: "Have you understood what a full stop is?" And then, transforming us all into rumbling coaches, turning herself into an engine, letting out a shrill cry, she'd say, "Look! There's someone lying on the tracks in front! *Chhook-Chhook-Chhook* the train is going, *Koo-Koo-Koo*, loud shrill horn, there's just an inch of space left . . . *Koo-koo-koo-koo-koo-koo-koo-koo – Chhook-Chhook-Chhook, koo-koo-koo-koo . . . chhook-chhook – chhook*."

A second later the man had jumped up and run off! "*Arré!* He's safe! His life's been saved!"

"How long will you lot go on staring with eyes wide open? Have you understood or not? This is what an exclamation mark looks like!"

She'd turn to me. "Fatty, if you blunder again between an exclamation mark and a full stop . . . !"

Anyway, after finishing the lime wash we all sat down to have tea with Kakka. Mother had made the tea a little too strong.

Next day, Shalu and Shiva finished the house's lime wash and went off to paint the dhaba. But Bai wasn't happy with the bits at home that she hadn't done herself, no-one else's work was good enough for her. She picked up the brush and started redoing areas that had been freshly painted. She climbed to the top of the ladder and took three steps down each time she needed to dip the brush into the pot, which was on my head, and carried on this way.

She was a fine painter!

Standing tiptoe on the ladder that day, she swung the brush so hard she disturbed a wasp's nest in the corner. The brush fell out of her hand and the pot fell off my head. A swarm of wasps came flying out and I yelled "Bai . . . Bai . . . Bai . . ." Somehow or the other she managed to clamber down the ladder and started dashing around. There were too many wasps. She flung off her sari. Seema and Bhaiyya tried shooing away the wasps. Nothing worked. Any number of wasps were now stuck to Bai. I ran and picked up the broom and began swatting at the wasps on her head, on her face, on her hands, on her feet . . . wherever you looked there were wasps . . .

Hearing our clamour the Aunt across the road came running and helped Bai lie down. With the attack from the broom, most of the wasps were dead, the remainder had disappeared. Bai had fainted. Seema ran and got Kakka from the dhaba. He brought a rickshaw with him.

Two days later was Diwali. We called it our Waspy Diwali.

The wasps must have stung Bai in a thousand places. Recalling the incident she often shivered. So did I – some of those stings in me had for a while turned sore. One night Bai, watching me sleep, said: "If Babli hadn't used the broom on the wasps, I wouldn't be alive. Her brain really worked – the fact that she went and got the broom . . ."

Like the stings of those wasps, the soreness within me vanished.

15

ALL THE SHOPS AT the bus stand stood on encroached land. The dhaba too was only half legal. The area where the oven was, where the pots and pans and plates and glasses were, the platform on which Kakka sat, and the area behind the dhaba which showed a little mound of ash and coal and the water tank – they were all on encroached land. Only the portion in the middle where the customers sat was secure and legal.

When an anti-encroachment squad arrived and began demolishing all the shops, we saw Kakka shaken for the first time in our lives. He ran to the house and gathered up all his papers. The town's bigwigs and lawyers all collected at the dhaba.

Some people started protesting while others, keeping in view the delicacy of the situation and the firmness of the squad, suggested that a solution be found through discussion. But the anti-encroachment squad was prepared to listen to no-one. They just carried on. Everyone was so bewildered – stunned beyond tears. The Deputy Collector and the Deputy Superintendent of Police, who was called the DSP, were both tough customers. People trembled at the very mention of the DSP's name.

When the squad reached the dhaba, despite Kakka and his friends being present, the oven was demolished. Both officers had looked through his papers most carefully. For the first time in our lives, Kakka pushed us all aside. A huge crowd had gathered at the bus stand. People held their breath as they watched shops turn to rubble. Seeing the crowd and the state Kakka was in, we felt our insides crumble too. Shalu took us away and made us sit on a mound of ash at the back, even though she herself was in pieces, and Shiva's eyes were turning red – she was near the tap, just frozen. The tin shed had been entirely destroyed – with everything in it.

Kakka came to where we were on the pretext of washing his face, but seeing us he panicked. Shalu and Shiva clung to him, panic-stricken and broken.

Where was the oven to be put? The middle portion was where all the remaining equipment was, so there wasn't space to position it there. At night no food was cooked anywhere, the whole bus stand had been demolished. People sat around in a stupefied silence on mounds of rubble.

At eight or nine Shalu came in running and panting. "Kakka! Kakka! The head priest at the temple is asking for you! Hurry up, come on!"

It was as if she wanted Kakka to fly, she was breathless, her words garbled: "Kakka, officers have gone to the temple . . . the head priest wants you!"

Before he could move, we had run ahead. Bai was

already in the temple and we nestled behind her. The head priest made Kakka stand alongside him. The Deputy Collector, after paying obeisance, went to the head priest and bowed before him. The head priest pushed Kakka forward, "*Arré!* He is our leader! He has a big heart. He has eight daughters and a son, the youngest. He has a dhaba at the bus stand."

The officer understood. Tremulous with anxiety, Kakka narrated all that had happened. The officer quietly told Kakka to put the oven where the ash mound was. Kakka thanked him with folded hands.

For the first time – yes, for the first time, ever – Kakka seemed entirely helpless. And how helpless he looked! The officer's car had barely left when Bai and Aunt bent to touch the head priest's feet. The priest looked at us all and said to Bai, "Why worry? God will make everything all right. Go tell your husband . . . get the oven going tonight." Then he gave us all some of his temple sweetmeats with his blessings.

The dhaba stood proud again. The food was now made on the oven – at the back. The youngest among us, Seema, Bhaiyya, and I, stood prominently outside so that people knew the dhaba was open for business. Shalu, Shiva, and Kakka slaved away inside. Because the shops were all demolished, our dhaba's sales were better than they used to be.

Rameshwar Uncle and various others resumed selling tea on handcarts. Uncle brought a variety of savouries from his home. His little wok lay unused – who was ever going to buy stone-cold savouries? So there was no option except just to sell the tea made on those handcarts. Well, there was at least a halfway decent chance of a tea cart selling tea, but how was one to run a hotel on a handcart when even the tea sellers found the going tough – for folks like to sit and drink their tea. They'd say, "If one has to stand and eat here, its best not to eat at all. We slog day and night to get some food into our stomachs, and then we're told we have to eat on the run . . . No way. Unless we sit comfortably crosslegged we can't eat, so it's no use all this talk of how fine it is to break bread standing straight up."

There was now only the dhaba, in the entire bus stand area, where people could sit and eat. And even us youngsters didn't need to hang around outside any more – everyone knew the oven had been repositioned at the back. Even the cow knew it and showed up at the back each morning, before the first sale of the day.

But, given the circumstances, the fact that the dhaba was running so well was no great occasion for happiness amongst us. All around were people perched on heaps of rubble, and there in the middle of that chaos was our solitary functioning dhaba. It sometimes seemed the bus stand had turned into a bizarre ground for lounging, and we were running the dhaba in the middle of it.

Kakka now took people to the court house turn by turn, and there the discussions with lawyers continued for hours on end. Then he took everyone to meet the MLA, a politico who handed everyone extra-sweet tea – not that anyone really wanted his tea. When Kakka was away on these odd jobs, people from the bus stand turned up to help us run the dhaba. The sadness on their faces left us even more morose.

Three or four days went by in this fashion with no magical outcome in sight. People went again and again to try meeting the Deputy Collector, but leave alone meet him, not even a glimpse could they catch of the fellow. Then, Kakka decided to take everyone off to meet the head priest. On that day, when the people of the neighbouring locality saw the entire bus stand's population at the temple, they laughed sceptically, "You never even look in the direction of the temple normally! . . . Better late than never . . . do keep showing up there after your shops have been rebuilt, else they might be demolished again!"

"Ram, Ram, Jai Siyaram! Radhe Krishna, Krishna, Radhe Krishna, Hail Hanuman, begotten of the wind" – the temple reverberated with a chorus of voices from the bus stand. The congregation at the temple anticipated the arrival of the Deputy Collector, people bowed low before the head priest, then settled down to wait with long faces, intermittently chanting in full-throated unison their plea for the priest's help to make their encroachments legal. After a couple of weeks of this, people simply started rebuilding their shops. Why they were demolished, how

they were rebuilt, no-one would dare say. The very phrase "anti-encroachment squad" had them petrified.

Kakka put his takht outside the dhaba. The bus stand went back to being exactly what it used to be; even the rubble disappeared, heaven knows where it went.

But the oven remained forever at the back. One day at teatime I overheard Kakka say to Bai, "Shalu and Shiva are now looking quite grown up. It's best they stay working in the back. Let the others remake their shops in front, it's better for ours to stay where it is."

16

AT HOME WE HAD A big, nice-looking maroon and light-yellow radio. For some unknown reason it was perched on a stone stand. Bai never listened to it but saw to it that everyone gave the radio the respect that was its due.

Shalu and Shiva had their tea at different times. When their quarrelling grew intense, they no longer yelled and shouted or hit each other. Instead, they'd worked out new ways of getting on each other's nerves. Shalu listened to the radio a lot – she always had it on while cramming. The logic she gave was that it helped her concentrate. God knows what they fought over, except, one day, Shalu pulled out the radio's wire, hid it, and went off to the dhaba. So when Shiva came home and tried to put the radio on, she couldn't get a cheep out of it. This rattled her. She swung the radio around . . . left and right, up and down . . . until she finally got it – the wire was missing. She said, "Bai, where's the wire?"

Bai kept her mouth pursed. So Shiva started hunting for the wire. Her tea went cold but she wouldn't stop looking for the wire. Peering everywhere, she came and stood in front of the stone stand, as if expecting the radio to tell her where the wire was!

After a while she found the wire somewhere amongst the quilts. Saying not a word to anyone, hiding the wire in her kurta, she went up to the roof and shoved it into the attic. Then, picking the cold crust out of her tea with a finger, she said, "We don't have to do anything now; we just have to turn into Bapu's three monkeys: no-one heard; no-one saw; no-one spoke. Let's see how Sourpuss gets to listen to the radio now!"

Shiva stayed mum. The radio stayed mum. And Shalu couldn't say anything because she knew she was the last to have put the radio on.

Bai said to Kakka, "Our radio's gone bust. Day and night these girls twiddle its knobs. I think Shalu turned it on last, after that it hasn't worked. Nothing's getting it to work."

Kakka tried putting it on. But how was it ever going to start? Shiva glared fixedly at me. God knows why, but we were all now scared of Kakka. There was never any question of him hitting us, or even yelling at us, but the fact was that we were wary of his temper. On this occasion he had only to look firm and say, "Hey, you . . .", and it was enough for Shalu to blurt out the whole story. Bai turned all the quilts upside down. Still no wire.

Kakka turned to Shiva. He said, "Go, get the wire."

But what an obstinate creature she was – it was two days before she fished out that wire. And even then, she just dropped it disdainfully near the quilts.

17

SHIVA PROGRESSED TO Class 10, Shalu to Class 11.

One night, Kakka was sitting around with his friends on the takht outside the dhaba when I, listening intently to their conversation, suddenly thought of Shalu. I looked around for her everywhere but could see no sign of her. Tired, I turned and asked, "Kakka, Kakka! Where's Shalu?"

"Must be around . . . at the back."

I ran towards the back, came back without catching sight of her, and said, "She isn't there either."

Kakka made no reply.

After everyone had left, Shalu shimmered in out of thin air. "Shalu, Shalu," I screamed.

She pinched me hard, "What're you yelling for? Kakka, I'd just gone round to the boundary wall . . . to shit."

Not much more could be said, it seemed best to end her story there. The difficulty was that the same thing began to recur every day. Every day she'd disappear, and then as suddenly reappear. Once, she disappeared for a really long time. Kakka hunted high and low for her at the dhaba and even sent me running to the house. I banged the door open, entered panting, and yelled "Shalu, Shalu . . ."

Bai saw my state and went into shock. I went running back to the dhaba. Father saw me and understood immediately that I hadn't found her. He went quiet, he looked around, a quivering floating leaf in a sudden heavy rainstorm. Seeing him in such a state, I said, tears in my eyes, "Kakka, she's not at Raees Bhai's shop either."

Hearing that, he placed his palm over my mouth. From the back we heard Shalu yell, "Babli! Help me wash my hands."

18

THE LONESOME QUIVERING leaf swam up again . . . Kakka's eyes filled with tears as he looked at her. I looked at her too – and I also saw Raees Bhai. He had quietly shown up in his shop and begun doing some welding work.

We shut the dhaba earlier than usual and went home. Kakka was very quiet, and as for Bai – well, she could tell even from the way we walked that something was seriously amiss.

No-one ever learned what transpired between Kakka and Shalu, what was said between them. Perhaps even Bai never got to know. All I was sure of was that Shalu started seeing me as her enemy. For a period she was very quiet. Kakka too appeared off-colour and irritable.

Raees Bhai continued working at his shop and carried on chatting with his friends, but he no longer looked in the direction of the dhaba. Occasionally, if a particularly sentimental song happened to be playing on his radio, he'd turn up the volume. At ten o'clock one night, during the Chhayageet programme, there was a man on the radio who sang, "I'll want you in the morning . . . I'll want you at night . . . But your name . . . never again will I call out your name." All the while, Raees Bhai sat quietly at a table, head bowed. And Shalu, who was at our window, wept. The moment she saw me, I ran off.

For a short period of time, all seemed well. Shalu tutored Bhaiyya and carried on with her studies – in fact she seemed a little too immersed in her books. The tension had eased, everyone had begun feeling relaxed because her mind now seemed focussed on her books. On lazy afternoons we freshened our faces with splashes of water. Kakka's hopes seemed to have blossomed, his tendency towards flights of fancy seemed ready to soar again like a bird.

He came home for tea one evening, as he always did. At the dhaba, the broom in the corner beckoned Shiva; the oven and the pots and pans waited upon Shalu; the floor needed watering. Heating the lentils and vegetables, sweeping the dhaba, drawing water – these three evening tasks had long been divided between the three of us. I reached the tap with a bucket when, suddenly, the two of them said to me, "Go! You can go off home this evening!" I got the feeling that my presence was irritating them, it looked like there was some reason or other for them to want me gone. They'd now begun chatting merrily, in fact they were soon a cackling and chuckling twosome.

What was afoot? And why was it afoot? How come Shalu and Shiva had suddenly become thick as thieves?

In my mind it seemed the Parasari had turned turtle and begun to flow the other way round.

19

ONE DAY, CHATURVEDI-JI'S daughter ran off with Raees Bhai's aunt's son. This stunned the whole town into a profound silence. Raees Bhai was locked up in the police station. The police caught hold of maybe forty or fifty people. When they were produced in court, the crowd stoned them. One of the stones hit Raees Bhai. He screamed, *"Arré . . . !"*

A strangely suffocating atmosphere shrouded us soon. The children around seemed to have grown unnaturally cocky, the world around had grown tense. People seemed to look at the dhaba, and especially at Shalu, with hostility. Kakka took to lying quietly on his takht. The conversation in every household was about nothing else. And complete strangers began apearing at the dhaba to eat – men we'd never seen before. Their eating, we sensed, was an excuse. They'd come to check up on us.

Some of these fellows started loitering around our house, as if to indicate that this was where they were going to catch Raees Bhai's aunt's son and the eloping girl red-handed – and that would give them a chance to attack Kakka in full public view. A strange silence fell over our home. Bai kept the doors open longer, as if saying "Come and see. Take a good look. There's no-one in our house."

And what could Kakka say? Over this time he grew almost unrecognisable. Shalu hadn't stopped seeing Raees Bhai, she'd just changed the timing of her meetings with him. Their rendezvous happened in the evening, near the well behind the school. It was Puran Singh who told Kakka about it. Puran Singh, who had a shop at the bus stand, rolled up his sleeves and said, "If you want, I can confront your daughter . . . what I say is true."

Kakka resisted, he was determined to stay resolute in wanting Shalu to finish Class 11 and Shiva Class 10. To Bai he explained matters gently: "This is the age . . . children make mistakes. I've explained matters to her. She won't disobey me. Our daughter is sensible, isn't that so?" His look in her direction was an appeal.

A mass marriage was scheduled to take place in Nagpur. It may have been tempting, but Kakka stuck to his guns and wanted nothing to do with it. His girls must first stand on their own feet, their marriages would follow. He gave Bai strict instructions to say nothing to Shalu – who kept her head down over her books all night, with the radio on.

The police finally caught Chaturvedi-ji's daughter on a Sunday evening while she was watching a film in a cinema hall, wearing a burqa. Chaturvedi-ji was an influential man, so the matter was hushed up and within eight days he married his daughter off to a Brahmin boy.

Raees Bhai's aunt's son, Salim Bhai, disappeared from sight. At the dhaba a lot of overblown gossip went on and on about the whole affair. Everyone had his own version of it, each story had twists and turns added on to the dramatic core.

One night, when Kakka, Shiva, and I stepped out of the dhaba on our way home, we saw a little boy hand over a letter to Shalu. Kakka began coughing and bent over the tap for water. When we reached home Shalu was bent over her books. The sky was covered with stars, some of them twinkling brighter than the others.

Asha-jiji arrived the next day. Stories about Shalu's doings had reached her village as well. She shut all the doors and windows of the house carefully, then spoke: "The whole village is murmuring, 'Watch out, her sister's going to run off with a Muslim.' Kakka, we don't have Chaturvedi-ji's clout . . . we can't just marry her off to some fellow from our own caste. The whole world's begun spitting on us. Kakka, she's going to let you down!"

By this time Asha-jiji was enraged and spluttering. She caught hold of Shalu: "Hey, you! You're still seeing that fellow every day, aren't you? And you won't change your ways? You can fool Kakka maybe, but there's no way you can fool me, you blasted good-for-nothing! I know just what you're up to . . ."

The four winds confirmed all that Asha-jiji was saying. Made even more livid by the silence, she proceeded to smash the radio to bits. "A most strange way of studying!

Listening to songs while concentrating!? When most people barely manage one task at a time!"

Here were Asha-jiji and Kakka, and there, by them, half comatose over the broken radio, was Shalu – broken too, and in tears. And suddenly a shriek from the lane. We all rushed out, even little Bhaiyya. Bai was shouting and pushing Shiva, but she had positioned both her arms around her head in self-defence and was refusing to budge.

"What's happened, what's happened?" Kakka sounded shaken.

Bai pushed at Shiva again, then explained, panting and breathless: "There we were, arguing with Shalu . . . and this idiot Shiva went upstairs with a bucket . . . I shouted to warn her against doing anything stupid, but would she listen? . . . So I banged on the door and it flew open . . . I'd no reason to think there'd be anyone in there." Bai took a long, deep breath. "And there under the stairs she was . . . hiding with Raees. And look at this, there's something in her hand . . ." Saying this, she hit Shiva.

Whether Raees Bhai had given Shiva a letter for Shalu, or whether Shalu had asked Shiva to pass on a letter to Raees, I couldn't figure out. Seeing Bai's panic, my world too had shattered around me.

Early the next morning Kakka left on a train for Nagpur. The dhaba stayed shut. Asha-jiji stayed on with us. Shalu and Shiva were confined to the house. Kakka had gone off to look for grooms for them. In two days he was back. The next day, the boys' relatives arrived and all the arrangements were finalised. The weddings were to happen soon. Once the girls finished their papers, we'd all have to go off to Nagpur.

Overnight, Kakka turned into a tragic figure, the embodiment of a dirge. He had only to glimpse Shalu and Shiva to turn away frozen, cold as his unused oven. Regardless of the oven's temperature, though, the people around Kakka began breathing freely once more.

20

SHALU'S RESULTS WERE out. Kakka opened the newspaper eagerly, searching for her roll number. He still hadn't given up hope – her result could still change the game. All he wanted for the moment was a little piece of land on which he might stand on his own two feet. But her roll number wasn't to be found.

Shalu took the torn newspaper and shed copious tears. The dhaba crawled on. The normally fast-moving Shiva, red-eyed from crying, hung silently around a dry tap. There was no water in that tap. Shalu's tears had used up every last drop in it.

Even the cow's eyes looked as if she'd been shedding tears. She just stood there, watching the torn newspaper. She just stood there, waiting for the earth to swallow her up.

Kakka looked as shrivelled as a dried-up well. He stuttered when he spoke: "Girls, I've done my best to see you have a good life. Now, my dears, your fate is out of my hands." He seemed to have fallen apart, a mountain was crumbling.

Shalu and Shiva could never have imagined his love for them boomeranging on him as a curse, a curse that would break his back forever. Suddenly, overnight, we saw Kakka turn into a very old man.

21

OUR AUNT, PHAPPHU, and Grandmother arrived with the usual hustle and bustle and customary wedding presents, but one look at Kakka, and Phapphu forgot all about the presents. Grandmother took Bai aside to figure out what was going on. Perhaps they hadn't heard something they ought to have? But how could that be?

Phapphu and Grandmother weren't to accompany us to Nagpur. They wanted us to observe all the wedding rituals right where we lived, but no-one else wanted that.

"Newfangled ideas!" Grandmother muttered, taking a deep breath.

Phapphu stuck to Kakka day and night but kept her mouth shut. "And have you seen what your Kakka looks like? Your Kakka's a diamond!" Irritable and stubborn though Phapphu was, strangely enough she wasn't condemning anyone for the loss of Kakka's lustre.

Bai now had a bandage permanently tied around her head. Our Chhoté Mama-ji stopped popping up to the roof to smoke his bidis; instead he just hung around Bai. "Jiji," he said, "shall I put a little Vicks on your forehead?" And when looking at Shalu, he averted his eyes, turning them away just as he had, long back, when staring unblinking at the sparks of the welder's rod. He'd won that bet, but no-one would have said now that his were the eyes of a man who had won any sort of bet.

There were now so many people in the house, yet no bickering over pillows, no shortage of sheets, no commotion over baths, no complaints on shortage of space ... it was as if everyone had shrunk a bit. And what of the radio on its stand? It wasn't just missing one wire, it felt like every last bit of wiring within it had vanished.

22

AND THERE WAS NO storm, no rain, no thunder, no lightning. A whirlwind blew in, and before we knew it, the wedding rituals were all done and dusted. Even the feet-washing was over without any of us having hidden the grooms' shoes! And the grooms hadn't untied the knot in the ceremonial area! None of the normal rituals had really been observed and yet the ceremony was over! The brides and bridegrooms had crossed the threshold without the brides' brother – our Bhaiyya – giving them his customary blessings.

At the ceremonial farewell from their home, Shalu and Shiva wept bitterly: there was no holding back the floodgates.

"Kakka . . . Kakka . . ." they wept, clinging desperately to him. And he, sobbing, stood before Shiva and Shalu's fathers-in-law with folded hands, wanting to say something but not finding the words. "Sahib, my girls, please . . ." – he'd start to say what was brimming over within him, but then he'd get no further.

Why was Kakka falling at the feet of these grooms and their fathers, over and over again? Why was he bending over backwards this way? Why was he weeping his heart out? We'd never seen him so cringing, so upset. It was clear to me that had Shalu and Shiva continued with their education, none of this would have come to pass.

No. Kakka should never have stooped before these people as he did. The grooms and their fathers, standing there proud and haughty. Whereas Kakka . . . a flood of tears.

And so in this manner we bade farewell to Shalu and Shiva. We bade farewell to their love. We bade farewell to all dreams of their becoming doctors. Kakka's dreams of making his girls stand on their own feet were over, they'd come crashing down like the poles on which the wedding awnings had hung. One needs to reflect on the past with patience, explain things coherently, just as they happened, because the breath grows faint when the heart is afflicted with uncertainties in telling the story of the shattered dreams of a man who never had any dreams for himself.

Nothing is left now. There is only this blank space, a blank page in place of those ephemeral ambitions that vanished in a trice – like a dream.

23

NOW I SAT BY THE oven and Seema did all the serving. I wasn't used to making rotis, but gradually I took over Shiva's place and the oven became a part of me.

I was fast with the griddle and the rolling board. If the oven was being used for other work, I'd make four or five extra rotis, doublequick. The heat didn't bother me. While making the rotis, the board stayed steady under my hands, and with practice I stayed steady too – unlike the old days. The dry flour for the roti was always just so. The dough didn't stick to the rolling pin. I learnt how to manoeuvre the roti despite using tongs that were hot. I could take the griddle off the oven with one hand while picking up a rolled-out roti with the other. After which, without my knowing how, the tongs would put the roti on the fire. And that griddle wasn't about to get even a moment's rest.

Kakka's friends took to remembering Shalu and Shiva. "With the girls gone, you're left all alone. It's hard for these little ones!" One thing would lead to another and then under their breath . . . "You got away! These are bad times. Lucky nothing unwanted happened, or you'd have been left with no face to show. Look at Chaturvedi-ji – he caved in at the first hurdle . . ."

Since we were hanging around there and listening, Kakka tried changing the subject. He seemed now like the stricken hissing embers of the oven when splashed with water – which had to be revived again next morning.

When I got to Class 9, he made me choose Arts, he was dead set against Science. There were occasional fits of rage now: "Children just aren't interested in their studies, Sahib. We may expect great things from them, but they'll do just what they want. I've now sworn that none of them will go in the direction of Science. This daughter of mine . . ." – he pointed animatedly at me – "this one will do Arts. *Arré*, those are a different species, the ones who go in for Science . . . not our kind of kids . . ."

"Yes, there are different kinds of coals that get to blaze in the oven."

Friends generously poured water not on the embers but on the fiery burning coals of Kakka's dreams: "We told you so. But you wouldn't listen."

People relished these victories; Kakka, on the other hand, was defeated and looked it. A Science student meant a bright student, an Arts student meant an idiot. Short of saying so in as many words, Kakka had made it plain that we were all idiots who'd be lucky if we managed to get through Class 11. He'd been singed. He wasn't about to take a step that he hadn't already thought through ten times in his head.

24

AND THEN THERE WAS for us the sight of the Science girls strutting around all over the place. There was no question of them talking to the Arts girls – in fact they wouldn't even deign to look at us! They went off for their practicals and during the recess they stuck to their books. Watching us play, they shrugged scornfully, "You're lucky! You only have to fill up some answer books! In the Arts section that's all you need to do to clear the exams. But for us doing Science, it's not so easy."

During the practicals they weren't even at the morning assembly. Watching us line up for the assembly, they laughed and showed off, discussing frogs and frogs' legs. We peered surreptitiously at their classrooms and labs out of curiosity. If those Science girls had had their way, they'd have turned us all into frogs, cut us up, and dissected each of our organs. "Look, look! Arts students look like this!"

My mind wandered, wondering whether they'd really have cut us up. Would they open up our brains and close them up again? How often would they do all this? Would they chuckle over the innards of us page-filling Arts girls? How long would they keep us in their labs?

What nutrients would they feed us? Quite likely they'd put nothing into our mouths – what's the point in feeding Arts girls, they'd say.

There were more basic and less fantastic questions in the air, though: how were Seema and I to go to school at the same time, given that our school timings were from twelve to five, and there were dhaba duties? Kakka's solution was: "Each of you go to school every alternate day."

Around eleven-thirty in the morning, the girls would all start out for school. The sight of them walking towards school made me miserable. How lucky they seemed, getting to go to school every day!

One of those days, it was Seema's turn to go off with them and mine to work at the dhaba. Kakka sent me off on an errand to the shop at Jai Stambh Chauraha – to pick up groceries. I looked longingly towards the schoolgoing girls till the very last turn in the road. The shopkeeper ticked me off for being inattentive. The twelve o'clock gong went – *tun-tun-tun*. I picked up the stuff and ran.

"Why, girl? You're late?"

"Kakka, I . . ."

Panting and puffing, I went to the oven and started making rotis.

The next day, it was my turn to go to school. The girls in my class said, "You come one day and don't come the next day. What kind of fashion is this, huh?"

The class teacher scolded me over my absence. Perhaps the same thing happened with Seema. So we said to Kakka, "We won't go on alternate days. The teacher gets angry . . . let each of us do ten days at a time."

He was quiet. Next morning he said, "Come on, hurry up and finish the work. Then both of you can get to school." We shrieked for sheer delight and got down to work with him.

Leaving him alone at the dhaba hurt us, though. He was stewed by the work, sweating from every pore. And though the work was unending, he'd laugh it off and say, "Go! Go! You'll get late." And so we'd both go running back to the house, where Bai was ready with our school uniform: somehow, pell-mell, we'd get ready and make a dash for school.

Over our free periods, the girls would saunter merrily up and down while my thoughts would be on Kakka, alone at the dhaba, making rotis, serving customers. I'd get a sudden and desperate urge to go running back to the dhaba, help with some of his work, and run back in time for the next class. But it was impossible.

The result was that a feeling of guilt built up in me. When in school I wanted to be at the dhaba; at the dhaba I wanted to be in school.

The problem was partly that both of us had afternoon school, but the problem was also the grain market: had that market run all year round, all would have been just fine. But crops ripen when they do and there's nothing to be done about it. Had peak season gone on the whole year, a helper could have been employed, and that would have come as a huge relief to Kakka. The alternative option – that we stop school altogether and work full-time at the dhaba – was not an option at all because Kakka would have none of it. Or else, had our neighbourhood been the sort that Kakka wanted – oh well, come to think of it, what earthly use was it to think of all these possibilities . . . what Kakka wanted, what we wanted, what the dhaba needed . . . Obstacles and desires have their own life. In fact, they have an interminable and continuously demanding life.

There was now another problem. The dhaba had only six tables. Kakka washed all the plates and utensils – he never let us wash the plates that customers had used. Bai and everyone else was full of admiration for Kakka because he did the dishes himself. At times when he was away on work, he could tell at a glance, when he got back to the dhaba, how many plates had been used by how many customers before settling down to wash the lot. Once, when he was away at the open-air market, all six tables filled up. We waited anxiously for Kakka when they'd emptied, fearing that fresh customers wanting to eat would be turned away by the sight of a pile of used plates on the tables. I told Seema to stand at the door: "Look! If you see anyone wanting to come in to the dhaba, just call me quick!" I picked up all the unwashed utensils and piled them at the back, near the water tank. Then I cleaned the tables and came and stood by Seema.

"Did you spot anyone?"

"No! No-one's looked this way . . ."

So I washed all the utensils and stacked them up. After which we got two more customers, and before more could arrive, Kakka was back. We were delighted. He looked at the tables and said, "Only two customers, girls?"

"No! We had eight!"

He looked at the tables, then at us, but said nothing. He just sat down quietly and washed the remaining unwashed utensils. After a while he said, "Don't you girls wash the dishes, is that clear?"

"Kakka, if we hadn't, the two customers who came later wouldn't have come in at all! In any case, nobody saw us."

Something changed within Kakka that day, but we said nothing about it to Bai or to our siblings.

In spite of his repeated admonitions, if he happened to be away when all six tables were full, one of us would wash up while the other stood guard at the door. It was all managed very deftly: we'd clear the tables, pick up the utensils one by one, and position them near the water tank. Then we'd put all the smaller used utensils into a large pot so that anyone watching us would think we were washing the big pot, not dirty plates. Then we'd stack the plates in a way which indicated to anyone eyeing the chances of getting a vacant table that there were in fact several tables going abegging, and that their custom would be very welcome.

25

OUR MARRIED SISTERS did not work at the dhaba. Asha-jiji lived with her husband in a village some distance off, so there was naturally no question of her even appearing at the dhaba. Usha-jiji sometimes stopped by to see Kakka at the dhaba on her way to the market. Over time, Asha-jiji started following Usha-jiji's example and paused briefly at the dhaba alongside her, but the trips made her uneasy and she'd barely show up before beginning to mutter, "Come on, Usha, let's go. Come on, let's go." Usha-jiji was soft natured and more affectionate. She'd see us slogging in the dhaba and start looking like she'd burst into tears – the thought that she'd done time there herself only made her feel for us all the more.

And now we'd reached the time when Shalu and Shiva too belonged very little to the dhaba and very much to their in-laws. Over the days that Kakka went off to fetch them from Nagpur, Bai fretted and looked dejected. So much so, she'd nod off sitting straight up and then jerk awake with a start.

Over those three days or so, Seema and I skipped school and Kakka hired a man to do the dishes at the dhaba.

At night Bai showed up to fetch us home. She'd stand far away, near Qazi House – which was so distant that some of the time we couldn't even tell she was standing there. Rameshwar Uncle or Mohan Bhaiyya would approach and call out: "Hey Babli! Your mother's standing there . . . there . . . !" We'd wave to Bai, finish the remaining work, lock up the dhaba, and head home.

When Shalu and Shiva came back from their in-laws' for the first time, tittering and bashful, we saw how completely they'd changed. Asha-jiji, Usha-jiji, and Anni, all three older sisters, came over as well. They took Shalu and Shiva to the market and on their way back the whole gang of them stopped at the dhaba. A couple of customers were busy devouring stuff and I was making the rotis. Shiva saw me and giggled. I cried out: "Shiva, Shiva, come along you . . . come and make the rotis! I'm tired. God knows how long I've been at it!" The whole lot of them ticked me off with *"Arré . . . arré . . . !"* If I could've walked away from the oven that moment, I would have, I was sorely tempted. But there was no getting away. The five of them went off home. I yelled after them, *"Don't any of you go off to sleep – we'll be home soon!"*

The next day Shiva came over to the dhaba and said, "O.K. – Hey, move! I'll make the rotis."

I looked askance at Kakka. Shiva didn't bother with his expostulations and started slogging at the oven without further ado. Settling down cross-legged, she said,

"Kakka, Nagpur's nowhere near us. No-one's going to see us here and carry tales all the way back to Nagpur . . ."

For as long as they were there, Shiva and Shalu slaved in the usual way at the dhaba. This suited me perfectly, in fact it made me feel just great. Seema and I went happily off to school and while there we never once felt like running right back to work in the dhaba over our free periods!

Shiva had some great stories to tell about Nagpur. Jija-ji had taken her to see two whole films. She told us their plots while providing information on how large Nagpur was. She spread out her arms, "Dear! Ten of our Basodas would fit into Nagpur! It's so . . . so big . . . that Nagpur!"

"Better than our Basoda?"

"Ah, that's another matter! Nothing compares with Basoda! Our Basoda's something else! There's nothing as fine as Basoda there!"

It came as the most delightful form of reassurance to us that nowhere could anyone ever find an improvement over our Basoda. It meant a lot to us to hear Shiva so categorical about Basoda's absolute superiority over everywhere, even Nagpur.

In Nagpur, she said, she whizzed around with Jija-ji on his bicycle. Sometimes she sat in front, on the bar, sometimes at the back, on the carrier. "There's a difference between the two," she assured us.

"And how's that?"

"Sitting in front, it seems one is going *ahead* of Nagpur, while on the carrier . . ." – she paused, and then, eyes laughing – "it's like the town's running with us, and sometimes we even leave it behind. *Arré*, so what if it's big, that doesn't mean one has to cling lovingly to it all the time . . . !"

In no time at all, their fetchers arrived to carry them back home. We trooped to the station to see them off. Shalu wept as copiously as Kakka – ". . . *Kakka, Kakka* . . ." – she wasn't able to stop her sobbing even while climbing on to the train. She sat by the window and just went on howling. It beat me clean how Kakka and Shalu managed to cry so much more than the rest of us.

As the train started trundling off, Kakka, still in his lungi and vest, ran along the platform and alongside the train . . . "Girl! Write to us! . . ."

This made Shalu bawl even louder.

When he could run no longer, Kakka stopped and carried on crying. This happened each time the train departed with Shalu. He was a sight! People at the station stopped in alarm just to look at a grown man weeping that hard.

Shiva was the exact opposite. She wasn't much given to weeping and wailing, and as time went on she stopped altogether. She was matter-of-fact about it all: "When the time's up, one has to go! Either one can go laughing or one can go bawling!" Not that her philosophy stopped her eyes turning red.

One time, before their departure, she roundly ticked off Shalu: "Listen! When tomorrow shows up, please don't howl and yowl. Listen, Sourpuss, when you weep that badly, you make Kakka weep too. Don't you feel ashamed making him cry?"

Shalu wasn't about to take this lying down. "Everyone's not shameless like you! I feel Kakka . . ." At this point she burst into tears so desperate they could've given a good run for their money to the tap she turned on over her departure days. Shiva was unmoved by the flood: "Well, if you miss Kakka so much," she said flatly, "why not refuse to go this time round? . . . Then I'd understand . . . Stay here with Kakka . . . Let's see how gutsy you are, Sourpuss!"

". . . And if you shed crocodile tears tomorrow . . . I'll show you . . ." – and with that Shalu ran squealing to Bai. *"Bai!"* she wailed.

Bai only yelled at her: *"Hey, you, take your fight to your father. Don't eat up my head."*

Shiva stuck her thumb out at Shalu. She was quiet for a while and then, bristling, went off to the dhaba to see Kakka.

I said to Shiva, ". . . Now . . . if she refuses to talk to you in Nagpur, what's going to happen?"

"Oh, let her not speak to me! I get very angry with that Sourpuss . . . makes Kakka unhappy each time . . . what a load of nonsense!" We nodded in agreement, then got lost in her Nagpur stories.

Shalu and Shiva's comings and goings were regular occurrences, they'd come and then go back together. But this time round Shalu went back alone. Shiva stayed with us for a very long time because she was expecting, and the first delivery was by custom at the parents'. She'd changed completely, developed a huge belly, but she still went on slogging at the dhaba.

At home Bai took good care of Shiva and stopped her from all work that might involve picking or carrying loads. She tried to stop her working at the dhaba too, but on that front Shiva was adamant because she felt much too fretful sitting around at home.

Early one morning she happened to be carrying a basketful of cowpats when, suddenly, she dropped the laden basket and squatted on the ground, grimacing in pain. Sobbing with distress, she asked me to pick up the cowpats, plonked the basket on my head, held on to my hand, leaned against me, and staggering forward we managed to reach the dhaba. In a short while she had recovered and seemed fit as a fiddle, though variations on this theme seemed to be developing towards a crescendo after that day. Towards the end she'd groan in pain, her face contorted and red as the coals that glowed in the oven.

Finally one night her discomfort levels grew extreme – she'd be fine for a bit, but then she'd screw up in pain again. She clung to Bai and Bai decided to whisk her off to the hospital. When day broke I didn't go to work at the dhaba . . . and before I knew it I was running from the hospital to the dhaba: "Kakka, Kakka! Come quick to the hospital."

I assumed he'd lose no time making a dash for the hospital, but he just hemmed and hawed. There were a couple of people at the dhaba. They seemed to understand what the problem was. Kakka only said, "The first delivery is always a bit troublesome, my dear . . ."

I was livid now, horribly angry with Kakka. ". . . I'm off to the hospital," I yelled.

"Oh, you idiot! You'll stay right here!"

I couldn't care less what he said, I ran to the hospital as fast as my legs could carry me.

Shiva was there, unable to walk. She was somehow, just barely, dragging herself around with Bai on one side and various sisters on the other. She was bawling at the top of her voice. Then I saw her taken into a room and the doors close. Bai and our two oldest sisters sat outside the door, their heads in their hands.

I ran to the back of the hospital and jumped up to the windowsill. Shiva's screams were getting louder. Two or three nurses had helped her lie down on a table, her sari lay some distance away. She was sobbing, the nurses were spreading her legs, tying them to something. I was driven crazy watching what was happening. I was aghast in a way I'd never been before. It was beyond all conception.

Her legs were being forced open further. She screamed, *"Help, Help. Help! Bai, Bai, Kakka, Kakka . . ."*

I screamed at the top of my voice, I couldn't help it: *"Shiva, Shiva, Shiva . . ."*

A startled nurse looked up and yelled at me, "Hey, Hey! . . ."

I slipped off the windowsill: hearing the commotion, Usha-jiji took me to Bai. After a while the screaming got fainter but the doors remained closed. Bai was muttering a prayer, her hands folded. Usha-jiji was praying. Anni said, "Actually she's very strong . . . do you think she's gone off to sleep? Perhaps she's not able to take the pain. Bai, what do we do now?" Asha-jiji sat quietly, her head leaning against the wall.

I saw Kakka come in but I turned away from him.

Shiva's screaming had stopped. Everyone heaved a sigh of relief and wiped away their tears. Then a nurse appeared and said, "All's well. It's a boy." Glaring at me, she turned back into the room. In her hands she held a big pan.

Kakka said to me, "Come on, come on. Nothing more you can do here now."

I wouldn't budge. He patted my head, laughed, and went off alone to the dhaba. Wrapped in a red blanket, Shiva was brought into the ward. She looked as though nothing at all had happened. She smiled and said to me, "Look! Look! Look at the little fellow! How he's shut his eyes tight . . . !"

The next day she came home from the hospital. Bai gave her such hot and bitter foodstuffs that she had trouble swallowing them. The moment Bai stepped out for her temple rounds, Shiva was ready to spit out what she'd been holding back: "Go, quick! Go throw this into the drain at the back. Quick, quick, Fatty!"

Kakka was entering the house that evening when Usha-jiji's five-year-old son, Billu, trilled – "Grandpa! Shiva Aunty's sown a baby." Everyone burst out laughing. Shiva covered her face, embarrassed – but she looked ecstatic as well.

Five weeks later was when she had to return to Nagpur. On the day before her journey, all the women of the locality showed up and their music and singing carried on till late at night. It was the first visit to our home for her husband, Jija-ji. So Kakka gave him a wristwatch.

That watch looked quite dashing on his arm. He said to me, "Come here, Babli! Let me show you what's inside the watch!" He showed me each and every component in that watch, then he shut it. When I told Shiva I'd examined his watch, she bristled: "Hey! Look out! Don't touch his watch, you! Kakka's given it to him with such love. What if you spoil it? . . . Here give it to me, my Kakka's given it . . . I'll wear it."

Jija-ji laughed it off, "O.K., O.K., let it be!"

Shiva made a face. She went off with her little baby boy and I was left alone.

Shiva's life at her in-laws was a happy one, but Shalu's was the exact opposite. Her whole complexion had changed and Kakka found her situation unbearable. She was deeply unhappy at her in-laws'. I wondered if perhaps some failing in her husband was gnawing at her like termites. When her departure day approached, Kakka went off and got her inland letter forms. The letters she wrote on those forms sounded like her fate now was to live in a vale of her own tears.

Shiva was a different cup of tea. She told us stories that we'd pester her to tell us again and again. One very funny story she narrated went roughly like this –

On their very first night together, Jija-ji said to her, "If I'd ever heard that any man had so much as touched you before I got hold of you, I'd just have abandoned you and left . . ." We waited with bated breath. Shiva laughed and continued: "'How can you do that?' I said to him . . . 'Before you got hold of me the bangle-seller had got hold of me. My hands were in his hands so many times! Why, even on our wedding day he took hold of my hands in his and put bangles on them . . . Now, say, are you still planning on leaving me . . .?'"

We loved her stories.

But Bai didn't. Marriage was no joke in her book. "You, Blackie, a curse on you!" she said, and glared ferociously at her.

Shiva told Kakka the same story and he enjoyed it thoroughly. "These Nagpur boys deserve it," he said. Shiva said she had no problem with Nagpur, but she did miss the dhaba.

"How much?"

"Desperately. Sometimes I miss it so much, I start to cry."

As she spoke, she looked towards the dhaba, her eyes brimming. God alone knows what her big round eyes had sucked into themselves from the world she had to live in.

26

IT WASN'T AS IF THERE weren't any fights around town. But if there was ever any likelihood of things degenerating from a straightforwardly venomous verbal spat to fisticuffs, someone or the other would jump in to pull the combatants apart. The gladiators would go on snarling – "Let me be! . . . I won't let go . . . Today I'll show this swine . . . Watch out, you, I'll skin you alive . . . The day I lose . . . I'll kick you and your arrogance out of here!" – for a short while, exchanges of ape-like aggression usually carried on in this charming vein. After matters had subsided sufficiently, people plied the fighting cocks with tea to soothe the animal glares with which they continued regarding each other through shrouds of bidi smoke. The spat's last stage was when everyone got engrossed in their own work and the fighters, in the absence of any audience at all, dusted themselves and disappeared.

Scenes such as these were regular around our bus stand. A twosome would start a fight, a third and fourth would turn up to part them, a fifth and sixth would hang around to watch the fun. "Come on, come to the police station . . ." – nobody used such words, and nobody ever complained to the police. If the battling louts looked like going too far, such as when they picked up sticks, a handful of busybodies grabbed the weaponry and stopped them mauling each other. The separated gorillas then ran around picking up stones but never actually chucked them – mostly, the stones served as side garnishings for a verbal assault – "I'll kill you! I'll kill you . . .," and sundry such empty threats yelled as they began circling each other.

The local policeman rode a throbbing Bullet motorcycle, and the faintest suspicion of its sound caused a current to go through the crowd and made the cobatants quiver like jelly: ". . . Oh, God, we were lucky he didn't spot us! Thank you, God . . . for making this our lucky day!" The policeman would saunter officiously for a bit and stare down the duo – who of course were by now quiet as church mice and struck dumb with terror.

We noticed the policeman's power and status, the fear his presence generated. It made us all want to become policemen immediately.

We'd never seen too many policemen and so, once, when truckloads of them began moving around, it gave us the shivers. All the schools around us shut earlier than usual. All the girls were sent home instantly, and those coming in for the fresh shift were turned around and sent back.

Meanwhile there was much weeping and wailing in town, and wherever you looked, smoke. The only store that sold wood was set on fire and the fumes penetrated through the pores of every home in the vicinity.

"What's happening?"

Everyone asked that question, their bodies trembling. Crowds collected on the road and forced the shops to shut. A few of the ruffians looked like they were looting the stores and chucking some of their loot on the road. In the blink of an eye the bus stop shut down and crowds surrounded the buses. People were now running helter-skelter. They broke windowpanes, they set buses on fire.

The owner of the store that sold wood, a Sikh in his vest and underwear, wailed inconsolably nearby, "... I'm ruined! I'm finished! ... Please, I need some help ..."

The rioting crowds turned suddenly on him. The Sikh was by now senseless with fright, which only made matters worse because the bullying crowd shoved him into his store, pulled the shutters down, and began baying for blood. "Come on! Come on! Burn it down!" There were people watching helplessly, holding their breath in a state of terror and panic.

Sanity prevailed for a few seconds when the Sikh was taken out more or less comatose and sent packing home. His wife saw his condition and collapsed to the floor.

Now the rioters moved towards the station, where they looted trains, burnt the station, broke all the lights there, and plunged the place into darkness.

Our world had been turned into darkness and ashes – who knows why. And who knows why the more dense the darkness, the louder the screams – screams different from any we'd heard in the past, unlike anything we'd heard before in our lives.

And then we heard the sirens of approaching police cars. The world blazed with shrill whistles and sirens. The schools were shut, the market was shut, the buses had stopped, the trains were dead caterpillars. The dhaba was shut. Life had come to a standstill.

Announcements were made on loudspeakers, they reverberated through our town: "No-one is to come out of their homes. No-one is to be seen out on the roads. The town is under curfew."

What exactly was a curfew?

We heard the sound of sirens and instinctively went running to the road to check. All we saw were vans full of soldiers with huge guns that made us plaster ourselves to the walls. The soldiers crossed Mill Road, they crossed the train station, they headed towards the bus stand. The moment they crossed Mill Road we yelled "Fire! Fire!" and went running home.

The women of the locality were scared stiff at the sound of the siren and grew roots where they stood every time it sounded. They did uproot themselves, though, when they needed to get to the temple.

Once, on a blistering hot afternoon during the riots, we ventured to the dhaba with Mukesh, Devu, Raju, Gudiya, and Pappi. The roads and lanes we traversed were all deserted. The bus stand was surrounded by soldiers.

We hid near Qazi House and gazed at the soldiers with their huge weapons, dumb with fear because of the siren and the silences after it.

And in the middle of it all, our dhaba, a lonely place now, utterly lonely . . . no-one near it, except soldiers.

Where was the cow?

We left the dhaba and came right back home, "We've seen the curfew! We've seen the curfew!" Everyone went straight back to their homes. The curfew lasted seven days.

We managed with a drill of our own over those days. The moment we heard the siren we rushed towards Mill Road and the moment we saw soldiers we yelled "Fire, Fire, Fire!" Once, they spotted us and smiled. One of the fellows pointed his gun at us, so we took to our heels. From behind us we heard his laughter.

"And if his gun had gone off? . . . Then"? Baby-didi warned us all. "Don't you dare step out of your homes again . . ."

And then, as though it had never begun, the curfew was over. Shops opened, schools opened, the market functioned again. Buses and trains started coming and going. The smoke disappeared, the ash mixed with the dust decided to fly around, the station looked happy lit up again.

Who'd burnt the Sikh's wood depot? No-one from amongst us, we knew, could have done such a thing. So who were the people who'd done it? Where had they come from? Where had they disappeared? Who were these strangers that gave us the curfew and blackened our town?

So many questions, all turning countless small Diwali diyas into a giant cauldron. That Diwali, every home in our town lit only one solitary symbolic diya. The festivities that year had no character, and even the local hunchback witch's curses we were used to hearing were silenced.

And Binny, who we were used to hearing maybe ten times a day, wasn't heard either, and wasn't seen for a week.

27

SHE WAS SOMETHING else, was our hunchback witch. There were times she loved the light, there were times she loved the dark. She was an enigma. Hiding in dark unlit corners of the lane, she waited for the diyas to die out; other times she was mad enough to make her way to each doorstep just to smother the diyas. Sometimes we heard her scream, "Come on light the diyas quick! *Arré,* where've you gone? . . . It's dusk, you idiots, dusk! . . . You haven't got the news it's dusk? Go on, light the diyas, get it over with." And if she still found no diyas by the basil pot, she'd start chucking pebbles. And if anyone tried shooing her away – "Hey! Hunchback witch, why such a racket this evening? Be off, get lost, witch!" – it was the end of peace for the whole neighbourhood, because that got her spilling out all her saved-up fury, and the abuse she spat out made folks rush into their houses, slam the doors shut, and stuff cotton wool in their ears. Even after that, there was no end in sight, her curses were a permanent shadow following people wherever they went. It had become almost a custom for stories about her to start with the lighting of the diyas.

"...What with household chores and sweeping and swabbing she's gone clean off her head..."

"No, Jiji! That's not it. She's suffered a lot too, the poor thing. Jilted, I hear...shown big dreams right in the middle of the day and then...so of course she went mad. She was cheated, I say, cheated in love...Poor woman, a curse got her, she thought from cleaning pots and pans she'd soon be a queen!..."

"Hey, really? Is that so?"

"Of course! Why else would she run around Banjani Babu's house in the middle of the night with a box and bag tucked under her arm? She goes all quiet and tentative up to the door and then suddenly starts banging her head on it. And when she sees the master of the house she makes these strange kissing sounds...though sometimes she just swears and curses!...Why, sometimes she even pulls her sari to her knees and trots around like a mare!"

"...Oof! Then this one's not plain mad, she's a fallen woman, and now she's up to no good, that's for sure..." – Pathriya-wali Aunt offered her opinion as beyond dispute, the last word on the subject. Her need to thrust her views down every gullet now made her turn on Suman Bhabhi: "Suman, you still haven't given up your habit of jabbering? You're a motormouth! Nine at night, and one can hear you snoring away in your house. So tell me then, how come you've seen the hunchback witch running around Banjani Babu's house in the middle of the night? Go on, spit it out!"

Suman Bhabhi wasn't about to step back abashed. "*Arré,* Aunt! *I've* not seen her. *He* was telling me. When he shuts shop and comes home, he sees the hunchback there, right there, in front. And yes, he was telling me . . ."

"Okay, okay, forget it! My ears can't take any more tittle-tattle. Just when it's dusk and prayer time and the diyas have to be lit, you lot start blabbing your nonsense!" The conviction was now changing direction. Pathriyawali Aunt was now berating anyone within her line of vision: "And you! All of you! If I find you here again on the porch gossiping about the witch, you're going to hear from me! Understood?"

The hunchback's curses happened to fall on Kakka's ears, once, as he sat drinking tea. "I say, Rajjo," he said to Bai, "that woman has a pretty foul tongue."

"She doesn't start any of it . . . it's when others start plaguing her and calling her hunchback witch, that's what sets her off. There's a whole gang bothering her, which includes that uncivilised Radheylal's son." This was Bai's view of the witch's uproar. The hunchback was just beginning to quieten down when I let out a shrill – "Hunchback witch . . . witch!"

"And look at this one!" Bai ground her teeth. "Tell me, what's the point in sending them to school, eh?"

Kakka, half-angry, half-laughing, knocked some sense into me: "Why bother the woman for no rhyme or reason, my dear?"

But Binny – she was an altogether different kettle of fish from the hunchback. She was something else, our Binny! Sparkling white teeth, complexion the colour of wheat, stark raving mad – and so stunningly beautiful -- Binny! The women of our neighbourhood often had long chats with her and took care to see she was properly fed. On festive occasions they kept aside a portion of rice pudding and some pooris for her, and if she happened to disappear for a longish stretch they'd be anxious and check on her whereabouts. Then, the moment she showed up again it was like she'd brought them relief and was spreading happiness among them all. She'd sit and eat absolutely anywhere she felt like, and if somebody'd made anything special that day, they'd go right home and bring it over for her to eat. She was everyone's darling, she absolutely was.

There was one time when no-one spotted her for maybe two or three days, and when she finally appeared Bari Kaki asked her, all sweetness and honey, "Come, Binny, come! Where were you yesterday? Binno Rani, how come you're all glowing today?"

"I went in a jeep, yesterday. Far, very far. Where there were lots of farms . . ."

The women were aghast, but Binny continued, innocent as ever, "And I got great food to eat too. And I had a bath with Lux soap. And look . . . look at my new dhoti and blouse! They're nice, aren't they? I'm looking good, aren't I?"

"Where? Where? . . . Where did you go, you stupid

girl? Who did you go with? Tell us, tell us!" The whole lot of them pounced on her. She laughed uproariously and, showing off her newly acquired colourful bangles, dashed right across the lane.

"That so and so! Always running away before we can get the truth out of her!"

"God knows where she goes whoring, the slut!"

"We shouldn't let her into our lane . . ."

"If she's mad, doesn't mean she should turn into a whore . . ."

They were all red-faced with anger that day, swearing at the louts who hung around Binny all the time, tongues hanging out.

"Turn into skeletons, they will . . . and perish at midnight! Snakes should've got them the moment they were born . . . carrion feeding on garbage, the whole lot! And that foul ruffian Ashok, he's riding high these days . . . Come on, let's go and see his mother. She should know what her son's been up to."

A lady with anklets stood up and urged the others to follow. Here they were, all the righteous women, so terribly agitated, and there at the top of the lane was mad Binny with flowers in her hair, merry and laughing. An elderly official's wife tried chastising her: "Hey, Binny. Take the flowers off yourself and get lost . . ." – this, being water off a duck's back, was followed up – ". . . You don't even have the decency to drop dead, you slut . . . at least then we'd get some peace around here!"

Binny was beyond caring but the old official's wife wasn't done yet: "If the poor thing had been normal her parents wouldn't have abandoned her in the middle of that hot day . . . She was with her relatives for a while but when she came back her mind was gone . . . but why this slut had to find happiness in our neck of the woods of all places is beyond me, and now these louts are after her . . . Oh Lord, before things get worse for her, Lord, take me away from this world!"

Her misery was quite genuine. Meanwhile, every now and then Binny put flowers in her hair, stood at the top of the lane, and trilled with full-throated ease: "Hey, friend! I'm madly in love! No-one knows my pain . . ."

On quiet nights her voice rang out for miles. When things seemed to be getting utterly out of hand, Muniman Aunty tried her best in a choked voice to get things back in order: "Hey Binny! Hey Binny! Don't go running around . . . Stay here, right here, in this area, my dear." Her voice sounded gentle to Binny, God knows why, so she'd put her head on Muniman Aunty's shoulder and weep the bitterness out of her heart.

Rekha Bhabhi had a different perspective. "Binny isn't mad at all, Jiji. She wants to have a good time, so she pretends to be mad. Look, just take a look at how dressed up and made up she is! Where does she get the brains for *that*? She gets free food, so she's cock-a-hoop all the time! We shouldn't let her anywhere near our girls!"

Muniman Aunty and the old lady made their disagreement plain to Rekha Bhabhi. "Don't go on with your rubbish about the girl," they told her. "If you find her so disgusting, there's no need for you to talk to her and give her things to eat . . . Understand? You're the eldest daughter-in-law, learn to manage your tongue."

In all this chatter there was one woman who never uttered a word. Bhaktu-jiji. She listened to everyone, and you could see a variety of emotions cross her face. Often it seemed as if her thoughts were being voiced by others. At other times it seemed the opposite – as if she were speaking herself but without allowing any emotions to show on her face. At those times it seemed there were emotional upheavals going on inside Bhaktu-jiji that she had to suffer all by herself. Sometimes it was as if her neck had a spring inside it which made her turn towards a person on the verge of speaking – but even before the person had spoken a word. I never saw anyone move their necks left and right as rapidly as she did. Her neck made it evident to everyone at those meetings on the porch that there was no better listener than the face it supported! And the darling of our locality, Binny, knew equally well that so long as this gaggle of mothers and aunts was around, no harm could come to her – she could safely go on being the mistress of her every desire!

Occasionally, on our way to school we'd see her following us, guffawing now and then for no reason we could fathom. Then she'd either swing back and return to our neighbourhood, or if her mood dictated that she spend the whole day behind our school, she'd hang around there, near a well. On such days we saw her again when school got over, swaying like a flower in full bloom, and she'd race us all the way home. There were other times when she showed up at the dhaba. Kakka fed her caringly, and if she happened to spot us around she'd burst into one of her guffaws.

Kakka never forgot to tell Binny of the sparkling white teeth to "either stay here or go straight home" – home for her being our neighbourhood temple and its environs. Binny laughed and glowed with happiness. "And I'll come right back here," she'd say. And singing the wedding songs she knew, off she'd go, strolling far into the distance.

28

THE SOLE PURPOSE FOR Shiva's in-laws to come into this world was to find a groom for me. In their book, suggesting four or five eligible boys was the same as firing a rifle laden with male pellets, the first of which, heading straight for me, could take the shape of a tea-shop owner, the second a puncture-repair man, and the third a mill worker.

Shiva's letters were completely unrelated to how I dreamt about life and they made me furious. My reactions were not Seema's: she thoroughly enjoyed those letters. She'd rib me about them while I pretended to be clueless about what she was driving at. Every fifteen days a new letter arrived, providing details of yet another batch of prospective grooms. Each of those blue-coloured envelopes gored my heart the moment it arrived and made me explode in anger: "Can't Shiva's in-laws discover *anyone* even vaguely suitable? Have they never encountered boys who aren't tea-sellers and savoury snack-sellers?"

At which Bai's snort was predictable: "Wow! You're running away with yourself, aren't you? You're from a family that runs a dhaba and you think some wealthy mill owner's going to come looking for you?"

"We aren't the kind you think we are, we aren't just some waitresses in a restaurant . . . we're different! You just can't understand this . . . you sit at home so you've no idea how different our dhaba is . . . There's a huge difference that you just don't get . . . Just like there's a huge difference between Kakka and the fathers of all these other girls around us . . . Can't you understand? You've got the wrong end of the stick if you think we're like you . . . we're not! Especially not me – *I'm different.*"

My voice got screechier and screechier as I railed. It had little effect.

"Whatever you want to say, say it to Kakka. You keep mum while he's around and the moment he leaves you start off . . . take a day or two to think things over and then let Kakka explain what'll make sense."

Hot on the heels of advice calmly delivered came battle commands at fever pitch: *"You better understand and you better explain matters to that no-good father of yours!"* And having let off steam, whatever came to hand she'd smash on the floor. I'd rush off for the dhaba, the blue of the sky turning in my mind into the torn-blue of those inland letters.

It was as if the very minute a girl finished Class 8, an alarm clock rang asking the whole world to start working on her marriage. God alone knows what made the world see all growing girls as best married off – and the sooner the better. No-one had any notion of a girl's life beyond this single idea that seemed to have been hammered into every head. The government had at least a twenty-point programme it wanted to implement; the people around us had a one-point programme. Marriage, marriage, marriage. Marriage was the universe's single-point solution to the problem that it saw taking shape as a girl.

This wasn't really a part of Kakka's worldview. In his steadfast opposition to girls being married off too early or before they'd reached a proper age, he'd disagreed with many and antagonised more. Now, though his arguments lacked the edge they once had, it was not as if he'd jettisoned his earlier opinions.

Meanwhile, my horoscope wasn't aligning well with someone or the other who'd been mentioned in one of Shiva's inland letters, while another fellow's dowry requirements were outlandish enough to leave even poor Shiva speechless with anger. Evident as a subcurrent through all this news of negotiations was Shiva's effort not to disclose a lot more of the sordid details that underlay them.

Her letters vexed Kakka too. His irritation was evident to me even from the way he'd start stirring a pot of daal – and because his frustration often made him flick extra chillies into the pot. "*Arré!* I'd rather spend money educating my girls than hand the money over to their grooms."

The Siyari-walla, adjusting his dhoti, was one of those who got hot under the collar when Kakka said such things. "How can this be?" he asked. "You can educate a girl as much as you want, but will you marry her off, yes or no? And I say one thing Sahib . . ." – now he sounded like he was addressing the public from the Red Fort – ". . . if your daughter is too highly educated, you'll need to find a boy equally well educated, yes or no? In our caste, even the *boys* aren't well educated, so this talk of yours about educating *girls* . . . ! Why, after educating her, would you want her to stay single all her life? We're not about to hand our girls over to some other caste, are we?"

The very thought of the imminent apocalypse made his mouth, crammed with tobacco, spew involuntarily. But he could neither stop himself talking nor spit out what was stopping him talking. "Sahib, adolescence is a dangerous time," he said. "Before things go awry, better settle them down." He was looking so incensed that Kakka ended up burning the roti he was roasting.

There were in fact far too many fruitless discussions of this kind at the dhaba. The reports of these irritated Bai no end.

29

A GIRLS' COLLEGE HAD opened near Jai Stambh Chauraha in the centre of town. Plenty of girls joined it after finishing school, but more than half of those eligible preferred just staying home. Their families became superfast express trains running on one track, searchlights on, looking for boys their girls could marry.

"Take your father's blessings; May you have a happy married life . . ." – this song was the national anthem of every household with a young unmarried girl. And with this anthem in their hearts, girls headed off to the Needlework and Embroidery Centre. Their embroidery on pillow covers and bedsheets often showed two green leaves and two big red roses with "Welcome" written above. Some of these women turned painters and some went off in the direction of the fine arts – just the things to smoothen the primrose path towards matrimony and floral expression: "I've sent you a flower in a letter; it's not a flower, it's my heart!" The pleasure of day-dreaming about the letters they'd write their husbands supplemented the embroidery.

We were delighted at the idea of starting college, but what delighted us even more was not having to carry school bags – now we could carry the books in our arms. You attended class if you wanted to, and if you didn't feel like it you could gossip or take notes or pretend to take notes while writing other stuff. You could just sit under a tree, deep in thought. Sometimes girls danced around trees, sometimes they flung leaves or played with them, lost in dreams. Sometimes they sheltered under a shedding tree, trying all the time not to let the falling leaves get crushed under their feet. It was as if the tree wasn't a tree but the prince of their dreams!

No-one dared, however, even to think of bunking college and going off to see a movie.

A stone slab at the back of the shops next to the park wall that separated us from the market had fallen off. The gap started to serve as a window. Samosas came through the window one way, and on the other side the shopkeepers minted money. There was no fixed time for hot crunchy samosas, no fixed period; their aroma suffused every period. The window became a bridge between girls and samosas. In time, the trees started shedding more than leaves, they began shedding little paper balls with scribbles such as "Eat samosas! Make your skin glow!"

The moment I started my B.A. I told Kakka, "I'm going to study. I'm going to finish my B.A." His answer was cautious: "O.K., my dear, study . . . But I hope I don't get complaints of any kind."

It was the Shalu Effect – that's what had happened to Kakka.

The students union elections were held in the college and I contested for the post of chairperson from a party called the Unity Panel. There were seven girls in the Second Year, four in the Final Year, and seventy-five in the First Year. So the posts of chairperson and secretary really belonged to the first-year students.

Before I arrived in college, I'd stood for the position of secretary in Class 11, where I'd lost badly because I hadn't bothered to canvass among the Science girls for their votes. But Vanshika of the Science stream and her friends showed up every day before the Arts girls, campaigning for votes. A day before the votes were to be cast, they came around to shake our hands and said, "Give your votes to Vanshu, O.K.?" After they left we were mighty amused – "Fat lot of good studying Science does if they can't even tell who to ask for votes and who to avoid . . ." We weren't all that amused when we realised the Arts girls had voted for the Science lot. Losing the elections turned us into wounded tigresses.

Roli gave us courage when it came to the college elections: "Come on! Let's all go eat chaat-pakora." With loads of hot and sour eats swilling inside us, electioneering got going in great hope and excitement. After a bit, it grew tiresome. There was no mud-slinging and name-calling, but much else was happening – behind my back, I was being called "Daal Fry". Along the same lines we discovered that Neeta, a competing candidate, came from a family that made papad. When girls from the rival camp went by, we taunted them:

"My dear! I can't fill my stomach without daal, say what you like."

"And papad?"

"Oh, get lost! Don't even talk about papad!"

The tug of war grew into a battle royal between Daal and Papad. Sometimes Daal fell, sometimes Papad was crushed.

Besides canvassing within the college, we went house to house. Often we reached the college late, but no-one ticked us off. In the college it was forever non-stop tea and samosas. To win was everything. From Daal vs. Papad, matters progressed to going off to watch films and taking voters to watch films. The whole cinema hall couldn't be booked to bribe the voters, but soon we discovered that the opposition were organising shows for all the girls at home on a VCR. Films for votes seemed a tigerish ploy. So, what were we going to do to foil it?

Our group got hold of certain employees of the electricity station and, hand in glove with them, we had the electricity switched off six times in three hours over the film show. Who was going to vote for those who'd shown them half a film?

I was fighting the election, but Kakka worked like he was my election manager. He said to all his acquaintances, "*Arré,* tell your daughter to vote for my girl!"

I'd tell Kakka everything that happened and he, an enthusiastic listener, taught me the ins and outs of electioneering. When he heard I was Daal Fry, he laughed uproariously and said, "That's terrible . . . but this kind of name-calling is normal during elections, my dear. Every candidate has to pull out all the stops, you see!"

Kakka was a staunch supporter of Indira Gandhi, an out-and-out Congressman. He had a great deal of respect for her and any time he spoke of her he called her "Indira-ji", and if those around him didn't add the "ji" after her name, he ticked them off. If ever there was a radio news item on her or an address to the nation by her or if she was addressing the citizenry, Kakka's view was that it did not behove even a leaf to stir. Not even Indira Gandhi's sternest critics had the guts to utter a word against her within Kakka's hearing. He jumped to her defence with such vigour and was so persuasive with arguments in her favour that every sceptic seemed ready to be converted by the time he'd finished, if not fall at her feet and pray to her. If Kakka had had his way, his political goddess would forever have been elected unopposed, or simply been asked to run the government with no opposition at all.

It didn't matter whether an election was big or small, to parliament or to a legislative assembly, to a village council or to the municipal corporation, Kakka was always at the helm of the electioneering. He believed in campaigning house to house. The dhaba turned into an election office decorated with Indira Gandhi posters, banners, and bunting.

On the day of voting and counting in the college

elections, a whole bunch of us sneaked into Sumita's house near the market. After a long wait, Geetu came and told us we'd won. We spilled out into the streets, delighted. It seemed to us then that the very existence of a girls' college had given us all wings – and we could fly for sheer joy!

And we heard celebratory drumbeats in the college!

Kakka was gazing towards the college. I ran up from behind and clung to him, "Kakka, Kakka! We've won, we've won . . . !" A plate fell from his hand. He hugged me and I felt a current of happiness run through him. He blessed all my friends and turned to Pappu nexdoor, "Hey Pappu! Go quick and get some of that sweet stuff . . ."

The whole bus stand crowded in. People regarded me with admiration and happy astonishment. Girls arrived from our college and boys from their college and the dhaba filled up with them – the drums were going, powdered colour was thrown on people, people danced. The four of us – chairperson, vice chairperson, secretary, and assistant secretary – were garlanded. Kakka was ecstatic. We started off in a procession, raising slogans . . . "Long Live the Unity Panel!" Kakka wiped his eyes with the edges of his lungi.

After the procession, friends parted with "See you! See you tomorrow! See you . . . !" It felt like we'd touched the sky and soared into the empyrean!

The whole neighbourhood arrived in full force and stuffed itself into our house. The moment they saw me there was hustling and bustling and shouting. Bari Kaki said, laughing, "You must be tired, girl . . . Look at all that colour on her . . . give me some of that sweet suff . . . your father got it all . . . they got to see the procession but we only got to dance to the sound of the drums . . . !"

In the evening, over Bai's visit to the temple, women who'd never before spoken to her said, "Hey, aren't you the one whose daugher won?" Bai reported their conversation to Kakka, putting aside a pot of rice pudding . . . Whom she was saving such a lot of it for, I wasn't sure. Maybe she was saving it to give to Binny. And some for the hunchback witch, perhaps?

30

KAKKA LOOKED HAPPY, his status amongst his friends had risen. Now and then he'd tell me to carry right on and bury myself in my books as much as I liked. Simultaneously, I lost all my inhibitions over working in the dhaba. Often, I'd head straight there after college. Other times I'd get there before college, and my friends would arrive to pick me up. Plus, alongside work at the dhaba, I started getting a lot of market chores done.

The moment the dhaba seemed free of customers, I'd get on my bicycle – my new passion! I fetched coal on it from the coal depot across the station. Another source for oven fuel, I discovered, was a passenger train: its engine stopped in front of the station and there disgorged bright red coals. As soon as the train departed I heaved a sackful of those dying but still usable pieces onto my carrier and carted them off to the dhaba. This way I prevented Kakka having to do some of his "marketing".

Riding my cycle, doing a few useful things around the market, these activities now gave me a thrill. They generated within me a tumult of excitement, and I sometimes wondered if what I now felt was what Binny, in her own demented way, also often felt. If I happened to see our mad beauty while cycling, a crazy impulse possessed me to take both hands off my bicycle's handlebars – and I did!

And the more she laughed, the faster I cycled.

31

THERE WAS MORE FUN and laughter around our college as well. The principal made sure things ran well and smoothly on the premises. No obstacles seemed beyond solution, the atmosphere was carefree, and the girls felt secure enough to roam where they pleased. It helped to know he was there, keeping a sharp lookout. His smile was benign and he'd join now this group, now that. Many a time he'd come in unobtrusively and stand around observing us, saying nothing.

"Sir! Sir!"

The girls were startled when they noticed his presence, and then his raucous laugh rang around the college. He was also a bit of a gossip: if ever a group of girls wanted to talk "private" stuff, they first looked around to make sure Sir wasn't hovering nearby.

Our principal believed in the law of demand and supply: he was always writing letters demanding more staff and other facilities for the college because there was just him, the head accountant, and the head guard – only these three – on the college payroll.

But no class went untaught. The principal himself was a jack of all trades who taught the political science class, the economics class, and the social science class. When a First Year class was on, the Second and Final Years lounged in the garden, ate samosas, and played badminton. In our free time, we *all* piled in to play badminton. There were all of four rackets to go around, so one of the principal's responsibilities, or should one say problems, took a new direction: "Come on, come on! Give it to her now." He proved himself an advocate of the *mot juste* as well – "Don't call it a bird, girls! Call it a shuttlecock!" – and a stickler for rules: "*Arré,* you mad girls, will you just keep adding points or will you learn how they're to be counted? . . . Come on, follow the rules!"

"Rules?" we asked, astonished.

"O.K., O.K., say it! Go on, say it – 'Rules are made only to be broken'."

"Oh, but Sir, our bird's fallen on the roof."

"Go on, climb on to the roof. Let me see how you do it without a ladder."

"Sir, can we get a chair from your room?"

No raucous laugh this time, only a smile to say "Go . . . do as you please." The result was a race amongst the girls to climb up to the roof.

He seemed to be having as much fun as the girls. Sometimes, perhaps more so . . . He'd come and stand near the chair which the girls were using to clamber up. "*Arré,* you are all monkeys! Monkeys! Careful, careful dears, else your mothers will break my head!"

Kabaddi, kho-kho, *ghoda maar khai*, carrom, and badminton – we liked playing all these much more than swotting. On the day of the slow-cycling competition we pestered the principal: "Sir, please let's have a regular cycle race." But he wouldn't allow it – on the grounds that "slow-cycling is more difficult than cycle racing!" We had a riproaring time anyhow, because many of the cyclists banged into each other and laughed so much that not even one cyclist breasted the tape.

Questions, questions: Are all villages like this? ... Are they really so pretty? ... What a lovely cool breeze ... Do cows bellow like this? ... How does a buffalo manage to stay so long in the water? ... Are these fields? ... Does the plough work this way? No-one was really keen on discussing astonishing classroom subjects like these. Instead, the girls were full of their own stories and gossip.

Once, an educational trip was organised – to a National Social Service Camp in Baitoli village. For seven days, we were all to be herded together there. I recall that on the first morning there, Archana was sweeping the place in a rather gingerly and la-di-da kind of way, as a prima donna might. Watching her, Sir exclaimed, "Hey! Is this how you sweep at home? ... I'll have to check with your mother!"

"No! No!" she said meekly, then applied elbow grease to the broom and swished it about more vigorously.

"Yeah, that's the way! That's a lot better!" he said, laughing.

That spurred us all to get involved in cleaning up the

whole place. We made holes to soak up standing water, we made outlets for the water, we cleaned up wells, we painted and spruced up a small road. The principal took the lead in much of all this, so there was a huge flow of enthusiasm and high spirits among the girls participating in these improving enterprises.

Plenty more stuff got done too: we learnt how cow-dung was converted to manure, and our house-to-house visits resulted in an informal census on how many kids had been inoculated and how many more still needed to get their shots. An idea of the sorts of illnesses people suffered from in the village, and how those infections might be avoided, coalesced as a kind of picture in our minds of our stretch there.

All this done, there was more – so said Sir. He handed us books for use in an adult-literacy campaign which involved teaching the elderly. This I had never anticipated as a requirement, and it struck me that Kakka, when told about it, would very likely be quite delighted ... and who knows, I thought, maybe even our dear Sir will soon start showing up at the dhaba ...

Evenings were for singing and dancing and storytelling with the villagers. One night we had a singing competition – it was us versus the village girls and the game involved giving clues. The principal showed himself most fair-minded, sometimes helping the rural belles with clues, at other times us. It wasn't easy to tell whom he favoured more! We could tell, though, that he had an incredible memory for all the great film songs. None of us had ever, until that evening, even the faintest inkling that this teacher of ours who spouted the philosophy of Aristotle and Plato was also a singer of our kind of film songs!

After a while, the village women took over: they sang and played to the rhythm of the local drums. It was all great fun when it began, but then the singing became raucous and high-pitched, and our ears had had their fill by the end of it. Still, those seven days flew by fast and the camp stayed in our minds as a wonderful new experience.

As time passed, vacancies in the college's teaching positions began to be filled. New teachers were appointed to teach home science, economics, political science, social science, and Hindi.

The principal kept himself unusually involved: "How many hours do you study at home?" he often asked. "Do you just cram, or do you really understand what you're reading? I hope you're not turning into parrots, the whole lot of you?" Or he changed the subject and asked: "O.K., tell me. What did you learn in class today? Which of your teachers do you like best? Was she teaching you out of a book or from notes?"

The girls mostly gave it to him straight: "So and so's no good; she just hurries it all up, any which way. We don't understand a word she says." About teachers that didn't teach properly, or who came late to class, or who left before time, the girls were frank too.

"Wait! I'll send her a memorandum. It'll straighten her out in no time . . ." – he'd even start getting a memo typed and conclude – ". . . now she's going to get a memo; then she'll shape up. She'll learn to behave . . ."

Resentment among the teachers was inevitable. The home science teacher was heard saying, "The principal's spoilt these girls. They're all idiots, and they'll stay idiots – they have no manners, this bunch . . ." The other teachers, some of them, nodded in agreement. Some rolled their eyes.

Some of us laughed at all this, some of us marched to the principal's office: "That madam was calling us idiots . . . Sir, are we idiots? Why do these *madames* talk this way about us?"

"Oh, you mean those madams, not *madames*!" the Hindi madam said, smiling.

The economics class ended early one day. The principal emerged from his room. "Hey! Why are you girls loitering around here? Why aren't you in your class?"

"Sir, Madam ended the class early, so we're chatting."

All hell broke loose in the economics class after this. The next day, class started bang on time and ended exactly at 8:40, in the middle of a sentence: "Adam Smith said . . ." Glaring at her watch, angrily slamming shut her book, glowering at the girls, the economics madam left in a huff, bang on time! The principal heard the noise and came round to the classroom, but we beat him to it: we'd already reached his office: "Sir, what's all this memorandum stuff? . . . You've straightened out economics, but not the *madame* teaching economics!"

He rang a bell, but before the economics teacher could be summoned, the girls ran away giggling.

Now, if there happened to be even a five-minute delay in a class starting, the principal looked agitated.

"No matter, Sir! Just send a memorandum and all will be well," we told him familiarly.

A library was to be opened in Room No. 5. The door to Room 4 and Room 5 was common – it was like a railway compartment: you could come and go from Room 4 to Room 5 and from Room 5 to Room 4. No-one ever did, though.

One day, Sangeeta and I reached the college early. Rambharosé Dada had unlocked both rooms and disappeared somewhere for tea or a bidi. We walked into Room 5 – the door opened easily enough but couldn't be closed. Two of the door panels were missing and the door frame was so weak that the moment we touched it, it fell into our hands. So we blocked the door: no-one could come after us now.

What bewildered us, what beguiled and enchanted us, was what we saw beyond this door – a wonderland, another world altogether, an unreal fantasy realm we had absolutely no idea existed within our very own ragged, dilapidated campus!

We were stunned by what our eyes told us we were seeing – a world of dry leaves within an unkempt garden. Not one or two leaves, the garden had thousands of dry leaves. The utterly unexpected sight of it bowled us over. We walked barefoot on those leaves, we climbed up and down those unreal trees. We ran around, and after a while our scarves slid off us, turning into little bags with dry leaves spilling out of them! The whole scenario that we'd chanced upon was a sort of mystery world awaiting discovery.

We made mounds of the dry leaves and a beautiful small path between the mounds. The sound of dry leaves as we ran around them drove us mad with delight. And it wasn't only all this. There were so many other things in that unbidden never-never land that drove us crazy ...

But then, all too soon, our delight turned to fear. From Room 4 nextdoor, where the economics class was, there came a voice, "Is there someone in there? Is there someone inside ...?"

We were struck dumb; the voices came closer.

The sounds we'd made seemed to have stunned everyone in the classroom too. We tiptoed to the door and hid behind it; peeped, and came right back. We sensed the stupefied silence in the classroom next to our out-of-bounds world right nextdoor to it.

Quickly, we spread all the leaves back again so that the mounds and the path through them disappeared. But there was so much rustling and hissing from the dry leaves that the girls in the economics class started shouting, "Ghost! There's a ghost! Run, run!" Before the girls could run, the teacher had grabbed her books and scooted. It was a good thing the two of us weren't wearing bangles, or else with the bangles jangling there would've been cries of "Witch! Witch!"

We climbed up a stone to look across: everyone had gathered in the playground. The head clerk ran to call the principal. Rambharosé Dada spoke of calling the police: Kailash, the constable, was a pal of his. We were so scared of what might happen that we froze where we were.

"Sir, hurry up! There's someone in the back, over there!"

The head clerk was more agitated than the others. Rambharosé Dada, lock in hand, said, 'Sir, I'll lock the door. Please hurry up and call the police station."

Now it was time to panic. The principal walked around, inspecting all the girls. "*Arré,* where are those two naughty girls?"

We screamed, "Sir, Sir! Please, don't lock us in."

"What're you doing in there?" he yelled, furious.

We were punished for two periods: made to stand in a corner. The principal announced the punishment and went off to his room. But before the first of the two periods ended he'd melted, "O.K.! O.K.! Go attend your class, but don't ever do this again!"

We thought the trees were looking at us and smiling.

32

BHAIYYA WENT TO A convent school. He took an hour over his tea: he was entirely uninterested in getting ready for school and we'd have to shake him hard even to make him get up. The moment the school bus came he went and sat on the ash heap behind the dhaba. Often he shut the door and shoved his shoes into the ash.

Kakka forced him onto the bus, which made Bhaiyya ruffle his well-combed hair and look dishevelled. A Sister from the convent summoned Kakka to the school quite regularly and complained of exactly the same thing each time: "Your son's not doing at all well with his books."

Back home, Bhaiyya said to Kakka: "Please wear proper clothes when you come to school. Everyone teases me about you when they see you in your lungi and vest. Why wear that to school? Wear a kurta-pyjama when you come." Not content with that, he made it known to our parents that he was also unhappy with their names: "Bai! Kakka! Can you please change your names!" he said. And to Bai: "Don't tell them your name is Bhanwari Bai. If someone asks you your name, tell them its Kaushalya." His suggestion to Kakka was on similar lines:

"And Kakka – you . . . Instead of Mohan Lal, call yourself M.L. Singh."

Bai laughed, but Kakka was less than amused and exclaimed: "What an idiot he is . . . What an idiot! Concentrate on your studies, you fool, and spare me your nonsense!"

Stories about the convent as an institution were a part of the local gossip. Anytime the Sisters emerged from its premises, a crowd collected around them, gawking at their clothes and the cross around their necks. Curiosity made people trail after them, but if they happened to turn around their pursuers melted away; then the moment the Sisters moved forward, the people trooping behind them were back again. If they went into a shop, they were followed in.

The garrulous and utterly useless Ajjan Chacha brought in his version of the gossip. The Sisters, he said, had placed a bucket of water in front of the school kids, and a stone image of Ganesh as well as a Christian wooden cross on a table. They'd then asked the children to – "Look . . . the real God won't sink in the water, the false one will." Ajjan Chacha enjoyed spinning such yarns, and his ridiculous inventions were far from the only ones circulating – some of the kids from the convent, sitting surrounded by women, would come out with more in the same vein, each sillier than the last.

This became in fact a new game for all the wastrels and layabouts: they spent animated hours talking about the convent and its supposed activities. Some were dead set against sending children to any convent school at all, while others offered an opinion even more drastic: "Just shut the school."

No-one was interested in the unconcocted truth. Nobody had personally seen any of the things they were ready to swear about. Ajjan Chacha was able to get away with stories that grew fancier by the day. He had apostles following him around wanting him to manufacture his version of the gospel, which made his mind descend into levels increasingly childish – he'd fabricate one thing one day and come up with something wholly at variance with it the next. Sometimes, the contradictions made him exclaim: "Oh forget it, friends! Why have you latched on to just this one thing . . .?" The funniest thing about him, however, happened a little later – his own kids started going to the convent! And so his earlier yarns disappeared suddenly down a rabbit hole from which they never emerged again!

Kakka organised tuition classes for Bhaiyya in his convent. The school closed at one-thirty but he stayed back till four. I cycled down every day to pick him up. Despite those tuitions, he failed repeatedly, and finally the day came when the school refused to keep him on. Kakka pleaded with them and gave them all kinds of promises, so finally the Sister gave in and said: "If he fails just one more time, there's no way he'll stay on in this school."

I picked a fight with Kakka every now and then on the matter of our education. I'd seat myself in a determined way right in front of him and start berating him about it: "Kakka, haven't you been a bit of a cheat yourself? . . . You gave Bhaiyya a convent education. So why not us?"

"There was no convent around in your time."

"What a whopper! –You could've sent us there after Class 8. Come on, give me a better defence – speak!"

"You're squabbling with me for no reason at all. This convent school goes only up to Class 8. *Arré,* this whole thing's been a blunder!" He struck his forehead with the palm of his hand to convey his extreme exasperation, but that wasn't about to make me let him off the hook.

"O.K., O.K. Let's say we agree with what you're saying. But then, there's Neera – why didn't you send *her* to the convent?"

"*Arré,* my dear, you're incorrigible!" By now he knew he was well and truly cornered and he wasn't able to stop himself laughing.

". . . And besides," I said, twisting the knife, "Bhaiyya isn't even remotely interested in his books."

His embarrassed laughter turned to genuine regret: "Oh yes, my dear. Yes, I confess, this is a sin I can't be forgiven for . . ."

Had I even tried to stop myself smiling at his admission, I wouldn't have been able to. "O.K., O.K. You're forgiven!" I said.

After which I desisted from raising the issue ever again. I knew how upsetting it was for him to have it constantly nagging there at the back of his head.

33

ONCE MORE, A LETTER from Shiva. This time round the "boy" worked in a bank. The boy and his family were all gems of the purest ray serene: she ran out of space praising them. Her letter was a stove stuffed with sawdust – every last bit of the paper was written on. *"The boy's family demands nothing, but they do want a grand reception."* This bit was heavily underlined. Her letter's arrival seemed to have created a flutter of excitement in the house.

After cleaning out the oven and pouring oil on a cow-pat, I reminded Kakka of his promise to let me carry on till the end of my B.A. He had a bucket full of coals in one hand and a matchbox in the other. He pretended he hadn't heard me, carried on lighting the cowpat, and put more coal into the oven. Smoke filled the dhaba and his eyes.

Then, suddenly one day, Shiva showed up in person. Having exchanged various photos and having had horoscopes matched, she had confirmation from the stars that it wasn't a mere sixteen to eighteen qualities of head and heart on which "the boy" and I were compatible. Apparently he and I were perfectly matched in all thirty-two!

Shiva's was the final word on my horoscope. By the evening, Asha-jiji, Usha-jiji, and Anni had marched in. It was a mercy Grandmother and Phapphu hadn't shown up yet.

It looked to me like it was a done deal, or almost a done deal. Ignoring the ash, the cowpats, the match box, and the smoke, I confronted Kakka, giving it to him straight: "Kakka, I'm not getting married. I'm going to carry on studying and then I'll get a job."

Water off a duck's back, because the next day "the boy's" family arrived – an eventuality for which I was wholly unprepared. So, now it was time for everyone to start working on me; nothing was more urgent than to get me to come around. Paeans in praise of "the boy's" various virtues – his house, his job – began to be drummed relentlessly into my ears. But my well-wishers had a problem on their hands: there was no way any of their pleas was going to make me feel ready to be presented to "the boy". He sat with his brother in the outer room and I heard him say "...The marriage will be held quickly."

"How quickly?" Shiva asked.

"You know how it is," he replied, "I'm the oldest in our family and my younger sister's married already. My mother now has a problem doing the household chores, so I want her to take it easy. She's worked hard her whole life, she needs a break. She gets tired working now, she needs to rest."

In short, the marriage was as usual about getting a daughter-in-law to do their household chores – all the things that I *couldn't* do; and as for work outside the house – all that I *could* do – that was entirely out of the question. I had no option except to dig in my heels.

Which then got everyone lecturing me on family honour – now, it seemed, clan prestige was at stake. When I looked stony-faced and turned a deaf ear to their pleadings, Kakka blew a fuse: "If you don't listen to me, our relationship ends here and now. We'll have nothing more to do with you . . . Go off and do as you please . . ."

I knew that tone of his. Every time he was really angry, he only ended up sounding officious. To Bai he said, "Understand, Rajjo, this is no longer her home, starting today."

I just stood there, motionless as a tree trunk. Bai was livid with Kakka in a way I'd never seen, she really let fly at him: "You've spoilt the girl rotten, and now she's dancing on your head! Go on, send her to college, take her around town, get her to fight elections! Father and daughter, both want to be leaders! You're great, aren't you, just like Nehru . . . so now you want to make her your Indira Gandhi? . . . *So suffer, now!* You've brought this suffering on our heads, and you're going to be the death of us all . . . Go on, call them – they're close to you, aren't they – people like Diwan Singh? Call him now and ask *him* to explain things to her . . . To hell with such children. You call these *children*? They're a curse on us . . . the misbegotten sins of our past lives!" Her tirades were like spasms, once begun there was no stopping them: "... *Arré,* she's turned wild! I'm telling you she won't rest till she's killed a couple ... !"

By this time, Kakka knew he was neither burning coal nor stoking embers – he was meant to be at the dhaba. Instead of which here we all were, burning down the house.

Asha-jiji carried on glaring at me. I picked up the keys to the dhaba; she caught hold of my arm and slapped me twice across the face. "And what kind of fancy job d'you think you're going to land? You think you're some big hotshot? Maybe you already have a husband who's offering you some big job? ... We should discover what's going on, shouldn't we?"

Finally, we were close to the last stage – when the weeping and the wailing took over. The "boy's side" had meanwhile sensed that something was seriously amiss. They called out to Shiva. Her eyes red, she gulped down some water and moved off to talk to them, then came right back and said, "They're saying 'send the girl out fast' – they have to leave." She sounded close to tears.

So then the last-ditch efforts began, everyone begged and pleaded – why was I persisting in my obstinacy, they wanted to know. They gave me water to cool me down. But I stayed adamant. "No means No. I've said it. That's it."

In my desperation, I tried a shot in the dark to silence

the harassment. I declared: "I don't like the boy and I don't like his name . . . if any of you do, go ahead and marry him." I caught hold of Shiva, "You think you're a firebrand, Blackie! Why don't *you* marry the fellow?" This was a bolt from the blue she hadn't expected from me. She stood rooted to the spot, looking aghast.

Then three bristling aunts, comprehending the seriousness of what was going on, tried their hand. I was tart with them too: "If he's as wonderful as you say, why don't *you* marry him?" At this, Kakka made as if he'd smack me one, but he didn't.

By this time "the boy" and his brother, curious to discover exactly what all the commotion was about, walked into the room. Shiva was the target of their opening taunt: "Did you bring us here to belittle us? You should've asked your sister first . . ." They'd seen enough, apparently; they left for the station, refusing the food prepared for their welcome though their train was not due for another four hours.

A pandit who'd arrived to announce the auspicious time for the marriage ceremony took a deep breath, folded his almanac, shoved it into his bag, and got up to go. Asha-jiji tore my horoscope to shreds.

The house fell into a stupor, it became silent as a tomb. There was darkness all around that evening. Bai wasn't bothering to light even a diya.

For fear of her in-laws, Shiva went out into the lane and sat by herself on some stairs. Dread of the piece of their mind that they were soon bound to give us stopped the whole lot of us being able to eat a thing. For days after, no-one spoke to me. Not even Shiva.

The day she was leaving for Nagpur, I broke down. "Shiva . . . Shiva," I cried, clinging to her. I felt her hesitation and her despair and said, "Now don't ever try finding husbands for me, O.K.?"

"Fatty, who's going to marry you now in any case? And especially from Nagpur . . . You talk big but you still don't know what's good for you. You haven't the faintest notion of when it's right to stop refusing and seize the opportunity . . . And have you even seen your own handwriting? It's like a spider's been wading in ink . . and then taken to dancing all over the paper!"

I looked at her in dismay.

Soon after Shiva left, both the older sisters, and then Anni, left for their in-laws'.

34

TO KAKKA I DIDN'T dare utter a word. I just went meekly about my business and did the required work. I was near him day and night, but, far from speaking to me, he wouldn't even look in my direction.

One night, when he and I were alone at the dhaba, I said, "Kakka, I'm not being wayward or perverse . . . Just let me go on with my studies. I want to be able to work – like the college madam . . ."

He looked at me for a fleeting moment: "Go, go, get the savouries. I'm getting the daal ready meanwhile."

Was he testing me? Perhaps he believed Arts students also needed to pass certain practicals, and that the whole sorry marriage proposal episode was some kind of performance I'd decided to put on – impromptu theatrics of some stupid variety. If that's what he thought, it must have seemed to him a very ill-prepared and amateur effort. No curtain had gone up or come down; the oven had neither been properly lit nor allowed to go cold; there'd been smoke and embers but no proper fire.

What I wondered was why I was the solitary person being tested. Shouldn't there have been a practical examination to test Kakka too?

I'd just started off to get the savouries, and Kakka had just about started to make the daal, when Chacha-ji arrived. The moment he saw me, he laughed. I cried, "Chacha-ji" and clung to him. Patting me affectionately, he said, "Study! . . . Go on . . . you just carry on with your studies and no-one's going to say a thing to you, and if they do, just tell them they'll have me to answer to. I'll sort them out. You go ahead with your books as much as you like, and we'll get you whatever you need to do well . . ."

". . . Chacha-ji, I need a table lamp."

"Certainly. We'll get you a grand table lamp. Whichever kind you want. And if we can't get it here, I'll get it from Bhopal."

To Kakka he said, "Hey Brother, our girl's looking crushed by these past few days."

I was near tears hearing him but managed to keep a grip on my feelings.

Diwan Singh Chacha ji and Ajaib Singh Phupha-ji weren't really Kakka's brother and brother-in-law, but their relationship with him was closer than that of siblings. There are in fact no words to describe the depth of their feelings for each other. Chacha-ji was hugely respected through the district. He was a big farmer, and he had considerable political clout. He'd been Headman, then Market Committee Chairman, and was now getting ready for the state legislative assembly. Kakka, who'd played a major supporting role at every step in Chacha-ji's life, thought the world of him. When Chacha-ji was around, troublemakers seemed to slink away automatically. Though unluckily not the cynics who muttered under their breath to Kakka: "He's a politician, after all, it's his job to keep the whole world smiling. If he'd educated his own girls and got them jobs he'd be practising what he's preaching, but he's married off his own daughters early – so he's just hoodwinking you . . . Friends should be peers, his type of fellow is way above your league!"

It seemed after a while as if the upheavals in my life were trickling back to normality, but I discovered soon enough that gossip has a way of reaching every ear, that my story had spread all over town. In college, virtually every day, her eyes widening, some girl or the other would come up to exclaim: "You said *'no'* to marriage?!" And she'd look at me like I was the Eighth Wonder of the World. How molehills are made mountains of and then carried around like display pieces for the world to see was something you could learn from this bunch!

The ladies of the locality weren't exactly going easy on giving me a hard time either. "Hey Babli! If you don't marry, what're you planning on doing your whole life? Becoming the modern Meera Bai, maybe? . . ." They were so taken up by their own witticism, and laughing so hysterically and rolling their eyes so sarcastically, they could hardly speak. ". . . And the temple's right nextdoor too, so our Meera Bai won't have to go far to sing . . . she won't need to go off into the forest searching for her beloved . . ."

Their outrage was infectious. It spread around me like wildfire: "Have you heard? Girls have taken to refusing marriage proposals! What's the world coming to? *Arré,* there's so-and-so's daughter . . . did you hear what she said straight off – she said *she didn't like the boy!*"

Things were bad enough for me, but they were terrible for my sisters. They were now constantly taunted because of what I'd done and cornered by their in-laws, for no fault of theirs, into a state of absolute abjection. Nor was there any sympathy or emotional sustenance for me at home. Shalu and Shiva had seen to the end of that: their love for me had, it seemed to them, been reciprocated only by my misbehaviour.

The love and sense of well-being there had been in my life had died even before it could really blossom. The recollection of this feels even now like the falling of autumn leaves.

I'd look at the moon for hours. There was a beautiful view of the moon from the dhaba and no need to take time out especially to look at it or to climb to the roof and look up. It was just so quietly visible while I worked, I could see it from near the oven, I could see it from the ash mound at the back. Sometimes it seemed the moon was at work with us in the dhaba. I could never have enough of watching that moon, and sometimes when it hid behind the clouds I'd get . . . well, all moony, and murmur romantically to it, "Again, O Moon, you are in darkness lost . . ."

All night I dreamt of the sea. The tide came in, it touched me, it went out. I saw my sisters, and their unhappy faces made me feel I'd been thrown into the deep end, right into the middle of the ocean. But though I didn't know how to swim, I struggled and worked my way to the shore.

All day, all night, visions of Shalu and of Kakka floated before my eyes.

35

SOME TIME LATER the Parasari was again in spate. No rain, no flood, but the college was going under: I was still a First Year student when the principal was transferred.

Seeing the girls weep, his eyes welled up. "Boys don't cry" never sounded more false: I'd seen Kakka cry his heart out, and now the principal looked like he was neck deep in tears surrounded by a bevy of girls who didn't know how to swim! To keep us from drowning our principal had all along been our boat, our saviour. And now he was going.

The railway station was a flood of tears . . . "Please write, girls . . ."

In the end, is all of life just a sequence of letters on paper? Will that train too turn into a missive some day? Possibly. Will books made from mounds of dry leaves, and the library in the lane, end up as letters written from some faraway shore? Will any of us ever see the principal again?

Maybe. Maybe not. Nothing endures.

36

TENTS HAVE BEEN stretched out all around. The fields surrounding them are being watered. Disposable plates made out of leaves are stacked on both sides. Some two or three thousand people have gathered. It's not a dream: Asha-jiji's mother-in-law is dead. A woman who lived life to the fullest – a full ninety-nine years!

People have arrived from the seven villages around us. Women in long shawls, groups of them, howling down the village lanes. Shrieking fit to burst their blood vessels.

"Oh my sister! Where have you gone? Oh my sister, why didn't you take me with you? . . ."

"Oh, your life . . . just gone! Oh, why didn't you take me along?"

"You saw no happiness! Not even briefly! You had to sit all your life on a mountain made of sadness! . . . How could Lala-ji leave you in the afternoon of his life! . . . And how you gathered your family around you . . . brought up your children! Oh, Aunt, why have you left us . . . ?"

"You kept an eye on the land, you supervised the farming; you flinched from nothing! Oh, Aunt, your house is bereft without you!"

"Oh my sister! How you deprived yourself . . . ! Oh sister, you should have taken me with you!"

Everyone crying in tune, chattering in tune. Then suddenly, silence. Followed by second, third, and fourth rounds of the same: the same lamentation, the same wailing.

With the exception of a single solitary corner, the entire field is covered in durries. The bereaved family's entire village, top to bottom, has been invited. The women of the household are seated within. The untouchables from the village have to sit in a barren corner of the field, where they squat crammed against each other, a fellowship of the humiliated, clinging to their leaf-plates, saucers, and mugs. The upper-caste men huddle closer to each other, fearful of contamination, as though the very earth were being polluted by the presence of undesired intruders.

Even those who have been serving food serve the lower castes from a distance. Sweets, apples, yogurt, and more – all of it is ladled out hastily, pell-mell, with a deliberate lack of consideration, so that more falls on the ground than gets on their plates. And, once served, these lower castes become undeserving of a second glance from those who have so carelessly been serving the food – for there are higher castes elsewhere, waiting to be offered their seconds and their thirds. And when the "untouchables" walk past, their hands respectfully folded, no-one bothers to acknowledge their condolences, or even their very existence. And the same performance is repeated a number of times over the course of this day of mourning.

Loud belching sounds emanate at a distance from the privileged, indicating satiety among those whose last serving has been paan, Puhara bidi, and Cavender cigarettes – all reverentially offered to them on oversize platters. From their remoteness in the corner where they have been positioned, the bedraggled look silently on, their eyes betraying fright at the prospect of trespassing space preordained as not theirs. Even the glasses of water they hold look somehow flustered. Their women have been shoved into a half-built makeshift house full of straw, cowpats, thatch.

The upper-caste women are seated in the courtyard.

All these notions – of those who are upper-caste and those who are out-caste, even in the time of death – came as a revelation to us on the day that Asha-jiji's mother-in-law passed away. Only once, before this particular feast for the dead, had Seema and I seen a spread as sumptuous. That had been when we were quite little and Kakka had taken us to the one laid out in memory of the late Umaukheri Grandfather. We ate in our designated caste area in Mahavir Maidan, when, all of a sudden, there was a dust-storm. Within minutes a huge brown cloud had descended and blown away everyone's leaf-plates. There'd been a lot of sweets on our plates that we'd been saving for the end. The whole precious lot – pheni, gulab jamun, imarti, balushahi, barfi, and chum-chum – were carried off by that dust storm. I remember that feast well. Anytime we go past a shop selling sweets now, I see dust clouds and sweet delicacies scattered all around it.

You don't have to be rich and well placed to stage this thirteenth-day ceremony for the dead. In fact, even those who cannot afford to observe it must borrow money on interest and invite the whole world – all in the name of preserving their family honour.

Kakka's tone became hard-edged at times like these: "Why ruin yourself imitating what others have decided they must do, eh?" But though people heard him out, they weren't really listening. He'd try talking them out of it and fail miserably, then he'd say exasperatedly: "You'll ruin your takings from not one but many harvests. Maybe then you'll come to your senses."

The time came when Kakka and his friends stopped attending these ceremonies altogether – unless family obligations compelled them to show up for those that had been organised by close relatives. But to make it clear that only a sense of duty had forced them to attend, they ate nothing, nibbled only for form's sake on the sacramental offerings, and then proceeded to expound on the folly of such rituals to anyone willing to listen.

Their reformist impulse has never failed to fall on deaf ears: there are no signs of this kind of ceremony dying out. All the same, Kakka, Chacha-ji, Onkar Singh from Nateran, and our Uncle from Gyaraspur resolved most ardently that they "will not allow any thirteenth-day ceremony *for ourselves*. We've sworn an oath, and we're putting it down in writing. In whatever limited way we can, we'll set an example to end this evil custom. We need to hack away its roots. The next generation needs to be saved from this ridiculous practice."

These four men stopped attending not just the thirteenth-day farce but also the "patta" ceremony prescribed as necessary three years after a person's death. For a change, this bit of good sense seems to have percolated into people's heads: there has been some coming round to the idea of ending patta. By refusing to organise a patta ceremony for his own father, this Uncle of ours set the ball firmly rolling.

37

SHIVA HAD APPLIED to take the Class 11 Home Science exams at a local college. One afternoon, after coming back from the college, she stood by the door at home, red-eyed and silent. The silence around her was like the hush that falls on a platform after the train has left, and seeing her looking so spectral I was filled with apprehension and began trembling involuntarily. A long stillness separated us, and then, when she told me what had happened, it was beyond comprehension.

Shalu had run away from her in-laws' house. For days, she had been alone and hungry, and then at some point, still in her old clothes, she'd ventured ticketless onto a train. She reached our home about eight that morning, clung to Kakka, and wept bitterly.

He said to her, "I'm still alive. What are you scared of?"

She was lying indoors when I reached. The moment she saw me she howled "Babli! Babli!" and broke down completely.

I couldn't cry. I was too stunned to say anything either. A huge mountain had crumbled over our heads: Shalu had returned empty-handed – and pregnant.

To collect myself, I went on to the dhaba. I found the cow standing there, under the electricity pole, her head bowed. It took no more than a glance to take in both Kakka and the cow. I wondered what had brought her there at this hour – she was never there at that hour, so why was she there now?

"Don't know what she's gone and eaten," Kakka said. He was filling a large pan with water from the hand pump. The cow's eyes were watering and her mouth was frothing. She didn't drink the water she was offered. Instead, she just collapsed in a heap near the hand pump. The roti on the oven stayed where it was. Kakka's eyes had filled with tears. As had the cow's.

Back home, Kakka made Shalu follow Shiva in applying to take the Class 11 Home Science exams. Simultaneously, Chacha-ji found her a job paying five hundred rupees which kept her busy doing something or the other in the Irrigation Department. She was due to deliver fairly soon, but there was no news from her in-laws . . . there was total silence, in fact. The cosmos seemed to have calculated how to put Shalu in the state of misery that surpasses understanding. In this state, one day, she broke every bangle on her arms.

She broke her bangles in the house, and outside in the neighbourhood the hunchback witch went berserk. The entire neighbourhood echoed with her curses, and not even by evening was there any sign of her stopping. In between swearing she'd shriek, "I'm being summoned to the cremation ground . . .", and it felt like she was herding the whole lot of us there before her. The ruckus she created went on for hours. She was found in a semi-conscious state next day in the lane behind Banjani Babu's house, still muttering the most foul curses.

The hunchback witch had never been in such a bad way before. And the cow? Though never an enthusiastic forager of rubbish bins, she'd taken to going nowhere at all, she just stayed put at the dhaba night and day – though she wouldn't eat a thing. I wondered if her mouth would ever stop foaming and frothing. And then I began to wonder how long it could be before the ritual of feeding her the day's first roti came to an end.

Had the hunchback witch also reached the end of her tether? Suman Bhabhi refrained from expressing her opinion, but Pathriya-wali Aunty, Muniman Aunty, and the old official's wife continued their mutterings against her. A bundle of clothes under her arm and clutching a tin box in her hand, the witch had taken to sitting at the well near the temple. There, for long stretches, she'd stare at the water in the well, and she looked down so intently that . . . well, some people came and pushed her away from where she sat. But being stubborn as a mule, she went off to another well, to the one near our school, where we could hear her foul-mouthed tirade. The well looked like it had been fated to swallow her up. It was only a matter of time.

In all this time of frothing and fearfulness which connect in my mind with images of a crazed woman staring into her well of doom and shards of broken bangles, Shalu gave birth to a girl. The baby was born with six fingers on her right hand. Usha-jiji went running home and rushed back with twine. She took the baby in her lap, tied the offending sixth finger tight, and verily it came to pass that, on the third day, the sixth finger swaddled in twine just fell right off . . .!

Some of us teasingly called the baby "Chhingly" because of her six fingers. Jiji warned us against all possible connections with ill luck: "Hey! Don't! . . . It'll become her name! Call her Preeti. Preeti. Her name's Preeti."

She dandled the baby in her arms, who off and on chortled with delight. The scenario was heart-warming enough to put a smile even on Shalu's face.

Where the baby's sixth finger had been there was now a little scar. A single small scar. A lot fewer than those branded on the heart of the baby's mother.

Being aware of how things had gone with Shalu, Kakka seemed to have decided that, come what may, he'd never insist on Seema, Neera, and I being married off in the near future, not even if any of us looked like we were going astray. He'd do everything in his power to make us self-reliant. Marriages could follow.

He blamed himself. Deep feelings of guilt rose within him. The recognition came as a blow to the core of his sense of self that he'd wrecked Shalu's life. A man who'd always thought "They're children, they can be careless" was now consumed by guilt at what he considered his own carelessness. A deep-seated fear had settled within him: had *he* made all this happen? In theory, he could have changed his view of the matter if he'd really wanted to, but the reality of it was that this was a constricting fear that he hadn't the strength to shake off. Whatever it was, it now plagued him incessantly to think that it was *he* who'd had both Shalu and Shiva married off without really thinking through the possible consequences of such haste.

Who else was there to blame? If Shiva was to be believed, neither Kakka nor Shalu were culpable. It seems Shalu had had a friend, Aradhana, who was carefree and fun-loving – and Shalu had hung out a lot with her, the consequence of which was now in evidence . . . And with regard to her own stupidity in marrying early, Shiva said: "Oh, I just wanted to see how much fun we could have! That's all. And then I got stuck because of silly Shalu's behaviour!"

"Oh yes! Then why didn't you say so . . .?"

"I saw the pressure Kakka was under, and I was scared." And then, immediately changing the subject, she said: "In any case, marriages are made in heaven."

I couldn't stomach this kind of talk. But she wasn't to be stopped: "It wasn't Shalu's fault, it was Aradhana's, she was the wayward one. That's the truth. And Fatty, shall I tell you another thing? There are people who fall so low, they're happy to dredge up stories about others. Just you watch – the dead will speak one day." Like a fortune-teller, she'd grown loquacious.

Shalu herself never uttered a word on any of this. Carelessness, waywardness, stupidity. Shalu's carelessness, her friend's sense of fun, the stupidity of supporting a friend. It wasn't some single lapse, it was many lapses, many causes, and a world of consequences – and, on the other side there was Kakka feeling he was wholly to blame and must now carry the cross of it all on his shoulders. Imagining himself the culprit for everything that had gone wrong. For no good reason.

In this guilt-laden atmosphere the barking of stray dogs, which started sometime after midnight, put the fear of God into my heart. Signs of sudden and dire trouble strike the animal world before the difficulties they've sensed can reach the human doorstep. All of us crept with guilt into our beds over those days. Bai and Shalu, more timid than the rest of us, sat bolt upright long into the night. They were more certain now than they'd ever been before that the world's worst calamities were reserved for them.

In the midst of the dogs' frightening howling, the hunchback witch appeared with her bundle and box. Windows opened as her cries drowned out even the baying of those stray dogs around her. "Light some diyas quick! *Arré,* where've the whole lot of you gone? It's late! It's late, you fools! Why so careless? Light the diyas, light the diyas!"

From our neighbourhood, all the way to our school, her cries shook everyone out of their slumber. Where we lived, a night more nerve-racking had never been known.

Will someone, anyone, at the end of everything, light a diya at the well near the school – for the hunchback witch?

38

ACHARYA-JI WAS A great help to Shalu in her office. He taught her the office routine and bucked her up so she felt better about herself, more self-confident. Off and on he'd drop in at home and praise her work and conduct. He was always most supportive.

But Shalu had forgotten nothing. She was unhappy deep down and in trying to appear happy and unaffected she sometimes looked utterly forlorn.

Acharya-ji wrote to her in-laws to initiate divorce proceedings and ask for maintenance, but he got no response. A month later he wrote again and waited two months. There was still no response. Not a crow in sight sat on the windowsill to caw. But one day, all of a sudden, Shalu's brother-in-law turned up.

Acharya-ji stuck around the whole time playing the lawyer. For three days there was a bewildering exchange of allegations and counter-allegations. The brother-in-law accepted their family had been at fault and swore "this will not happen again". But Shalu wasn't budging, she refused to go back. On the fourth day, he went back empty-handed.

The time came when there wasn't one crow, there were many crows, all cawing on the boundary wall. Shalu continued going off to work. Preeti was unusually exuberant, chortling and dribbling all day long. She'd begun crawling and could lean against a wall and have fun with toys. Luckily she'd also sleep on hearing a lullaby and smile in her sleep and laugh through her tears.

But, there was no letter and no-one appeared from her father's family. Till one afternoon, suddenly, Shalu's mother-in-law, her sister-in-law, and her husband all arrived without warning.

It was a blistering afternoon. Her husband had drunk cold water at Ketan Bhai's water dispenser. He apologised for not needing to drink any more. There was much crying and howling. Shalu's mother-in-law picked up her granddaughter and said to Shalu, "Come, come! Don't be so angry! Come back with us to your home. Look at poor Sunil there – he's suffered so much all this time."

And that was it! Shalu went off, back to her husband's home.

Spaces empty in no time, as do lives. An emptiness within an emptiness – a void that nothing can fill with any meaning ever again. Who can do anything about the emptiness left by a large, white, beautiful, black-eyed cow?

Each time Kakka fell into a black hole such as this, Chacha-ji instinctively arrived at the dhaba. He'd chat about goings-on in the world. It was his way of helping Kakka to forget the void. Every time he came by, Kakka cheered up. And this cheered me up even more than it cheered up Kakka. Because for me there was no better proof of Chacha-ji's devotion to my father.

39

DREAMS THAT CAN NEVER come true are invariably the most alluring, like long-lost things. Some of these, like places emptied out, seem so doomed that you know they're meant to be lost, to be parted from.

The convent Sister occasionally sat at the dhaba, awaiting her bus. Her presence there seemed to fill some of the emptiness, but sometimes filled-up spaces can look like they're about to empty. On one of those days, she sounded like she wasn't so much filling an empty space as trying to empty a filled-up space, for she said to Kakka, "You're a very good man, you work day and night, but your son is no good at his books. Our school's reputation goes down when we keep such a poor student on our rolls."

This news from the Sister was enough to get Kakka and Bai arguing:

"How will he go to Vidisha after Class 8?"

"He can just live in Vidisha."

"No, he'll have to commute every day."

"Oh? And how early will he get up? . . . And how will he come back home at night? . . . And when's he going to be able to study?"

When Kakka got going with this kind of argument, Bai held her head in her hands.

And so Bhaiyya was switched to the Babu Tapriya School. He couldn't bear the convent in any case, whereas we girls dreamt about being in it night after night . . . a necktie, shoes, socks, school bag, water bottle, smart uniform, going to school and back in a bus, plus those swings! But the very school we dreamt of had been sullied by Bhaiyya's presence.

His eyes had only to fall upon a book for him to fall asleep. Kakka had to force him to go even to the Tapriya School. Left to his own devices, he'd have played hooky on his way there! Each time his exam results came we found he'd scored exactly the same in every subject – a straight zero.

We, the girls, were all steady Second divisioners. This fact hit Kakka one day and he said, "So many kids get First divisions . . . What's your problem, girls? How come not one of you ever manages a First."

Shiva, peeling peas, piped up: "Kakka, I'll do it . . . and to top it all, in Science. Only, just remove the 'Home' before the 'Science' . . . well, come to think of it, Kakka, when have you ever given me the chance to get a First in Science? All because of that heroine Shalu . . . she ruined herself and she ruined my life too . . ." And saying this she popped a few peas into her mouth.

Before she could swallow them I intervened: "Oh really! You – Blackie, you, a Doctor – hah! Have you forgotten our fair doctor's Class 11 results? Zero in Physics, zero in Chemistry, zero in Biology! And only just pass marks in Hindi and English!"

"Quiet! You B.A. wannabe! You donkey!"

"Ho! Ho!" was Kakka's response.

His full-throated laugh got me cramming full tilt for my B.A. Final exams. It was for his sake, and nothing else, that I'd resolved to try getting a First.

40

EVERY EVENING, SEEMA and I parked ourselves near the tap and spent hours watching people come and go. Getting in and out of the bus, shoving and elbowing, pulling and pushing, laughing, chattering, gossiping, guffawing – their world of general merriment. "Hey, Patel, Patel, you've taken offence? I was just pretending to be angry! Swear on Ganga-ji, Patel! Here, have a quick cuppa and some tobacco . . ."

It felt like free entertainment staged just for us. We'd stare at everyone coming and going and comment on them aloud:

"Oh, look at that affected fellow! How disgusting he is!"

"Yeah! Just look at him!"

Or we'd spot someone and say, "Wow, isn't that a stylish fellow . . .?"

Bellowing cattle sauntering home. Herds of goats. The loud horns of buses. Rickshawallas, their legs stretched, singing with gusto. Hand-cart pullers. Shopkeepers washing their hands and feet, hand-combing their hair. Paan-wallas sipping tea, tired of making paan all day for their customers, now making masala paan for themselves.

The evenings were charming, evenings to savour. Dusk descending, turning into darkness, a sense of well-being like managing to come back from the well with a full bucket of water!

When the sky belonged to the bats, it ceased belonging to the birds, the time when birds searched in fear for other corners. Those changing colours of the sky filled us with joy. The moon a slice of watermelon; long lines of birds in flight, crows cawing, bats covering half the sky, clouds looming over swaying neem leaves and the peepal. We could never tire of watching this evening show.

The contentment would last from about five-thirty to seven or seven-thirty every evening – our time free of customers. If one happened to turn up, we'd dish out some outlandish excuse, suggesting how much better off he'd be if he came back an hour or two later. We got caught out turning them back this way, once, because one of the returning fellows later innocently asked Kakka, "Hey, Brother, how come dinner's delayed these days . . . what's the reason?" There was nothing we could say in response. The evening panorama was just so heavenly, it wouldn't do to have anybody around. It was all-important at that time of day to finish the work and then to just stand and watch the sky. The water tank needed filling up, true – a really arduous task – but that done, the evening show seemed doubly soothing.

Other times of the day, other things: for example, if anyone happened to leave the tap on, we'd be wild with anger. It left the tank half empty when customers were careless, and then Kakka would let flow some rather choice abuse. I suppose it was pointless blaming a happy customer, happy in his own world, unthinking . . . still, if he happened to run the water to wash his hands for a duration we thought too prolonged, we'd glare at him. Which was nothing to what Kakka did – he boiled over and his voice became acid: "I say, do you do this at home as well? *Arré*, shouldn't a man live within his means? . . . You spend four bucks on your food but you behave like you're the District Collector . . ."

It was much the same if a customer over-ordered, because even then, despite it being to Kakka's advantage, he took offence: "You're going to eat daal-fry *and* potatoes? How much did you manage to get for your harvest? Better go away, you ass! You'll waste all your money here, and all year round the rats in your house will go hungry and lie about in a coma! Get off, you clown . . . go back to your village. You'll miss the last bus and then you'll hang around here all day. Have a heart, think of your wife and kids, my friend!"

Most customers felt thoroughly browbeaten by these blandishments and squeaked out some timid justification or the other – such as, "*Arré*, Brother! *Arré*, Brother! I only get the chance to indulge myself once a year, after a good harvest . . ." None of this would wash with Kakka, who liked turning a ten-buck customer into a four-buck customer. "Hey friend, cut your coat according to your cloth, that's my advice . . . Be off, go, get lost! Your bus driver's honking . . ." And if a customer proved a show-off, he'd be roundly ticked off: ". . . At home you eat what you're given, but here you behave like you're the state Governor? *Arré*, just fill your stomach, man . . ."

And then there was the situation with onions. Kakka counted out the slices of onion he felt was each customer's due, but when the price of onions shot up he charged two rupees extra for the garnishings. Or, well, he charged most customers, but not everyone; some he chose merely to rebuke: "*Arré*, onions don't grow on trees . . . why d'you want to spend two whole bucks on onions? *Arré*, why not just do without onions for a few days? Or if you must eat them, eat them like tongue fresheners, to vary the taste in your mouth . . . Hey, you won't die if you don't eat onions for a few days, will you?" At times like these he seemed to believe valour was the better part of discretion and let fly the mild expletives, calling people "Idiot" and "Laat Sahib" and so on. His vocabulary irritated Bhaiyya: "Are you running a business or an almshouse?"

"Ah, these are all decent citizens from hereabouts. If they're spendthrifts, it'll ultimately hurt everyone. They come to the market, get seduced and spend all they've got, and then they rue the day the rest of the year. These are fellows who manage just one harvest after a full year's slog – so if they go about squandering what they've earned over just four days in town, what's going to happen to their families?" This made Bhaiyya bang his hand on his forehead and mutter through his smile, "Oh . . . my *dear* father . . ."

When Bai laughed at Kakka's antics, her face shone like the shiny scrubbed floor. She hardly ever went out – even her brother she visited only very briefly, and only if there was some special occasion, because Kakka missed her terribly. He wouldn't drink his evening tea at the dhaba because he'd be keeping a vigil for the buses coming in, all the while anxiously chewing tobacco.

"Kakka, you feel so lost without Bai around!"

"Yes, my dear! I don't know how other men manage. I don't feel like going home at all."

Once, Bai said she'd go to her brother's for two days but she got back after all of four. Kakka was so upset, he didn't talk to her for days. That made Bai sulk in turn.

I said, "Bai, don't ever do this again or else Kakka will lock our door and you'll have to live at Grandma's forever."

Bhaiyya said, "Yeah, and then what's going to happen to Kakka's evening tea? C'mon, Bai! Let's you and I both go off to Uncle's for a month. Come on, come on, let's be off right away."

"Ho, ho, ho," we yelled, and Bai and Kakka both laughed, and the evening tea regained all its flavour.

There was never any sulking or pampering at home. If either parent happened to tick us off, or if we fought amongst ourselves, we'd just end up eating more than normal! On such occasions Bhaiyya had a standard line: "Kakka's fried my brains. Move off, I need to eat!" And then he'd arrange his plate most prettily and proceed to tuck into daal-fry, six or so rotis, chopped onions and tomatoes, pickle and salt, red chilli, lemon, a jug full of water. He could spend an hour and more contentedly eating, sitting comfortably cross-legged on the floor.

One summer day, Kakka asked for some tea to be brought in for his friends. He forgot to include Bhaiyya in the headcount of tea drinkers, and for some reason it made Bhaiyya go berserk. The moment the tea-boy brought in the tea, Bhaiyya said to him, "Go on back, boy! Quick, go get a glass of lassi." And when it arrived Bhaiyya proceeded to make a great show of enjoying the lassi – for Kakka's benefit. After his friends had gone, Kakka yelled at him: "Hey, you! *We* drink tea and *you* have lassi?"

"But did you ask for tea for me? Did you? Tell me, did you?"

Father cursed and swore at him, but Bhaiyya laughed it all off, and in fact later told us the whole story quite gleefully. When we cross-questioned Kakka – "What did Bhaiyya do today?" – Kakka began cursing at Bhaiyya all over again. But Bhaiyya looked like he couldn't be bothered.

Tall and broad-shouldered like Kakka, and fair-skinned

like Bai. Tough physique, large, deep, dark, heavy-lidded eyes. Bhaiyya was a thing of beauty who had none of his father's vigour or suppleness – not the merest hint of them.

Everyone called Asha-jiji's oldest brother-in-law Baradi, but I called him Badé-dada. He had a Rajdoot motorcycle which he once parked at the dhaba and went off on some errand. I put a piece of welding rod into the keyhole and kick-started it. And then I panicked.

When Badé-dada came back and put his hand into his pocket for the key, I showed him the piece of welding rod and said, "Look, look, Badé-dada, one more key," and I started the motorcycle.

Stunned, he said, "You want to ride the mo-bike?"

I rode around a lot, with him riding pillion. I'd accelerate and he'd yell, "*Arré*, not like this, not like this . . ." Gradually, I learnt to change gears, and then one day sped way beyond the bus stand. Soon, I was riding the bike not in the maidan but in the bazaar.

Once, he made me ride a Bullet mo-bike. On this one I would, every now and then, land up at his village, Muradpur. On the way we passed stone quarries, red-hot mines, searing summer heat, mountains of stones, scores of labourers, and enormous machines. Those mines didn't yield stones, they threw up gold.

"Look, Babli, look, look! So many different coloured stones. The fellow who owns these mines must be rolling in it! But it's not everybody's cup of tea . . . some hit gold, others just hit barren rock. They also ruin people's lives, these mines. And if one's lucky and discovers a gold mine, there are thugs and crooks waiting to armtwist you out of what's yours."

"How's that, Badé-dada?"

"What d'you mean, 'How's that?' In this day and age everything goes."

Through all this gossiping I'd sometimes press the accelerator, and sometimes we'd crawl, or I'd forget to change the gear and the bike would stall. And we'd chance upon conversations.

"O.K., tell me how much you've leased this mine for . . . Here, take this money and get lost! Go!" All the tough old thugs of the mining world had settled on a charpoy with a bottle of liquor. They yelled at the labourers, "Come on, you! Start digging fast! Maybe we should prod you guys to work, or maybe we should just bury you in these mines? . . . Half of you'll imagine you've seen ghosts and run off yelling 'Ghost! Ghost!'" They'd take out country-made pistols from their pockets, stretch their legs, and get down to inspecting work in their mine.

"This isn't for the poor and the meek, Babli, this mining business! No-one can stand up to these three or four fellows. Together they've got dozens of mines and there's a huge demand for our stone across the world. All the huge buildings, the sort we see on TV, they've been built with these same stones. If these mines were owned by the people, it would be the end of poverty . . . God knows, but it would change the fortunes of so many villages . . . Basoda, Kurvai, Shamshabad, Sironj, Lateri, and Vidhisha." I'd swing around on the bike and look at Badé-dada, jaw dropping.

"Yes, yes! What I'm telling you is bang on! Look straight; look ahead," and he'd grab the handlebar.

Those stone quarries were Badé-dada's endless obsession, his unending raga. Every stone in them got baked in his dreams; every stone in them made him see villages and towns. Those stones were all his heart's desire, he badly wanted them to go forth and become the homes of the many, not of just a handful. ". . . These gold-spewing mines, they'd change the fortunes of our whole district if they were freed from the clutches of these fat-cats!"

In the middle of one of these conversations, back home, I laid a playful bet with him. Seema and Bhaiyya were both around at the time. Badé-dada declared: "Whoever spits and then licks the spit, I'll treat them to a lassi."

"Oh? How many?"

"Two. For four days."

"Bet on it?"

Banging the table with his fist, he said, "Absolutely."

I spat like lightning on my palm and licked it up.

Everyone said, "Yuck! Yuck!", but Badé-dada couldn't stop laughing. "Babli! You're really something! You pig! Go, go wash your hands and face."

I'd won the bet and eight glasses of lassi appeared over time. But Badé-dada went on laughing non-stop, thinking about it. He said to Seema and Bhaiyya, "Don't tell anyone, O.K.?" But of course Seema couldn't keep it to herself. She had some of the lassi and went and tattled to Bai, who was livid: "To hell with her and her ways ... Get her married off fast, that's what I say! ... And stop her riding around on that mo-bike with Baradi."

Then she turned to me: "And I forbid you to tell Baradi any of what I've said!"

But how was I to stop riding that mo-bike? Now, every few days, I was on a Rajdoot or a Bullet, riding all the way to Muradpur. The gold-spewing stone mines had sucked me into themselves, hook, line and sinker.

But I'd never been to the Ambanagar Chowk, Gured, Johad, and Nateran on the bike. Because to get there one had to ride on *the* road – the road which everyone absolutely refused to mention or talk about. When we went to Asha-jiji's village, Kagpur, you could see that road.

It was the road with a whole lot of women roaming around, hair loose, or women just sitting on doorsteps. Most of the houses on it were temporary and makeshift. The women looked at themselves in hand mirrors and chewed paan. There'd be a titter in the bus from which we saw them, and the mirth wouldn't subside. God knows why that tittering went on and on – I haven't been able to figure it out to this day.

And on our journey back we'd see the same women

ready, all dressed up, sitting on their thresholds in shiny outfits. Some not very old, some middle-aged, some really young. All the men grabbed the window seats in the bus and leaned out of the windows, smiles on their faces. The Parasari and the peepal tree, which was so completely green then, were witness to this spectacle.

And at the village liquor shop were people stumbling around. Some would go in with their chests puffed out, others went in stealthily and emerged with bottles wrapped in paper. A fellow looking ecstatic climbed into a rickshaw like he was mounting a royal carriage; a fellow sozzled to the gills was rolling around on the ground. He staggered to his feet, stood for a second, and promptly fell face down into a gutter. Some rogues of the same feather sloshed water all over him, some made him smell a shoe. The drunk growled at them, making as if to get up and thrash the lot and then set fire to the whole place. Some squabbled, others turned philosophers and made it known to those nearby that the world had never contained men of greater learning. This same bunch went into hiding each morning, but come evening they were back at the liquor shop . . . This was a sight I saw as a child, and later as an adult, and every time there was something new, something colourful to behold.

But I only ever saw it from the window of a bus. I never ventured on to that road on the mo-bike, nor did I ever go to that liquor shop.

In any case, the bus stand near the dhaba was always there for me. My kaleidoscope of life, the world, the universe. And that left me precious little time for all those other sights that, now and then, I was fortunate to catch glimpses of.

41

THERE WERE TWO TYRE shops at the bus stand. One was Raees Bhai's, the other belonged to Pheneshwar. Pheneshwar was the youngest of four or five brothers. There was a kind of jauntiness about him, something weird in his demeanour. He listened to the radio at top volume and when the songs started he sang along and swayed to the music. At night everyone crowded around him and asked him to sing. He shied away behind his tyres, but people chased him all the way, surrounding him till he came around, not letting him shut shop. And then, after all their begging and cajoling, Pheneshwar sang.

His audience enjoyed it thoroughly and pulled his leg: "Pheni, you should sing on the radio." Pheni was delighted by their compliments. People asked him to send a postcard to the popular Binaca Geetmala so he could sing on it. He wrote out a postcard and popped it into a postbox. Everyone listened to his singing for months on end and went on pulling his leg endlessly.

I was part of this crowd. The moment he began singing I'd jump into the small gathering around him, push my way to the front, climb to the top of a stack of tyres, and sit cross-legged – right on top. This way I sat away from the crowd and listened to him sing from up close.

The crowd fixed the postman to ensure Pheni got a reply. For three days the postman was bribed with tea, tobacco, a plateful of Rameshwar Chacha's savouries and accompanying stuffed chillies. After which our honourable postman was a happy man. People then handed him a return-paid postcard to give Pheneshwar.

When the postman did as persuaded, the crowd hoisted Pheni onto their shoulders. He started crooning "Dance and Sway, Sway and Dance, This way, That Way, You Worshippers of Wine . . ." Every day, now, the crowd around him made him practice for hours so he could be ready and fired up to sing in the Binaca Geetmala.

People who knew him, people unknown to him – he went around showing everyone his postcard from Binaca Geetmala, crooning and flailing delightedly, swaying and swinging more than singing. Which was precisely what the crowd loved about him. Now, he put on two shows per day, at night and before nightfall – he wanted to regale his devotees every evening as well. So, now we all had a walking-talking Binaca Geetmala at our doorstep that we could more or less switch on anytime we wanted! All we needed was the time.

Pheni wasn't alone among our madcap buddies, we had three other equally important fun-time friends: Bookbinder Khateek Dada, One-and-a-half-legged Signal, and Red Bull.

Little Khateek Dada stepped out most days for a matutinal stroll. He wrapped himself in a dhoti-kurta and cap but was even more wholly wrapped up in himself, head bowed. We taunted him so mercilessly it took him an hour or more just to cross the bus stand. We'd say nothing except just yell "Hindustan-Pakistan" as he was about to step forward. And with that all hell would break loose! He'd scream and the imprecations he spewed in our direction from the middle of the road were fit to make the underworld blush. Then the moment he turned his back we'd shout again in unison, "Hindustan-Pakistan". That would make him come running towards us, a threatening stone in his hand . . . The evenings passed without us noticing their passing when we played those street games.

And then there was the dog we called "One-and-a-half-legged Signal". Off and on, he showed up to listen to Pheni's songs. Some folks liked teasing him, and he'd stare viciously at them, but he never barked. No-one ever found out what had got him so disgruntled. What he was really good at was running – he ran faster than any hare. All you had to do to get him going was to say "One-and-a-half-legged Signal", and he'd be off the blocks, showing off how fast he could sprint by running around the bus stand. He never left the area around the bus stand. His meals were fixed – he was such a terror that no other dog dared venture near his turf. People called him "Moti" when they were being affectionate, but when they wanted to needle him he was always "One-and-a-half-legged Signal".

Red Bull was frightening. No-one knew where he'd come from, but every eight days he showed up and stood bang in the middle of the road. Once he parked himself there, no-one dared cross the road. Everyone just stood around looking at him and a whole evening could pass with folks just waiting for him to move. But he was docile, he never hurt anyone. Nor was he a dog in the manger – at no time did his bulk in the centre of our universe ever suggest he was trying to bar customers from entering a shop. It was just that he was so incredibly happy standing still in the middle of that particular road. Sindhi Kaka fed him vegetables and roti and provided him all the water he needed to drink. No-one else went as close. Those keen on making him an offering always asked Sindhi Kaka to make it on their behalf.

I don't know how it happened, but one day it became clear that Red Bull had lost his sight – he'd gone completely blind. He could no longer see the buses and was terrified of their honking. It took a lot to move him on from his chosen spot. His day would go by perfectly well because people shifted him around, but what worried his well-wishers was the dark. What if he lost track of where he was and landed up near the railway tracks? He had often been seen at the Batauli Road, where the railway crossing was. Luckily, they worked out how to confine him at night in Qazi House and release him again for his rounds in the morning.

But with his vision gone, Red Bull began to decline. It made a lot of the neighbourhood very anxious on his account. His friends kept an eye out for him, and if he happened to stray ever so slightly, someone or the other would lead him to the bus stand. The amazing thing was that people tended to his needs not just in their free time, he was one of those rare beings that people looked after even when they were busy. I think caring for Red Bull kept us calm, soothed us somehow, and kneaded the sense of feeling responsible into our everyday lives. Even our little One-and-a-half-legged Signal had an eye open for Red Bull's well-being. And that made folks pet him in a kindly way and whisper sweet nothings – "... *Arré*! Wonderful Moti! What a nice chap ..." And that was a Signal to Moti! He'd rush around performing his showing-off antics, rolling on the ground and stretching himself. And that made full circle, it kept us all amused and giggling.

How Moti loved being called "One-and-a-half-legged Signal"! If he suspected anyone at all of having failed to notice him, he went rushing around the bus stand and then waited to be noticed and called by his name. That was his all-time favourite game.

42

VINITA MALIK MADAM taught us Hindi Literature. All the girls were crazy about her, she looked so gorgeous. Thin, graceful, a watch high on her right wrist. She wore starched cotton saris, one prettier than the other. Before we saw this walking wardrobe, we knew only synthetic and silk saris. She was no dumb cluck either, her teaching was spectacular. There was never any need for her to repeat what she'd explained the first time round because she was so clear – every girl instantaneously understood everything she taught.

She was the first to make us understand that it was fine to wear a watch on either wrist. Until this change to our conceptual horizons we'd always just dumbly followed a dumb rule – that a watch had to be worn on the left wrist so we could figure out which was left and which was right by looking at the wrist adorned by the wristwatch. Which is why, for a long while, we'd gone on thinking her right hand was actually her left hand!

One day she asked the girls in her class, "Have you thought of what you're going to do after you've done your B.A.?" This came as news too. None of us had even vaguely conceived the notion that such a thing could actually be planned. So, none of us could really respond to her question. All we did was gape at her open-mouthed. "Think, all of you, and then tell me quickly," she said, suppressing a smile.

But around this time all of us girls had got into a biggish fight between two groups. Things went beyond the cursing stage and there was a regular brawl. I pushed a girl. She started bleeding from the mouth. Things got so bad, there was talk of calling in the police. But the Principal didn't register a police report, preferring to see the incident as an internal college matter.

The next day the group opposing ours declared a strike in Basoda. We couldn't risk going to college, so my friends and I stayed put at home – in fact we weren't able to get to college for several days. To my surprise, Vinita Madam visited us at home, and soon after, these turned into regular visits. They even took a new direction, because she'd often stop by at the dhaba to chat with Kakka.

Meanwhile, the Principal made both parties – meaning our respective fathers – sit face to face, and somehow matters got sorted out. All of us were quite petrified because we could've been rusticated for our most unladylike scuffle. Anyway, the very thought of that dire consequence had put the fear of God in us, and it was not long before those who'd fought like cats were fast friends once more.

Vinita Madam commuted daily to Basoda, all the way from Bhopal. Anytime her train was delayed, she turned up at our home. And on her way to or from college she took to dropping in at the dhaba, chatting nineteen to the dozen with Kakka and his pals.

On such days, a few months after the fisticuffs and our near-rustication, her scheduled time of arrival tended to be 1 p.m. after the end of day at college, and her estimated time of departure to catch the passenger train was 4 p.m. At times she taught me stuff at home over those hours, and then I'd accompany her to the station where she'd climb on to her train.

There were other times when she reached the dhaba after 4 p.m. for a session with Kakka to give him the lowdown on all that had transpired over the course of her life during the day. She got on famously with Bai too, and the whole locality was practically whooping for joy the moment she arrived, with all three aunts giving her their warmest "Namaste". If she got delayed coming, or if she didn't make it some days, they were disconsolate and went on at me: "Why? . . . Why hasn't your Madam come till now? Is she O.K.? . . . Now your Madam's one of us. So if she doesn't show up we're at a loose end . . . our day picks up the moment she's here!"

At the station, once, Vinita Madam said to me: "You want to study and then work too, don't you? . . . Don't you? Tell me?" I nodded. "Come to Bhopal then," she said. "You can do an M.A. in Hindi there."

When I reached the dhaba, I raised this delicate matter with Kakka, deploying my most hesitant voice:

"Kakka, d'you think I can go off to do an M.A. in Hindi literature . . . with Vinita Madam?" Later, I said the same to Chacha-ji. Neither man responded.

But Bai did. When she heard what I'd said, she looked stunned out of her wits. And there the matter seemed to rest – or rather, it didn't rest at all. It sat like a rock on their chests.

The trains passing by our house made the pots and pans rattle – and this despite our station not being one of those through which super-fast trains hurtled, siren blarings, green flags waving. Our station was one of those where no train thought itself too weighty for pause. Even if for just a brief rest, our station made every train stop. And then for a while we savoured the ambient silence.

When they resumed their journey, the sounds of those trains filled us with romance and hope. The Delhi–Mumbai rail line was our heartbeat. It woke us up if we were asleep, and as often as not lulled us back to sleep. The regular passing by of those trains wouldn't let me rest, their passage became a pulsation within me about the possibility of leaving with Vinita Madam.

After a huge tug of war at home, Vinita Madam took me off with her to prepare for the B.A. Final exams. She took me in hand most thoroughly and tutored me in every subject, not just Hindi Literature. Those couple of months that I stayed at her place before returning home to do the exams were a day and night struggle for her over me.

Some of Kakka's friends were of the view that I should go on to do an Ll.B. Anytime we siblings quarrelled with each other, Kakka, hugely exasperated, said: "You argue just like lawyers, you lot!" He was fairly keen himself that I do an Ll.B., but that was not an area of learning of much interest to me – in fact its sole advantage seemed to lie in the fact that because law classes were held in the evening, my helping out at the dhaba and pursuing law could go hand in hand. In any case, Vinita Madam taught Hindi Literature. Had she been a teacher of law, it would have seemed a sound reason to switch. The sad truth was that none of us college girls had much connection with Hindi Literature – our connection with it was that we loved Vinita Madam. We'd dropped out of Social Science and switched to Hindi Literature only because of *her*. I recall our response in one of those Hindi classes early on when she said, "Come on, tell me, which poem or poet do you like best? The one you want to read again and again . . ." Without batting an eyelid we chirruped in unison: "*None*, Madam! Those fellows are all happily gone . . . leaving us with all this bilge that we have to mug up!"

She felt genuinely annoyed that day and threw us all out of her class. And then, for days at a stretch after that, she made us read the same poem over and over again, as punishment. But not to be outdone, we told her with sweetness and innocence written all over us, "Madam, *now* we love poems . . ." And it wasn't me, it was Vanmala who said softly from the back, "Madam, just the way we like *you* . . ."

The truth was we couldn't cope with poetry. We couldn't make out head or tail of what a poem was. Vinita Madam would read a line and we'd parrot it dutifully. Then she'd set about explaining the poem's subject, its meaning, its interpretations, and God alone knows what else. Our response to everything she outlined was to continue parroting what we'd heard her spout, and for good measure we assured her, "Madam, we think the same as you . . ."

"Is that so?" she said with a tight smile.

We must have looked sheepish. "Er . . . Madam, that is not exactly what we meant . . ."

"Again you . . . *again* you don't understand! Why not at least try!? O.K., now repeat this sentence ten times. Only then will it enter your thick heads."

But all this explanatory stuff was nothing to the difficulty we had pronouncing "sh" as opposed to "s", which was colossal. We only knew how to pronounce the "s". Getting us to hear the difference in the pronunciation of "s" and "sh" made Madam break out in a sweat. Often, when "sh" was coming up in a poem, we said, "Madam, 'S' for 'Sakkar' is on the way . . . We won't be able to pronounce it . . . Madam, can you just read out the line with this 'S' in it . . ." But she wasn't so easily taken in. Had she been, she wouldn't have been Vinita Malik Madam, would she?

One time she took us on a tour from college to Sanchi. For us this was another first, so she taught us all about getting on the train, getting off the train, how to sit in the train, how to figure out which train was ours.

In Sanchi she was enraged when she saw our tiffin boxes. "Do you girls eat food, or d'you eat just chillies?" Thereafter, not a day passed without her badgering us to not eat too many chillies because of how badly they'd burn us up inside.

Our group of friends discussed her a lot. "This Madam's good for us! We'd never have known anything of the world outside . . ." Then they'd look at me and say, "Well, she's sure great for you! She visits your house and takes you everywhere. You don't need to do anything at all now. You're through . . ." So I strutted around a bit, but they wouldn't stop. "Hey, listen! All the stuff Madam teaches you at home, why don't you teach it to us? That'll work out well . . ."

An issue on which we got punched big time was our pronunciation. "Feel free to talk whatever way you like at home . . . Speak Bundeli or whatever . . . But when you're here, you're going to say things the way they should be said. None of this mixed-up pidgin stuff here, because if you don't learn to speak straight here in college, you never will."

She treated us to coffee once, and I said, "I won't have tea right now, no thanks . . ." – and I'd barely said this when Hemlata butted in – ". . . See, Madam, she doesn't even know the difference between coffee and tea! What does she know!? I'm sure she doesn't know the difference between ash and dust either." Vinita Madam said nothing, she only laughed. But her laugh said a lot.

And the mysterious garden with mountains of dried leaves and the magical walking trails we'd made through them that the Principal had converted into a library – from that very same library, she picked up Maxim Gorky's *Mother* for us to read. We'd never read a book that wasn't prescribed and in our syllabus. *Mother* was the first.

The day arrived when even the rattling of the non-stop trains stopped! I danced round Kakka. "Look, Kakka! I've got a First Division!" And immediately, excitedly, I followed that up with, "And now I'm going to do my M.A. from Bhopal. I'll stay with Vinita Madam . . . of course."

He laughed. "I shouldn't have to hear any kind of complaint about you, my child!"

I sensed at once that this was my opportunity. "Kakka, I'll never do anything against your wishes. Just don't force me to get married. I won't run off or elope . . . All I'm asking is that you let me go on with my studies with Vinita Madam."

His glance contained the whole world. Our eyes met and for a moment we were transfixed by mutual understanding. Coming out of my trance, I said to him straight: "If people gossip to you about me, check the facts with me first. I can never lie to you, I'll never do anything to hurt your self-respect. Just ignore people who can't mind their own business and don't recall me halfway through my course."

The deal was as good as signed with that frank exchange: he would not pressure me to marry and I'd never do anything that might make him feel small. The underlying meaning didn't need spelling out: I was not to get involved with a man and run off over a love affair. Kakka nodded. "O.K.", he said.

Groups of pigeons that had taken flight came back to settle down again. Rail lines in the distance shone in the sunlight. And the red light at the back of the last bogie of a passing train flashed for a long time before turning green.

43

I MISSED HOME, KAKKA, and the dhaba desperately. At night, wrapped in my blanket, I'd sob my heart out. Yet I didn't want to go back. If I heard a bus honk, I longed for the dhaba, and the *chhook-chhook-chhooking* of every train made me yearn for those two – Kakka and the dhaba. Given the feeblest chance, I'd have clambered on to a train heading home.

That journey of 165–170 km away from home had taught me a myriad startling things, some of which fuelled me with courage and emboldened me, and as many others that made me cautious and feel I might land flat on my face. The train, for a start, showed me two worlds. One was the world contained in shining air-conditioned bogies which I couldn't enter but only peep into – where all I could see were my own distorted face and features reflected in the tinted glass windows. Even to try entering that world meant risking becoming the laughing stock of the world to which I sensed I was restricted, to suffer disgrace. A primal fear turned me away from those darkened glass panes.

The feeling was mutual: the first-class travellers behind those panes, cocooned in their shining first-world bogies, had no desire to come within sniffing distance of the second- and third-class compartments. Their perfumed hankies went straight into protecting their noses and stopping them retching when passing near our inferior compartments. Those rail journeys – the to-ing and fro-ing that my life now involved – were like admission to a new school. At times I forgot to buy a ticket and heaved a sigh of relief when I reached without getting caught.

Bhaiyya did not like his sisters sitting around at the dhaba, but, he being the second-youngest, none of us cared what he thought. His view of the dhaba – "Kakka, let's shut the dhaba and start some other business" – made Kakka livid and curse more than was normal for him. In the end, Bhaiyya managed all the same to do some of what he wanted: he stopped Seema and Neera from following in our footsteps and working in the dhaba. On this subject he thwarted Kakka conclusively: "They will not go to the dhaba any more. And I mean that."

Bhaiyya also turned the whole dhaba upside down. The oven at the back was demolished and a tandoor installed in the front: rotis were now not made on the griddle but in the tandoor. The six existing tables were removed and new furniture made to accommodate twenty-five or thirty customers at a time. The dhaba was painted cream. Four tubelights and two hanging lanterns appeared as new fixtures. Curtains were hung to create partitions.

Four ceiling fans, two large coolers, a big fridge, a water cooler, and four large water pots came in as part of the refurbishing. The tandoor and the coal-based oven got two whole table fans to themselves.

Now the dhaba served matar-paneer, shahi paneer, palak paneer, dal makhani, dum aloo, malai kofta, tandoori roti, and tandoori parathas. Curds, rice pudding, halwa, cold drinks, and ice-cream were on offer too in the new menu. It was Bhaiyya Babu's philosophy that even a dung-heap's fortunes change. So why not a dhaba's?

And along with the dhaba's fortunes, those of the market, the farmers, even of the roads, changed. The roads were still dust-covered: there was always a special relationship between the market and dust. We had all – in fact the whole town had – consumed tonnes of dust thanks to the market, and all without much idea that we'd breathed in so much of it, or even that we simply lived in a dust bowl. Only when outsiders covered their faces with their hands and tied a handkerchief over their mouths saying "Ugh! So much dust!" did we even understand this physical fact of our daily life.

The grain market had expanded and the bullock-carts had given way to tractor-trollies. To start with, only the large farmers had tractors, but soon even the middling cultivators had them – though they didn't use them only to plough their fields: if they had, the loan instalments they were having to pay out for their tractors would have stalled. So, those tractors had to sing for their supper, and the singing consisted in carrying sand and bricks and ploughing the land of other farmers.

Kakka's sympathy for the very small farmers ran deep. They had no tractors, so he thought up a co-operative scheme: those of them who couldn't afford a tractor needed to pool their money and buy one jointly. He explained the benefits of the idea to the farmers and tried convincing Baijnath Singh of the tractor agency. "Visit the villages, my friend . . . try providing tractors to our brothers . . ." – Baijnath Singh being a small farmer himself. Not having managed to eke out a living from farming, he'd become a mechanic and started his own workshop. From that he'd grown into an agent for Eicher Tractors. Everyone made fun of his Eicher tractors, especially of the noises they made. Every time one went past on the road, people looked at it and laughed. Often, to tease Baijnath Singh, they mimicked the sounds it made.

Baijnath Singh was a daily customer at the dhaba. He sat for hours with Kakka on the takht. Gradually, Eicher tractor sales had begun to pick up, and with that he'd prospered. Eicher priced its tractors competitively and the farmers saw them as an attractive purchase. The Eicher tractor's body was also designed for tasks in urban areas. Before these tractors showed up, the market had been under the thumb of Ford, Kirloskar, Massey, and Escorts. Farmers who owned these brands were much envied.

Baijnath Singh was non-committal about Kakka's

co-operative scheme. He was, in any case, a man of few words, whereas taciturnity was not, to put it gently, among Kakka's most prominent virtues. "*Arré, yaar!* Your Eicher is going great guns. You're making good money. Now, my friend, all you need to do is this – set aside three or four tractors for those who have none – for their sowing, ploughing and harvesting . . . Small farmers face big problems, Brother! You've got to help them keep their farming going . . ."

Silence.

Kakka, now more aggressive, and in full swing: "I know one thing, *yaar*! You can do this . . . You have the wherewithal. You can charge them a minimal rent . . ."

Most everyone scoffed at Kakka's idealistic notions, but the smaller farmers looked hopeful when he voiced them because they knew he'd been a huge support to Baijnath Singh during the tractor agent's days of struggle – and that Kakka had even provided him a little financial aid. So those petty cultivators hoped against hope that the nouveau Eicher bigshot wouldn't have the heart to decline Kakka's proposition.

The day finally arrived when Baijnath Singh took Kakka's advice to heart and began running a few of his tractors on rent. And what was even more heartening, he started selling tractors on small instalments.

Bhaiyya resented what he saw as Kakka working to improve other people's ventures while himself staying put in the rut that was the dhaba. "He's spent his whole life doing this . . . If he'd used his brains to grow his own business he'd have been a magnate now." In fact, if Bhaiyya'd had his way, the takht Kakka sat on would've been removed and the daily newspaper discontinued. The moment Kakka's back was turned he'd say, "Customers turn away when they see the gathering of his pals on the takht. *Arré*, a bunch of oldies lying sprawled on the takht lecturing the chaps trying to eat! . . . Are they paying for their food or for being lectured? . . . Half the customers run away for fear of an earful of free advice from these layabouts."

The nature of the dhaba's customers was changing too. Bhaiyya had given his tacit approval to those who wanted a quiet drink at the back, on the ash mound. Two round tables and eight chairs were now positioned there. On the tables, people found paneer tikka and cold drinks; under the table, a bottle of liquor. It was an investment in incentive: more and more customers streamed in and our takings at the dhaba were vastly up. People from the world beyond began frequenting the dhaba alongside the local populace, so now there was no longer an unending season of lean months alternating with four months of extraordinary sales.

But the difference was also that earlier, with Kakka at the helm during our four months' peak season, the dhaba was walled off by his presence against louts and suspicious customers. Those we'd served in the past were all in some sense gentlefolk. The scoundrels and vagrants kept clear because Kakka's firmness against every variety of delinquent was known far and wide. His nostrils would flare at the first hint of vulgarity: "There are girls around . . . This place can't be a bad influence on children. Business isn't everything here . . . there are kids around studying and trying to live decent lives . . ."

But the old order had changed, giving way to the new. The older generation's worldview had to make way. Bhaiyya had no time for Kakka's homilies.

The shops at the bus stand had started to change as well. They'd turned glitzy. New people were opening new shops. Raees Bhai's welding and puncture-repair shop was now servicing cars and selling spare parts. His shack had grown into a very crowded establishment. People had developed a taste for getting their cars washed at his service station. Bhaiyya called it the "Glitz Lovers' Service Station".

All these fancy changes were the result of easy bank loans becoming suddenly available to practically anyone wanting them. Even the folks living near banks were strutting around, as if to say they owned the banks! And those whose premises were on rent to the banks didn't know what had hit them – they'd never had it so good!

Like the big farmers, the middling farmers had started settling in Basoda. Wherever you looked, you saw shops selling spare parts and hardware. If the stars happened to align well and a harvest or two came out good, these middling farmers began dreaming the dreams of the big farmers: of becoming chairmen of the Marketing Board, of the Land Development Bank, of the Zila Parishad. And people who looked like they were born the day before yesterday fantasised about becoming the heads of municipal committees. Regardless of whether they were city folk or people living near a city, the whole world dreamt of the day when there'd be a flashing red beacon revolving on the roofs of their cars.

"So much hard work for pushing others ahead! . . . Why don't you do all the hard work to get ahead yourself? Where's the need to waste precious time on others?" – this was Asha-jiji's Tinnu. "Aunty, don't underestimate Basoda's men. They're really smart; all they need is opportunity. Show a Basoda man a spot outside any door from where no-one else can enter, and sure enough, next morning, our Basoda man will be right inside," he'd say, and laugh out loud.

Bhaiyya's response was: "Shape up, you, Tinnu. Mend your ways. You're turning into a politico, are you?"

This made Tinnu double up laughing. "Look Aunty, Uncle is discouraging me from finding the golden goose! In this day and age, only two people have any status – the cop and the politico. The rest are irrelevant. Uncle, go where you like and find this out for yourself if you don't believe me. The moment a politico arrives, the whole village stands before him, hands folded. And not just the village . . . The same thing's true in towns. Today, no-one gets ahead of a politico."

"Live a life of simple decency, Tinnu! Get into this politicking world and you might end up losing all your land . . . or else . . ."

"Or else what? Come on, tell me."

"Or else you can stop calling me Uncle."

"Oh, and I thought you were going to help me get a ticket for the next Assembly election!"

Frustrated and angry, Bhaiyya poured a jug of water over him.

Tinnu got along better with Kakka than with Bhaiyya. He called him "Father", not "Grandfather".

Meanwhile the poor farmers remained the innocents they always were, and looked, if anything, more worried. The same endless rounds of the courts to get justice against traders who picked on them – traders who were canny enough not to try going after the big farmers and the middling farmers. So, despite all the visible progress, the bullocks, bullock carts, and small farmers had to carry on much as they had all along. In their lives there was no visible change. The banks gave them no loans, and for the most part the tractor agencies showed no inclination for selling them tractors on easy terms. The big farmers made progress using pesticides to reap harvest after harvest, godowns filled up with their produce, and they had the resources to wait it out and sell when prices peaked. The small farmers, on the other hand, were reduced to taking loans at high rates of interest from the large farmers. This further broke their already broken backs. They had little option except to sell when they could and at whatever prices their produce could fetch. No-one stood by supporting them saying "Fight for your rights, we're with you."

44

THE TRAIN IS A MAGICAL thing, it shows me something new every day! Since when has Mad Binny with her sparkling white teeth started coming to the railway station? And how she runs, swaying and swinging on the tracks! Has she started fancying the empty track? Or has she decided to give her life to it? The more she laughs, the faster she runs . . .

My commuting became more frequent in that train, which stopped at the Ganj Basoda station for a few seconds as if in need of a resuscitating breather. The moment the train moved off again, the dry leaves on its lonesome tracks flew up in the slipstream and stirred a short breeze, a sad unfinished song; and with an incoming train the same fallen leaves shivered as if just out of a winter bath.

Like Seema's shivering and quivering! It was difficult to tell whether Seema learnt her quivering from the leaves, or the leaves learnt it from her. Seema began her B.A. First Year when Neera began school. I'm not sure why, but an incident connected with Seema that happened years ago has stayed in my mind.

She was desperately fond of pooris – as much of eating

them as of hoarding them. And each time she stacked them preparatory to hoarding them, her chin quivered like jelly. And the moment her chin quivered we knew something was wrong. One day, we said to her in jest, "Bury a poori under the ground and it'll grow into a tree. A great big happy poori tree. So then, anytime you feel like having a poori, you'll be able to pluck a poori off the tree and eat it." We dispersed and awaited her next bout of chin-quivering.

Sure enough, in a little while we saw her creep into the back lane and plant a poori within a broken basil pot. We laughed till we cried; she stood in a corner and sobbed. Ever since, on every festival day, Bai fried pooris and saved some for Seema to eat over the course of the next few days.

Oh, and one more Seema recollection of some years later. It was when Kakka had gone out of town on work. At ten or eleven at night, Bai was as always standing at a distance, waiting to escort us back home from the dhaba. We were almost home when Seema said to her, angrily: "Bai, from now on I'm going to get my own sheet and sleep separately. You don't make the bed properly."

This irritated Bai thoroughly: "What! You think you're in some hotel? Have you gone off your head? . . . You want to go off with a separate sheet to sleep now . . .?"

I burst out laughing at Bai's apoplexy and Seema, now eighteen years of age, sobbed like she had when she'd buried that poori as a four-year-old. Only now she was ready to put up a fight and she hollered at Bai: "I don't go to the dhaba because I want to . . . I go because you make me. Tomorrow on, I'm not working there, I don't care what happens . . . Why did you call me names?" The more she cried, the more I giggled. Her tears and irritability were impossible to placate, they just went on and on.

Another story, also from a long time ago when I was little: the dhaba had no door, so, when it came time to lock up after hours, Kakka usually put two tables together, piled them high with chairs, and made a makeshift door for the night. Over those days he slept overnight at the dhaba, and occasionally I stayed there with him.

One night, I heard him call out *"Ricksha, ricksha, ricksha!"*, which startled me out of my wits. Then I saw, on the road in front, two women holding on to Bai – who was writhing in pain. I screamed and ran towards her, but before I could reach she'd got on to the rickshaw and gone off with the two women. I'd have run after them but Kakka held me back.

He tried distracting me to quieten me down. But I was a past master in the arts of screaming and crying, and though Kakka looked like he'd whack me one if I didn't, nothing could make me stop. He shoved me off into bed, where I went on sobbing the whole night.

Early next morning he took me with him to where Bai lay – on a bed under a red blanket, surrounded by women. One of them held my hand, and then Bai called me lovingly to her side. I stared at her for a long time. A woman came forward laughing and shoved me right next to the bed, where Bai cosseted me and reassured me and let me in under the red blanket to suckle her . . . And now, anytime I have a spat with Seema, she yells, ". . . and you! You even drank my share of milk in the hospital!" Seema had arrived as Daughter Number Seven.

Life was all hunky-dory till Seema grew up and started dreaming her technicolour dreams. She fell in love with a fellow called Manu Chaurasia and their affair soon became the cynosure of all eyes. The lovers met quite openly and Manu could be seen wandering around our house day and night.

When Bai saw Seema's Romeo, she burned up inside, but this had not the slightest affect on the cooing lovebirds. In fact they didn't care two hoots what anyone said, and Kakka, knowing all, pretended he knew nothing. He'd immerse his face deeper and deeper into his newspaper while the two of them waltzed their way towards becoming the talk of the town.

Bhaiyya tried stopping Seema from stepping out of the house, but that didn't stop her seeing Manu. So, after a few days, Kakka told her to get back and attend her classes in college. This made Bhaiyya see red, so once again there had to be a family conference.

"Get her married," Bhaiyya said.

Seema's riposte was immediate: "First Babli, then me."

Asha-jiji said: "Babli is still involved with her studies. But *you* we will marry off!"

Seema – chin now quivering: "I'm going to marry Manu, no-one else. And if you pester me otherwise, I'll drink poison. *Poison!* And understand this – we won't marry right now, we'll marry two years from now . . ."

Kakka's lips stayed sealed.

So now the heavens crashed straight on my head. *"The whole family will live to rue Babli's sins."*

That was where it ended, and it was back to status quo. Bhaiyya carried on hating the idea of Seema meeting Manu, and she carried on seeing him. Kakka wouldn't stop her going to college. In fact he became our rock by the sea, and we the many waves endlessly lashing and scarring him.

One year, Bhaiyya refused to let Seema tie a rakhi on his wrist. Everything then circled back to the same old hackneyed family arguments. Kakka, sitting on an emotional mountain, said, "Look! Shalu and Shiva's lives have been ruined. Rajjo, we made a wrong decision then. See what's happened to the two of them." He looked at Bai and wept. Setting aside notions of Right and Wrong, he told Seema: "Child, you must first finish your studies and stand on your own two feet. Then you can do as you see fit." He stood before her with folded hands and pleaded: "Why're you hell-bent on ruining your life?"

Bai interrupted: "You've gone mad in your old age. The world's going to spit on you."

But Kakka wasn't going to yield an inch on this subject – his tone grew defiant. "I'm certain of just one thing: get yourself a job and then do as you like." Stretching his hand over his head, he said, "I don't agree with your mother at all. Times are getting worse by the day. It's vital for women to stand on their own feet."

Bai's explosion at his obstinacy was caustic. "Jobs are baking in your oven, are they?" she said. "To hell with these kids, I say! They've left us hanging mid-air. Each one of them is a source of endless problems. *Why don't they just drop dead?* And pray, tell me what kind of ambrosia has been touching *your* lips?" The veins in her head were stretched to breaking point, but there was no stopping her. "Other men rise higher in the world with each new day! And there's you, falling deeper into the ditch with each passing day, for God's sake! Don't be so shameless. Are you planning to marry our girls off into some other caste? . . . Have you no shame left at all? *To hell with jobs for them* – are *they* going to keep you in food? I'm sick up to my neck listening to your endless raga about wanting girls to work . . . soon it's going to be only the two of us left growing old, coughing and spluttering . . ."

Kakka, unperturbed, turned and said to Seema: "Stand on your own feet, and then do as you please."

Asha-jiji looked like she'd become a zombie. Usha-jiji quietly walked away. Anni began muttering God knows what. Shalu, skulking in a corner, stared open-mouthed, now at Seema, now at Kakka. Shiva picked up her clothes and went off to wash them. Bhaiyya's face was flushed. He sat in a chair and cast sidelong glances at Kakka. "I hate all these girls. The world over, girls get married after they're through with Class 11. It's only our home that puts on these infernal dramas."

In the midst of all this, someone called out to him, "Mukul! Mukul!" Bhaiyya said to us, "Hey, one of you, go tell him I'm not home. The whole lot of you've ruined my name: I can't invite anyone over, I can't go over to anyone's . . ." Then, something struck him and he got up and went close to Bai. Hands on his waist, he asked: "Why, Bai? When our land was being auctioned, what were Kakka and Grandfather up to? They probably just hung around, watching the fun?"

What was Bai supposed to say to that, given she wasn't even there . . . and Kakka, poor man, was practically a babe in arms at the time! And here she was, facing our dear Bhaiyya who was intent on blaming Kakka for auctioning the family's land! There was no stopping him either. "*Arré,* if only Grandfather'd fallen at their feet and begged forgiveness, he might have saved his land and we wouldn't have had to face all this today . . ." He was brimming over with resentment and anger: ". . . The land wouldn't have been auctioned and he wouldn't have come to this town . . . *Actually, it's not the land that's been auctioned, it's my life!*"

Seema was fixated too – on making me the excuse for doing as she liked. "Babli! Think of Babli! All of you keep coming after me . . . She's older than me. If you have the guts, get her married first, then I'll follow. You've let her go free and are harassing the life out of me . . ."

Like a script never to be completed, there were reels within reels playing out at any given time in our home. Seema's unwritten diary, Bhaiyya's aggressive posturing, Bai's story of neglect, Kakka's vicissitudes. There was no question of any one coherent film emerging from this melange. Each of us was writing his or her own script.

Watching Bai at her prayers invariably brought a lump to my throat. She'd had to endure so much, so many unanswered prayers, yet she stuck with them. Every year, on the auspicious festival of Dev Uthni Gyaras and the start of the marriage season, she prayed with all her soul. Under a canopy of sugarcane stalks she'd first anoint Saligram and Tulsi; then prepare a pudding of pumpkin and water chestnuts, brinjal, and rice, and feed the gods, circle them, chanting: *"Arise, Dark God, With these offerings of berries and gooseberries and veggies! May the unmarried marry, and may the married be happy . . ."* Her gods were obviously asleep, and there was she, trying desperately to awaken them. She was dying of worry over Seema and me not being safely married.

Kakka's friends made things worse. Deeply serious and thoughtful expressions lined their faces as they explained it all to him. "You're over-educating your girls. In our society there aren't many boys as qualified, Ramji. You'll only get into problems later this way . . ." These were the sorts of people who hadn't changed through the generations, whereas Kakka was changing by the day.

Our older sisters tried their hand at the same game too – one at a time. I could never figure out on whose side each of them was, or what they really thought was right and wrong. The fact is that their lives had obscured the distinction between right and wrong, so how likely was it that they'd convince us? They'd come and go, and I always had the feeling that the home they were leaving was theirs no longer, and the one they were going to wasn't either. Our sisters returning to their natal home from their in-laws', wiping their tears – this too became a ritual pilgrimage, like ritual bathings in the Ganga. Get back home, get stuck back in domestic drudgery, in the daily chores, in the innocent belief that perhaps this time's pilgrimage, like the one after the purifying bath in the Ganga, will cause life to turn around into something better, get us back on track.

Relief sometimes came in the shape of our stunning-looking grandmother! Each time we repaired to her, how she pampered us! She'd offer us milk and bread and stop us doing any of her housework. Grandmother and Bai – both short, both beautiful.

Short, fair Grandmother said to Bai, "No point crying, Bhanwari! Tears are never any use!" Once, when I visited, she was so preoccupied chatting that she didn't know I was around. She was busy telling Bai that "Kallu Uncle from Bakhar thrashed his mother in anger once . . . With great difficulty, the villagers dragged him away. There's a huge spat going on between him and his brothers over property right now. I'm telling you, Bhanwari, just watch, there's every chance of a murder or two." Then she chatted about our oldest and youngest uncles. Neither of these brothers were what they used to be: for no apparent reason now, they'd lose their cool with Grandmother and broach the subject of a partition of assets and getting their rightful share. Grandmother said she intended separating out her own kitchen so she could cook her meals away from theirs, their attitudes had grown too combative for her taste.

With Grandfather's passing, it was as if her sons had come into their second manhood. With Grandmother now alone, they wanted to keep her under their thumb. Every other day there were fights at Kallu Mama's. Grandmother was coming round to accepting that maybe it would be best for the partition to happen before things got worse.

What does all this mean, I wondered. Was my grandmother scared that her eldest-born might . . . No, no! He'd never do a thing like that . . . Badé Mama-ji is now very old and gets along so well with Kakka, how could he possibly do the dirty by Granmother? And Chhoté Mama-ji has always been so good and sweet. And besides, he's scared silly of Kakka. I told myself all this and then said, "Grandmother, there's no need to feel frightened. Kakka is around, and Kallu Mama is only a bit eccentric, not like our other uncles . . . Why get into cooking just for yourself? You could move in with us . . ."

I meant well saying what I did but found Grandmother turning on me: "Hey you, if you're such a bigshot, why're you hell-bent on making a nightmare of my daughter's days and nights? . . . You've ruined her life, the whole lot of you. To hell with you, you worse than worthless things! There's no peace to be had anywhere . . ." She was agitated and waving her arms and she rose to her feet to tell me, ". . . You, you! If you think you're such a hotshot, why aren't you married? You won't give my daughter peace till you . . . Useless creature . . . you're a proper witch! God knows who's put this curse on my Bhanwari!"

I felt like telling her to quit calling me bigshot and hotshot, but she was red with rage and I kept my mouth shut.

Phapphu was next. As always, she got going with her litany of grievances on Kakka's behalf. "He's been working from the day he was born. No-one's harder working. Not in the seven surrounding villages will you find a man like my brother! I've never in my life seen him sit on his haunches or sit around doing nothing.

His whole life's a work in progress. And at the end of it, look at the kind of children God's given him . . . To hell with such a home and this non-stop drama that goes on in it. Don't other folks have children? Aren't there other parents in this world? *May you all burn in hell for chewing up my brother.*"

Her next ploy was affection. Her tone became soothing as she tried to explain the eternal verities. "Children, do think a little of your father's plight. He's the only one without land or property. He has no brother, no uncles. Because your grandfather had such a big ego, our land was auctioned off. Even then, your father never lost heart. Everyone abandoned him. And when he started his dhaba, the whole village laughed. I've seen his courage and determination, and he's earned such prestige and status with his dhaba! Even the well-off pale in comparison with what he's earned."

And finally we'd get the swelling tones and the concluding crescendo: "At first everyone taunted us by saying our land had been auctioned, and that since we couldn't afford to buy land Brother was reduced to running a dhaba. I wanted to weep when I heard those taunts, my child, but I didn't – I wanted so badly to cry out loud but I couldn't. And it was only when he became Headman and visited our village – only then could I walk tall again." It was a sight – Phapphu trembling with emotion and in full flow!

Then one last tactic: a sudden change of subject. "You

too have only one brother, and as luck would have it he's the youngest. So if something befalls your father, I shudder to think of what may befall you girls. In our entire clan, your father's the most mature." Severe breathlessness and tears concluded her solo performances.

Mahendra Bhaisahib, an outstanding wit who was around occasionally, sometimes butted in when Phapphu had reached fever pitch with his own list of Kakka's – i.e. his uncle's – virtues. "Sister, don't underestimate my uncle . . . he can take on all seven villages – all by himself. The day he loses his cool, he'll have the entire population of those villages running for their lives. For the moment, he's dug himself into a hole because of this bee in his bonnet about wanting his daughters' noses to be stuck endlessly in their books . . . So why run around starting this waterfall of tears, all of a sudden? Shouldn't you have restrained your crazy brother and his one-track mind long back? . . . And another thing, could you stop singing that favourite song of yours about the land being auctioned? I'm sick and tired of you playing the same tune, like a needle stuck in the same old groove. If that blasted land's been auctioned, it's been auctioned. That's it! Will your howling and singing restore his land to Uncle? Learn something from him – have you ever seen him wailing and gnashing his teeth?"

By now his oratory had fired him up into becoming declamatory: "*Arré*, it was Uncle's land that was auctioned, but does he moan and groan about it? He doesn't.

He just carries on living in the busy part of town – a New Age man! And as for you, who's listening to you anyway? You're boring us out of our minds . . . your idle mind's become quite a workshop . . . !"

There wasn't much Phapphu could say in reply to this blast. She went off and sat by the door, waiting for Kakka. But despite the fact that she'd put a distance between them, Mahendra Bhai wasn't quite done, he had flourishes up his sleeve: "Hey, Phapphu! How was your land auctioned? How old were you and Uncle at the time? And don't forget to tell us how your father turned around and boxed the official's ears . . . And did the Brits arrive at his farm too? And was the local official white like the Brits, or was he the same colour as Uncle and you? . . ."

This kind of taunting was the last straw. It burst a dam inside my aunt. She lost all self-control – which meant she turned her venom on *us*. The result of the fracas was always us getting such a mouthful that our ears went up in flames.

Bai defused matters with tea and sat Phapphu down for a tête-à-tête about Fate that made both women tearful. Phapphu was the more disconsolate. Her idea of the end of the world was the day on which Kakka's head would hang, defeated.

45

NEERA WAS BAI'S blue-eyed girl. Her share of everything was the best and the biggest. She never worked at the dhaba, which was partly because she was younger than Bhaiyya. She occasionally stopped at the dhaba on her way to or from college, just to see Kakka, but even this irritated Bhaiyya. "Watch out! I don't want to see you around the dhaba. What's brought you here anyway, tell me . . . It's this dhaba that's ruined everyone. I've had enough! Enough of Kakka, enough of this dhaba."

His words were full of foreboding. It was just as well that Neera's habit of talking to trees had ended – when she was young she'd stop on the road and chat for hours with trees. If she did that now, Bhaiyya would turn *her* into a tree!

A time came when Bhaiyya stopped meeting his friends. He spoke to no-one. And what was worse, he lost all interest in working at the dhaba. The fans grew querulous, the cooler gave up on work, the tubelight was in two minds over whether to come on, the bulbs blew a fuse, the ornamental lights looked dishevelled, the armrests of the chairs got the palsy, the spoons disappear-ed into outer space, the dust got into a relationship with grime and settled down, the curtains wore a perfume drawn from oil and vegetables, empty cold drink bottles huddled into a stack, the ice cream caught a cold, the freezer converted and became a bed, people threw decorum to the winds and sat anarchically where they pleased. The dhaba was all set to lose its lustre.

In May and June, when all the sisters got together, they tried explaining things to Bhaiyya. It only got him hopping mad: "You people haven't the faintest idea. It's easy to talk. Go and see what's what in the market – everyone's laughing at us."

Usha-jiji put in a word of advice to Seema: "You should stop seeing Manu." She looked nervous and weepy, her voice was a whine: "Look, if he doesn't marry you, what's going to become of you . . . ?"

Seema had no second thoughts. There was no doubt in her mind about her Romeo: "I believe in him. Far more than any of you."

"Then marry him. Marry Manu. At least this daily squabbling will end."

"I will. I'll marry him. But he says we'll marry once his little sister is married."

Asha-jiji didn't care for the sound of this at all: "He can consider his sister's future, whereas you can't think of your brother's? Can't you think of anyone else?"

Seema's chin would then begin its silent quivering. Shalu was the silent audience. Red-eyed Shiva had an observation: "What's happened to our family? How has this happened to our family? And how Kakka has aged! . . ." Which of course made her think of me: "Fatty, this is all because of you. If only you'd married that Bhagwan Singh, none of this would have happened."

During this whole uproar, Kakka lay peacefully on his cot, like a cow chewing the cud. Someone said, "What's happened to Kakka? He's not the Kakka we knew." Bai had an opinion on this: "He's discovered the virtue of thrift! This addiction he's got from Babli . . . He thinks, why spend money . . . *Arré*, marriages happen with money, not with idle chatter! He thinks, once these girls are educated, they'll manage life on their own. I say, do away with this confusion and get them married. Why are we cursed with this load on our heads?"

Bhaiyya, spilling over with aggression, was ever ready for a fight. "Yes, sell off the house and the dhaba. I don't want it. We can starve. We'll beg. We'll do the dishes in someone's home. At least we'll earn some self-respect. Does anyone understand?"

Trying to find a via media, I attempted bringing Seema around: "Look, you marry when you want, but don't meet him . . . or at least see him less often. Think of Bhaiyya – everyone plagues him over you."

Her high-pitched response to this suggestion was, "Whatever happens, I won't stop meeting Manu."

All this sparring within the family was probably the cause of her doing badly in her B.A. She got admission for an M.A. in Economics, but focussing on it was the last thing on her mind. She had to bide her time before the night of her nuptials and the interval had to be filled up with life in a college. We learnt that instead of two years, she had now to wait five years to marry Manu.

46

AND THEN THERE WAS Binny, who had a new obsession. Now, at four every evening, she was bathed and ready and arrived with a metal bowl. And what did she have on her mind? "You're all dirty. Don't pollute me. Give me the rotis from a distance. Don't touch me." If anyone so much as touched her or her bowl, she complained to the solicitous old aunties of the neighbourhood. "These people touch me. I'll beat them – they haven't had baths, but I have. Tell them not to come near me . . ." And the aunts, trying hard to mollify her, yelled at us.

One day, Neera touched Binny while giving her the rotis and vegetables. All hell broke loose. Neera had to run for her life with Binny chasing her all round the neighbourhood. Chhoté Mama-ji rescued her from Binny's clutches, she was on the verge of being slapped around. It took a lot to stop Binny, and Chhoté Mama-ji needed all his powers of persuasion: "*Arré,* Binny, these women are all mad – you're sensible. You're a queen! Don't get upset, Binny . . . come on . . . Here, take this quick. Why let your food go cold over these mad women?"

Glaring at us, she sat down on the porch to eat. Chhoté Mama-ji stood guard by her, stick in hand, and the old aunties gathered to sit protectively around her while she muttered, "... now don't touch me. Give me the roti from a distance. Don't pollute me. If you do, I'll hit you with a stick."

Chortling, teeth sparkling, she scampered off towards the station.

47

WHAT A REMARKABLE THING the General Compartment of an ordinary train is! Such a thrill to see people like us all around! I was enthralled by it and had many trains speeding around in my head. It was comforting to know I wasn't alone, that there were thousands and hundreds of thousands like me out there. It gave me confidence of another sort.

It was much more fun standing in the General Compartment of a super-fast express than getting to sit in a passenger train. The problem was that the speed and shrill siren of the superfast train frightened Bhaktu-jiji and gave her an ear-ache.

Bhaktu-jiji, whose spring-like neck betrayed her strong and avid reactions on the porch, had a son called Maheep Yadav who'd married for love soon after finishing Class 12. Kamini Jain of Gwalior visited her aunt off and on, which is when her friendship with Maheep blossomed. Actually all the aunts of the Yadavs were Jains. Close to the Naulakhi temple was the Jain temple, so even the non-Jains of the locality were considered half-Jains. And Kamini came from a large and broad-minded family.

She hung out quite openly with Maheep. In the evenings, the two of them sat and chatted on the roof for hours.

Bhaktu-jiji tried to make them understand what life was all about: "Don't sit together that way. Listen, don't talk to Maheep this way – when everyone's looking ..."

Though he was her husband, Kamini called Maheep by his name – sometimes Mahi, sometimes Maheep, leaving everyone who heard her open-mouthed. They even ate their food out of the same plate. Bhaktu-jiji tried putting a stop to all this, but Kamini's response was, "*Arré,* he's my husband, so where's the shame in talking to one's husband?"

When people in the neighbourhood heard her shouting "Mahi! Mahi! Maheep!" they gasped through their laughter: "... Like she's the only one with a husband, no-one else has a man!" And the various busybody aunts sang in chorus: "To hell with these love marriages! ... Or maybe we need to find out a bit more about these *love-shove* marriages ... What the hell! Our whole lives have gone up in smoke cooking in the kitchen with those pots and pans, serving our lords and masters ..."

Kamini and Maheep had become the objects of curiosity, merriment, and anger. Kamini showed no signs of shyness or embarrassment in dealing with her father-in-law, his older brother, his younger brother – anyone from her in-laws that she encountered. She had no qualms at all talking freely with Maheep despite the august and forbidding presence of the elderly, putting her arm around Maheep's shoulder, holding his hand. She became a walking-talking movie show in the locality.

The women sighed heavily and said: "Now there's no need for us to go see a film. The film's come right here and is playing all the time without us having to pay for it . . . Seeing it day in and day out . . . I've seen it all!"

Then, one day, Kamini and Maheep had a huge fight. Their voices reached every home – they were really having it out, the two of them. They came to blows right in front of the local audience; people intervened and pulled them apart. After an hour or two they were in love with each other again.

To celebrate the arrival of peace, they went off to Sanchi to have some fun, they ate together, they hugged and kissed, and the next day Kamini in a new suit of clothes was beaming, laughing, and deliriously happy. A few days later, one more wildcat fight – followed once again by kiss-and-make-up.

One hot Sunday afternoon, with various women sitting outdoors doing their chores, the two of them started a fight. The old official's wife lost her temper, ". . . And you call this a love marriage? *Arré,* this is a shit-marriage, a shit-marriage."

In the midst of this pantomime, Mad Binny of the Sparkling Teeth arrived and had lots of fun. She stared wide-eyed at Kamini, she peered at Maheep and hooted. But he wasn't discomfited. In fact he said to Kamini:

"Come on, you want to be friends with her? Let me help you."

But the moment Kamini arrived, Binny traipsed away, swaying, swinging, laughing, and disappeared across the lane.

Today, standing and laughing at the top of the lane, what is Binny eating? She's up to something . . .

What has she in her hands that she's devouring . . . what is making her glow with such radiance? . . .

"Come, come, Binny . . . Come, you must be tired of running around. You run and jump like a deer all day, and yet your legs aren't tired?"

Bari-kaki called out to her. But if she wasn't going to come, she wasn't going to come.

"This she-devil . . . she's desperate to get to the station! She's so keen to go to the station, it's like her placenta is embedded between the tracks!"

Binny, laughing. Bowl in hand. She went across the lane. She disappeared from sight.

48

A FEW DAYS LATER, IN a flash, like a firefly, our happy-go-lucky days disappeared. The four directions of the sky had been turned upside down. The trees had begun looking for space elsewhere. The dust rose up in the sky and hovered above, shuddering. Walls came up as new frontiers. All the symbols raged and cried. The air went on strike. It stopped moving. It crawled.

After many years of calm, our town was cloaked in dark, ominous shadows. With one swift bolt of lightning, all the shops owned by Muslims were reduced to ashes. Why?

No-one knew why. Even those who lost their shops had no idea. Neither did those who, dousing the fires, singed their fingers.

There were no riots. So how had such change become possible when, in our little town, the question of Hindu versus Muslim had never existed? We were not even conscious of the fact that by eating and playing together, and not quarrelling with each other, we were setting some sort of example.

Thank God Raees Bhai's shop at the bus stand was

spared. Bhaijan Sahib escaped. And Maulana Chacha stayed three whole days at Mathur Sahib's house.

A curfew was in place across the town.

Binny's teeth no longer sparkled. Did all this happen only to destroy her? Her running around the station at midnight stopped, of course. But even in broad daylight, her carefree runs along the tracks had come to an end.

"Lord, You have, before my eyes, destroyed this young girl."

The old official's wife looked with contempt towards the temple.

In our neighbourhood that day, there wasn't a soul who took the time to decorate her gods.

Evensong, the time for prayer and the lighting of diyas, came and went: not a single diya was lit.

The temple was no longer the temple it had been. It had been denuded of its serenity.

49

I TOOK UP A JOB that paid a thousand rupees a month. I went running to Kakka. As always, he was supportive. He had never given up on me, not even when the world all around was swearing at me and gossiping about me. He had a supremely blind faith in my decisions. In Seema on the other hand he saw a second Shalu, which made him shiver. "What am I to do with this girl? She's made life hell for me. Your brother turns nasty over her all the time." Kakka was growing old.

It is difficult to describe how I felt each time I went home and saw him. Old age was not for my father, it did not sit well on him. If only I could have caught hold of his years in my hands, pounded them to dust with a pestle and mortar, fried the result and scattered it to the winds ... I so wanted to see Kakka young and strong again.

I scanned the papers for a job. I wanted a job. Desperately. Any sort of job. I didn't care where or what – just *any* job. I didn't dare dream my dreams of teaching in a college. I just wanted a job. I applied for every kind of job.

I finally passed the tests for one permanent position.

Before the interview, I went to Kakka. His eyes welled up when he saw me. Usha-jiji was with him.

Her people from Siwni-Malwa said, "You don't get jobs just because you want them! You're wasting your time. How does one explain things to you? You'll spend your life doing odd jobs. And then, after a certain age . . ."

God knows, I couldn't make out much, there was such a variety of emotions on their faces.

Sounding irritated, they said: "In two years you haven't moved beyond a thousand bucks. We're anxious about you all the time. You've ruined our family's reputation . . . we can't show our faces anywhere. *Arré*, we can't even look our own relatives in the eye! . . . Because of you, our children's future is in jeopardy . . ."

They did their best to destroy what little courage I had left. Jiji gave me sidelong glances and in a voice dripping sorrow said, "Let people say what they will, you keep your nose to the grindstone."

Usha-jiji never did curse me like some of those others. But then she never took up the cudgels on my behalf either. She was always a bit of a cry-baby. Asha-jiji had a set formula for ticking her off: "You finish crying first. Then we'll discuss the problem."

Kakka, after conversing about this and that and about nothing in particular, decided to get down to brass tacks: "Child, if not today, you'll succeed tomorrow. Or eventually. Remember, don't be frightened, don't go off course, don't go off track. In those big cities it's easy for children to lose their bearings."

I left for the city the next morning, to the place where my dreams might fly. At the door, Kakka said: "Child! Don't lose hope. Whatever happens, we'll face it." Because of his unflinching support, my self-confidence sometimes burst and blazed like the oven at our dhaba. It felt like he was using every ounce of his strength and willpower to stoke each nugget of coal inside me into a roaring fire, as he did with his oven.

I discovered that, as one among the innumerable unemployed, looking for a job was like trying to cross a railway line with a train impending – only a few would manage to go over. And that there can be so much support from people when you're looking for a job, but when you've found a job it can take but a moment for them to turn on you.

Those out of work formed a kind of community within which they could share their problems and grievances, even their dreams and hopes, but on the day of the exam or the interview we'd avoid each other, adroitly hiding our notes and question papers! In fact we even took care not to disclose what we'd been asked in the interview! "First things first: I need this job, after that you or the deluge . . . I don't much care!" That seemed to be the attitude. And it wasn't just one or two who were implying this: everyone was.

What should I do? What should I not do? Which is the best way forward . . .?

A plague of questions. What if on my account the

whole family were destroyed? Had I aged Kakka before his time? Was I the laughing stock of the whole town? How about Bhaiyya? Had we sisters given him nothing except curses and reproaches? For as long as there'd been just five sisters, Kakka had had respect, status, self-esteem. And now?

Now there happen to be three young girls waiting unmarried in his home. Their mother is shrinking physically because . . .

Even now she trudges to the temple twice a day but speaks to no-one. She no longer spends hours at the temple because she feels stared at by other women.

Muniman Aunty tried soothing Bai. ". . . Don't take all this to heart. These are children, just children. They'll put you on a throne one day, and the next day they'll . . ."

Bai hadn't the courage or the strength to listen to any more.

If only. The number of "If Onlies" staring me in the face was legion, the story of my life.

If only I'd never set eyes on that dark-complexioned Madam. If only she hadn't stopped and asked me with a laugh about the precise position of her bindi. If only she hadn't been carrying books in her arms. If only she hadn't been a college teacher! If only, at that very moment, my head hadn't been laden with a basket of cowpats. If only I had never seen Kakka beg Shalu and Shiva's in-laws on that fateful wedding night.

If only my college Principal hadn't converted a barren space into a library. If only we'd never played badminton there. Why did he have to tell us "Life's not a zero-sum game!" He was right when he said, "It's easier to ride a bicycle fast. It's very difficult to ride it slow."

Obstacles, and then more obstacles. How many more? And will they in the end stop me before I've achieved what I want?

If only I hadn't thought of life and poetry as one and the same thing, I might have realised Kakka's dreams. If only Vinita Madam hadn't made us read Gorky's *Mother* and then *Asadh ka Ek Din*. If only she'd never asked, "What d'you plan to do after your B.A.?" If only I'd never thought of any of these things . . .

For how long can I carry on staying at her place? For how long will she try giving flight to my dreams by looking up job advertisements for me, day and night? How long can she go on helping me fill up application forms and send off payments with them? I can't begin to seem a lifelong burden to her . . . If only I'd never met Vinita Madam and been like my sisters, compliant and married. Seema could never then have said to Kakka, "But Babli! What have you done about Babli? Doesn't she do as she pleases? . . ."

I'm dog tired trying to work out what's in store for me. If I don't get a job, will I have to crawl back home? *Never, Never, Never.* The very thought makes me start trembling with apprehension. Fright at the thought that my whole life will end in an endless walk, that I'll just walk, walk, walk on a never-ending road . . .

And then I begin wondering if people aren't off their heads at all when they say I'm good for nothing. *Que sera sera* is all very well for me, *but nothing is just me,* everything I do has a bearing on my unmarried sisters . . . have I left them with no future prospects? Why has Kakka taken to being so stonily silent? Has he too lost all hope? Is he a broken man? And Bai? Her whole life gone just giving birth to children and then growing them up . . .

Are we the sins she says we are from her past life? Grinding masala, grumbling away – could all she muttered have been true, somehow? Was it so wrong for a girl to find love that her brother felt he could no longer face his friends? Was Seema's affair responsible for Kakka's condition? The romance in books as against the romance visible in our lives – how could the difference be so absolute? In the book version, love is the pinnacle of life's beauty. And in the cinema . . . well, don't even ask! And in the version at home, love means a whining mother and desperate sisters. And relatives who spit on you. So, it seems the real meaning of love is that it's life's biggest mistake, the losing of one's way, the sneers of the world, suppressed laughter that stings like whiplashes, a bone you can neither swallow nor spit out. My sweet Basoda, this is the variety of love you've given us!

Why?

Why do people not leave Kakka alone to live in peace? Why do they turn up with stories about Seema and Manu? Why do they go around telling Bhaiyya: "If you don't have the money, we'll collect it. But marry the girl off within her caste. After all . . ."

Perhaps they think Kakka's tight-fisted, he's not marrying off his daughters because he doesn't like spending. If anyone had dared say this to him twenty years ago . . .

Is dishonour inescapable in old age? I was consumed by all the things I regretted, and some of the rancour I felt within myself even made me blame Kakka. No-one really understood me, not my sisters, not their in-laws. Seema least of all. Not even Chhoté Mama-ji, who'd taken me to listen to the orchestra all night long.

Except for Kakka, no-one had stood by me. And because of me, only because of me, he was having to swallow the bitter pill of social disgrace in his old age. How can my sisters remain silent when their husbands spout rubbish about Kakka and me?

Had the dhaba's smouldering oven become a curse in my life, and in Kakka's? Had those cowpats set fire to our lives? What kind of earthquake was this, what kind of fire – consuming me and Kakka and our family, annihilating us, leaving nothing in its wake but forgotten desire and tired failure?

Kakka, I longed to give you so much . . . and what, in the end, have I ever given you? I wanted to see you stroll on a high road with Bai, like the parents of other girls; sit in an armchair in the sun, relaxed, reading your newspaper. I wanted to see you wear new underclothes with not a tear in sight. I wanted to see you shine and glow with contentment in the autumn of your life.

Because of me, Kakka's only starched yellow kurta lay as it was – unused. And Bai – she wanted none of it – "What will people say! Marriageable girls at home, and he's going about in bright-coloured clothes?"

As for the relatives in Muradpur, God alone knows what they thought of me. Perhaps Badé-dada there too thought of me with curses on his mind, like his younger brother . . . No, no, that cannot be . . . he taught me to ride a mo-bike!

I closed my eyes, thought of him, and sobbed: Wherever you are, come and meet Kakka! . . . Come and spend time with father as often as you can . . . Chhoté Mama-ji, abandon your playing cards and look after Bai . . .

I imagined Bai too, howling in pain, head wrapped . . . Munna Bhaiyya, Munna Bhaiyya! A pill for a headache, quick, please! And Bai praying for her children, walking around trees, ready to believe every djinn, every superstition, sitting quietly, statue-like, waiting, waiting for us to come back from the dhaba when Kakka was away, standing at a distance, waiting, standing with our school uniforms at the door to stop us being later than we already were, wiping our dripping hair when we sat out in the rain, keeping places in reserve for customers, Bai so quiet at times, wiping our heads with her sari . . .

Why am I plagued by thoughts now, by such thoughts? Why, why? It was never like this before.

And the dhaba?

Who knows, maybe the birds have stopped flying . . . those cawing crows, flying in from far away, coming to the aid of their comrade wounded by the current in a live wire . . . to his aid, never to mine.

My throat goes dry with thirst. Does the old hand pump sense my thirst? Am I forgotten entirely . . . that enormous peepal tree, does it recall the shade it gave me under its canopy of leaves?

An interview date: 20th March. Getting closer by the day. Day and night, it allows only a single thought: *What if I don't get this job?* All night I lived in a miasma of despair over this thought.

Questions chased me. I slogged day and night. If they ask me this, if they ask me that . . .

The nights grew short, the afternoons long, full of foreboding. *May that day never come* was all the feeling I had left inside me as the day got closer. I covered the calendar with my hand. Irritated by the moving needle of the clock and its unceasing tick-tock, I switched it off. My fear of failure was manic. I needed Time itself to stop.

Over those cataclysmic days of turmoil I clutched at straws, at any glimmer of hope in the horizon. I told myself things: "Just remember the dark-complexioned Madam and the basket of cowpats . . . You'll find the strength, partner! You may not get this job . . . there are a thousand others . . ." Some of these were voices mimicking Kakka in my head.

"May I come in, Sir?"

The moment I said this, I saw the people on the interview panel. To say I was scared would be putting it mildly; it was a fear I felt I'd never be able to shake off. The Board members seemed to take forever. They asked me my name and kept turning over the papers in front of them. No doubt they intended it to give me time to calm my nerves. Kakka's words came to me at an opportune moment: "Don't be scared. There are more good people in the world than bad." I smiled. My fears vanished.

When the interview ended, they smiled and said, "O.K."

Que sera sera.

My response to them was also quite a smile.

50

"IT DOESN'T FOLLOW THAT everyone must want what you want." This remark of Seema's really rankled. On the other hand Kakka's constant refrain – that girls must learn to stand on their own two feet – left me distraught.

Seema's relationship with Manu had caused havoc. The chaos had spread everywhere: people who knew us, people who didn't know us, everyone was swearing at the goings-on of Seema and Manu. They cursed her family more than her.

"If she were my daughter, I'd have killed her."

"Oh, it was all with the family's blessings . . . else how could anyone keep a grown-up daughter unmarried *that* long?"

Some said this, some said that. Some said stuff it was best to ignore. The bottom line was that the whole universe had conspired to turn our lives into a living hell. Most specifically Kakka's life. His life had become a nightmare. And over what? Over trivia. Over what should never have been an issue.

Bhaiyya had decided to take on Kakka. "So, they've all got jobs, eh? Our town should pin a badge of honour on your chest, Kakka!"

He came menacingly close to Kakka. Two sisters had to quickly intervene . . . "Bhaiyya, Bhaiyya!"

After a while, Kakka rose and left for the dhaba.

Bhaiyya was scarlet with fury. "Look! . . . He's absolutely shameless! There he goes, utterly unrepentant. *What can he say?* . . . He has no answers."

He looked like he was about to start smashing things around.

What things? Well, he'd have destroyed us for a start. Gobbled us up. Except he knew we had Kakka's support. And that he himself was almost the youngest born.

It was the only thing that had saved us – so far.

51

As always, Kakka went off to the dhaba in the morning and did all the work. Bhaiyya followed in the afternoon between noon and 1 p.m., but while there spoke not a word to Kakka. He seemed to go only to pluck around twenty-five rotis from the oven and then disappear to lounge in some establishment or the other. Kakka had to re-heat cold rotis on the griddle and serve those to his customers – who grumbled. When the rotis had finished and more customers were in, Kakka yelled for Bhaiyya to come back. But Bhaiyya couldn't be bothered. If Kakka sent a messenger to summon him, his response was, "Tell him I'm not coming . . ." He had a new bee in his bonnet: Shut down the dhaba. Open some other kind of shop right here. Go find work in the grain market.

Kakka's choicest expletives were all saved up for his son and regularly spat out, but come hell or high water Bhaiyya wasn't going to do his share of dhaba work.

Kakka wasn't ready to give in either. He shut down the big tandoor and restarted the smaller oven. This made Bhaiyya see red and he stopped going to the dhaba altogether.

From morn till night, Kakka ran the dhaba all by himself. It made him desperately tired. He carried on his incredibly taxing routine for as long as he could, but in the end he was done in – ironically, by the pitying consideration of his customers. Why trouble the old man, they said.

52

THAT THIS MIGHT HAPPEN to the dhaba was beyond our imagining. It may not have been our home, but it had given us a home.

Should one have spread out a chessboard and worked out a strategy? Diversified? To what end? Running the dhaba was no game.

The dhaba had taught us more than a thing or two. If you can't stop crying, try laughing. Don't make it too loud. But not so soft that it stops your eyes from lighting up and reduces your comely blushes . . .

So, what was the dhaba going to do for itself now . . . go into ventilator support? *No.* There was fire in the old dog yet. Trembling but still breathing . . .

Back bent double, Kakka stood up. Was he now preparing for a deep and permanent sleep? Why was he wobbling so terribly? The moment Kakka got up looking shaky, the questions came tumbling out. Did the fire need more coals in it? Who'd shovel them in? What if there was a storm? Would the aromas ever come wafting back out of his oven? Questions, followed by a load of wishful thinking . . .

Crackle, Crackle, Crackle. The coals were crackling. Inside whom?

Kakka assumed a watchful posture. He watched the world quietly. He spoke not a word to anyone. No-one could tell what was going on within him.

When will this end? How will this routine be broken? Will the big oven break first? Where will its ash be dumped? Will all the remaining coal have to be sold? And what of the pots, pans, tongs, hand pump, water tank, plates, saucers, glasses . . . will they go? And with them all, Kakka? *This cannot be.* Will Kakka take the dhaba with him to the world beyond? Things that had once appeared so difficult had happened all too easily. Well, that being so, misfortune might turn overnight to good fortune! A threshold might be crossed without anyone having to shed tears.

Will he come into our dreams, or shall we go into his?

Morbid visions of the future. Instead of the early morning roti for the cow, a hammer. Kakka's hand coming in the way, trying to stop it, and then . . .?

Where is the ash to go? People charging off with bucketfuls. God knows how many pots and pans the ash will clean. Will some of it fly into Kakka's eyes . . .?

Will Kakka cross his Parasari?

Will he end up sorting out what's left of the dhaba? God knows how many drums of rubbish he'll fill, his back bent double. Perhaps he'll place a mountain of leavings next to the mound of ash. Has he forgotten that if he does, a truck will come and take it all away? Where does the truck dump the things that it takes away? Will Kakka pursue the truck?

What next? In all the confusion that followed, one leg of the takht was found broken. And one of Kakka's knees was hurt. He wasn't able to follow the truck that came.

Now, Kakka's knees give him trouble all the time. They stiffen. When he sits, he finds it difficult to stand again; when he stands, his legs quake. Under his feet lies a gaping hole. It is filled to the brim with what's left over from the dhaba. The dhaba lives under Kakka's feet now.

How many years were the dhaba and Kakka married to each other in that peculiar harmony? How long was the dhaba a living being before it left this world? "Don't count the years," someone had said, "Counting will shorten your father's life." Who'd said this? Who'd spoken those words? The dhaba gone, could there be any sort of residual fire still burning in Kakka?

He cannot cross the river now. He cannot cross the bridge. He stands on this side and watches the other end. On this side where he stands, his knees shake. Across the river, the remains of what sustained him beckon.

Does he want to say something, hear something? Or is he now like the Sardar who once owned a wood depot? The Sardar whose son once hid in a train's toilet where he cut his hair and his beard, unfurled his turban, threw away the things that made him who he was, to escape a mob? And all for what? Trapped in the space between two bogies, he slipped. He was brought home in a box. And when the Sardar saw his son packed in a box like luggage, what did he do? What could he do? He did not go mad. He did not go across and throw stones at moving trains. He lived in a world that lay far beyond shock. The state of being that lay in store for Kakka with the end of his dhaba . . .

And if I don't get that job, will the trauma consume him?

The dust hadn't settled on its remains before Bhaiyya opened a cycle shop where the dhaba had once been. His world spinning around his head already, Kakka now had to face seeing cycles being repaired and sold right there, in the heart of our small town. At his insistence, the new shop started hiring out cycles as well. Bhaiyya preached caution: "Rent out cycles only to those you know." Whereas Kakka's habit was to throw caution to the winds. "*Arré,* they're all people known to us. All good citizens! Why suspect every third fellow without good reason?"

So, he rented out cycles to everyone – to the known and to the unknown. In a fast-moving world, some barbs flicker, others rust. In his rusted state of mind, Kakka rented out four cycles. Only three came back. Bhaiyya was furious. "Don't you dare come back to this shop. There's no need for you to work anyway. You've done enough. Go home and take it easy. I'll take care of your needs."

Bai tried intervening. "*Arré,* he feels lonely at home. He's spent his whole life working. If he sits around at home his whole body goes stiff."

"O.K., so give him odd jobs to do. He can fetch the vegetables and milk. He'll get to stretch his legs."

His dealings with rust and polish, speeding and braking, had made Bhaiyya cold and hard. "Kakka, you will not come again to the shop. *You will not.*"

Kakka, bearing his memories, his newspaper, and his walking stick, struggled his way out of what had been his dhaba.

Will the walking stick straighten his back? Will he burst out laughing again as he did when he heard words mispronounced?

Will I cross the threshold and find a career?

Every night it feels like I'm chasing after a departing train. Or that I'm trying to get past a railway crossing with a train impending. And there's no-one now to help me across. I dream of Kakka and his dhaba, my sleep a heap of dying embers.

Every night I break into a sweat, dreaming of an appointment letter in my hand. Of finding a gazetted officer to attest my character certificate. Put seal and signature on a medical report. I sweat like I did when making rotis in the dhaba. Fear of failure brings me close to tears.

And then, out of the blue, I'm blessed with a vision of the never-ending train tracks with Mad Binny of the Sparkling Teeth, swaying and swinging and laughing, running along the tracks. She tries to make me laugh. I breathe her in. I wonder where she is now. Still running around? Or across the tracks in no-man's land?

How does Kakka spend his time now, who does he chat with – Kakka who asked four rupees from customers when he should have asked for ten. What does he think of bicycle thieves? Kakka who started his dhaba at seven – does he now get out of bed? Has he taste enough left on his tongue to enjoy his evening tea?

I had never thought of life as a series of giant leaps, it was all I could do to manage chasing a couple of fleeting dreams. How long would I be able to go on chasing even those? Kakka's life went in giving us children a life. A desert of shattered dreams was the price of just getting on with the daily grind. Big dreams? Where was the question? The road ahead is barely a small track for me to walk on. There seems little point thinking about roads and bridges and traffic lights.

Do dreams discriminate between village and small town, city and metropolis, as they seep into people's lives? Do they see small towns as sleepless and slow?

In the deepest darkness
I saw the moving wheel.
But in the darkness so dense
I could see neither potter nor form.
Sorrow and joy are one . . .

Out of old habit, the sun rose from the east. A job. *The job.* It might instil some hope in Kakka yet. With that little job what might I not . . .

I caught the train. Had I wings, I'd have reached Kakka sooner. The birds, how easy and graceful their flight, enough to put a smile on my face.

Why does this train taking me back stop so often today? *Shall I get off the train, appointment letter in hand, and make a dash for Kakka?*

At the outer lights I jumped off that crawling train. And I ran faster towards my home that day than I'd ever run through my whole life. No-one could have run ahead of me.

Running. Panting. Banging on the door.

"What's happened? What happened?"

Bai looked shaken.

"Kakka . . . Kakka . . . Kakka . . ."

I'd have reached him first, but he dropped his stick and enveloped me in his arms. Shaking, quivering like my heartbeat. Now standing tall. *"Arré, Oh my dear! . . ."* His booming voice was back.

I wanted to say to him: Kakka, you can tell everyone your daughter's on her own two feet.

I couldn't. Before either of us could say another word, a vision of the dhaba came between us. Kakka's tears shone like dew. How good he looked having cast away his walking stick!

All we needed then was for his dhaba to have been with us, to share that precious moment.

Translator's Note

MY FIRST FEW YEARS in the I.A.S. saw me stationed in small towns like Jind and Jhajjhar in Haryana. These were market towns, much like Neelesh Raghuwanshi's Ganj Basoda, and my work and life there as a twenty-two-year-old were experiences never to be forgotten. Which is why when my friend Vasudha Dalmia suggested I read and translate *Ek Kasbe ke Notes*, it was not long before I found myself utterly hooked. There it was, the world of my early years, with insights and encounters added that could only expand my horizon.

Translating Raghuwanshi's world has been a heady experience. I found myself diving deep into it, living with the trials and travails of the family at its centre, for almost two years. Those two years turned out both hugely rewarding and therapeutic, trying to cope as I was with a traumatic bereavement. This novel brought me back to the world for long spells of the day.

I hope I have been able to do justice to the funny, feisty, flawed, but ultimately touchingly human characters of this lovely novel. Read the Hindi original if you can. As one translator put it, every language has its own way of thinking, and to that it seems worth adding that the flavour, the atmosphere, and the larger world implicit between the lines in the original can only be roughly approximated, not replicated, by the idioms of a very different language.

This translation is a collaborative effort, if ever there was one. It would not have happened without Neelesh Raghuwanshi's permission to translate and her instant responses to my many queries; Vasudha Dalmia's encouragement and brilliant Introduction; Rukun Advani's wizardry as editor; Shalini Bose's computer skills. To them my most profound thanks.

Thanks also to many dear friends: Kiran Aggarwal, Suresh Chand and Komal, Renu Sahni Dhar and Billy, Anupa and Darshan Lal, Meera Malik, S.S. Mukherjee, Kiran Sahni, Ranjana Saikia, Brinda Singh, Manmohan Singh, Charusheela Sohoni, and S.Y. Quraishi.

On a more personal note, my love and thanks to my stepchildren Anjolie and Himmat, and to my brother Deepak for seeing me through the worst years of my life.

And at all times, and above all, to Kamal, all my love.